Contents

ACKNOWLEDGMENTS

I'm forever giving thanks to those who have helped me over the years to become what I am—radio personality, author and retired nurseryman. There are some people I would like to acknowledge; the most important are my wife Beverley and my children Bill, Kathy and Edie, who worked their buns off for me in the business. There are a couple of others who have also helped over the years: Vincent Virgel, who was my financial mentor; Cliff Nelson, who allowed me credit when no one would; and Gordon Courtright, who encouraged me to write about gardening. —*Bob Tanem*

The authors and the publisher gratefully thank all who were involved in the project, as well as the many gorgeous private and public gardens that provided the setting for photographs in this book. Special thanks go to Strybing Arboretum and Botanical Gardens, Filoli Estate, Elizabeth F. Gamble Gardens and Golden Gate Park.

Don Williamson would like to thank The Creator.

The Trees & Shrubs at a Glance

A Pictorial Guide in Alphabetical Order, by Common Name

Bog Rosemary
p. 112

Bottlebrush
p. 114

Boxleaf Azara
p. 116

Butterfly Bush
p. 118

California Lilac
p. 122

Camellia
p. 128

California Pepper Tree
p. 126

Cape Plumbago
p. 134

Cedar
p. 136

Chinese Pistache
p. 140

Coast Redwood
p. 142

Common Quince
p. 146

Crape Myrtle
p. 148

Cypress
p. 152

Daphne
p. 156

Dawn Redwood
p. 160

Dogwood
p. 162

Douglas-Fir
p. 166

Dove Tree
p. 168

False Cypress
p. 170

Fir
p. 174

Firethorn
p. 178

Flannel Bush
p. 182

Flowering Quince
p. 186

Forsythia
p. 190

Fringe Tree
p. 194

Ginkgo
p. 198

Goldenchain Tree
p. 202

Grevillea
p. 204

Hardy Hibiscus
p. 208

Heavenly Bamboo
p. 210

Hebe
p. 214

Holly
p. 218

Horsechestnut
p. 222

Hydrangea
p. 226

Japanese Pagoda Tree
p. 232

Kalmia
p. 234

Kerria
p. 236

Lilac
p. 238

Loquat
p. 242

Magnolia
p. 246

Maple
p. 254

Manzanita
p. 250

Mimosa Tree
p. 260

Mockorange
p. 262

Monkey Puzzle Tree
p. 266

New Zealand
Christmas Tree p. 268

Olive
p. 270

Oregon Grape
p. 274

Photinia
p. 278

Pineapple Guava
p. 280

Podocarpus
p. 282

Pomegranate
p. 286

Redbud
p. 292

Princess Flower
p. 290

Rhododendron
p. 296

Rockrose
p. 302

Russian Olive
p. 306

Salal
p. 310

Spirea
p. 312

INTRODUCTION

Trees and shrubs are woody perennials. Their life cycles take three years to decades to complete, and they maintain a permanent live structure aboveground all year. A tree is generally defined as a woody plant having a single trunk and growing greater than 15' tall. A shrub is multi-stemmed and no taller than 15'. These definitions are not absolute because some tall trees are multi-stemmed, and some short shrubs have single trunks. Even the height definitions are open to interpretation. For example, a Japanese maple may be multi-stemmed and may grow about 10' tall, but it is often still referred to as a tree. To make matters more complicated, a given species may grow as a tree in favorable conditions and as a shrub in harsher sites. It is always best to look at the expected mature size of a tree or shrub to judge its suitability for your garden. If you have a small garden, a large, tree-like shrub, such as a bottlebrush, crape myrtle or photinia, may be all you have room for.

To make matters even more complicated, many small shrubs are trained or grafted as small trees, known as standards. For example, rhododendrons trained as small trees are referred to as azalea standards.

Some shrubs act like herbaceous perennials and die back to the ground each winter. Many tropicals and semi-tropicals fall into this category. The shrub may be in a colder zone than what is suggested for it, or it might have experienced a colder than average winter. The root system, protected by the soil over winter, sends up new shoots in spring, and if the shrub forms flowers on new wood, it will bloom that same year. Such shrubs act like herbaceous perennials, but because they are woody in their native climates they are still treated as shrubs.

Woody plants are characterized by leaf type, whether deciduous or evergreen, needled or broad-leaved. Deciduous plants lose all their leaves each fall or winter. They can be needled plants, such as dawn redwoods, or broad-leaved plants, such as maples. Evergreen trees and shrubs do not lose their leaves in winter and can also be needled or broad-leaved, like spruces and rhododendrons, respectively. Some plants are semi-evergreen; they are generally evergreen, but in cold climates they lose some or all of their leaves. Mimosa tree falls into this category. See the Quick Reference Chart (pp. 342–47) for which category each species in this book falls into.

Golden Gate Park (photo on facing page)

The climate of Northern California provides a wide array of growing conditions, from cool summer/mild winter coastal areas to cool winter/baking-hot summer areas in the interior valleys to genuinely cold winter/short summer areas in the northeast and mountainous regions. Each of these regions presents its own unique climate challenges.

The diverse climate makes it possible to grow plants from around the world. We can grow Mediterranean plants such as rockrose, olive and cedar, which thrive in the hot, dry interior. Great choices from Australia and New Zealand include bottlebrush and many of the acacias. We can grow many wonderful flowering trees and shrubs from China and Japan, including camellia, bluebeard

Bluebeard & ornamental grass (above)

Dawn redwood (below)

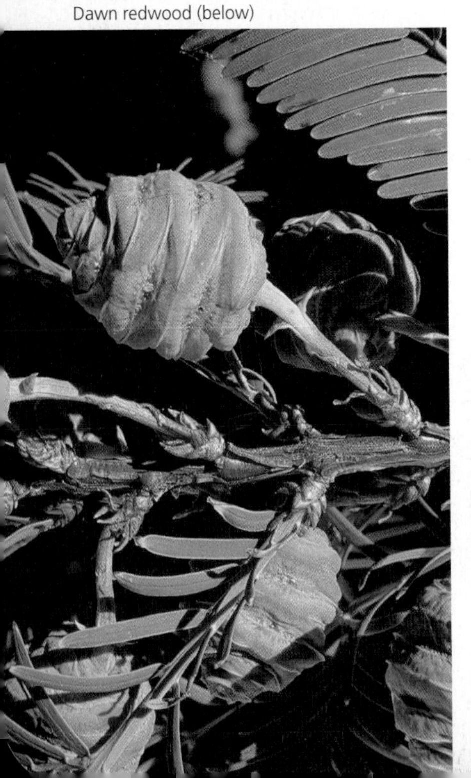

Mediterranean strawberry tree (below)

and common quince, the latter providing a deliciously sweet fruit. Also from China are the ancient ginkgo and dawn redwood. From the tropical and semi-tropical climates of Mexico, Central America and South America, we grow exotic plants such as angel's trumpet, bird-of-paradise bush, monkey puzzle tree and yesterday, today, tomorrow. Northern Europe has provided the European beech, English holly and Russian olive. Along with all the great plants from elsewhere, we have a good selection of native California plants we can work with, including the graceful coast redwood and giant sequoia, several varieties of manzanitas, flannel bush, salal, western redbud and California lilac. Many trees and shrubs from all over the world will

Purple weeping beech (above)

grow well somewhere in Northern California.

It may seem like a daunting task to choose trees and shrubs for your garden from the ever-growing list of plants that do well in our climate. Fortunately, Northern Californians are supported by an active and hospitable gardening population with many gardening and horticulture clubs throughout the state, as well as many fine garden centers and nurseries. Outstanding garden shows, public gardens and arboretums in San Francisco, Sacramento, San Jose, Palo Alto, San Mateo and Luther Burbank Gardens in Santa Rosa attract gardeners and growers from all over the world and are sources of inspiration as well as information. The chief resources of any gardener, however, are imagination and enthusiasm.

Norway spruce (above)

Enthusiastic crowd at outdoor plant sale (below)

A trip to the local arboretum or public garden that has labeled plants and unusual specimens is a great aid in helping select a tree or shrub that will grow well in your garden. Keep your eyes open as you walk or drive through your neighborhood. There may be a tree or shrub that you haven't seen before or that you were told couldn't grow where you live. If you are prepared to open yourself up to the possibilities, you will be pleasantly surprised by the diversity of woody plants that will thrive in your garden. You may want to plant only tried and tested, dependable varieties, but don't be afraid to try something new, like a tropical or semi-tropical. Gardening with trees and shrubs is fun and can be a great adventure if you're willing to take up the challenge and ask a lot of questions.

Japanese maple (above)

HARDINESS ZONES MAP

Average Annual Minimum Temperature

Zone	Temp (°F)
4b	-20 to -25
5a	-15 to -20
5b	-10 to -15
6a	-5 to -10
6b	0 to -5
7a	5 to 0
7b	10 to 5
8a	15 to 10
8b	20 to 15
9a	25 to 20
9b	30 to 25
10a	35 to 30

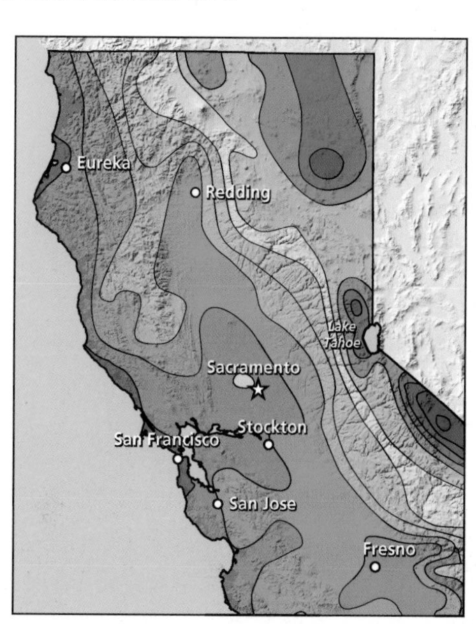

WOODY PLANTS IN THE GARDEN

Trees and shrubs create a framework around which a garden is designed. These permanent features anchor the landscape, and in a well-designed garden, they create interest all year round. In spring and summer, woody plants provide shade and beauty with flowers and foliage. In fall, leaves of many species change color, and brightly colored fruits attract attention and birds. In winter, the true backbone of the garden is revealed; the branches of deciduous trees and shrubs are laid bare, perhaps dusted with silvery frost, and evergreens keep color in the garden.

If carefully selected and placed, woody plants are a vital and vibrant element of any garden, from the smallest city lot to the largest country estate. They can provide privacy and keep unattractive views hidden from sight. Conversely, they can frame an attractive view and draw attention to particular features or areas of the garden. Trees and shrubs soften hard lines in the landscape created by structures such as buildings, fences and driveways. Well-positioned plants create an attractive background against which other plants will shine. Trees and shrubs can be used in groups for spectacular flower or fall color shows, and a truly exceptional species, with year-round appeal, can stand alone as a specimen plant.

Woody plants help moderate the climate in your home and garden. As a windbreak, trees provide shelter from winter cold and reduce heating

costs and protect tender plants in the garden. A well-placed deciduous tree keeps the house cool and shaded in summer, but it allows the sun through in winter, when the warmth and light are appreciated. Woody plants also prevent soil erosion, retain soil moisture, reduce noise and filter the air. Erosion is of particular concern to people whose homes are next to open space or steep hillsides. The proper tree or shrub is a must in these situations.

The attraction of wildlife is an often overlooked benefit of gardening. As cities expand, our living space encroaches on more and more wildlife habitat. By choosing plants, especially native plants, that are beneficial to the local wildlife, we provide food and shelter to birds and other animals and at the same time fulfill our obligation as stewards of the environment. We can bring nature closer to home. The unfortunate difficulty is that the local wildlife may so enjoy a garden that they consume it. It is possible, though, to find a balance and attract wildlife and at the same time protect the garden from ruin. In this book we note which trees and shrubs are least likely to be damaged by deer.

When the time comes to select woody plants, give careful thought to the physical constraints of your garden and the purposes you wish the plants to serve. First and foremost, consider the size of your garden in relation to the mature size of the plants in question. Very large plants are always a bad idea in a small garden. Remember, too, that trees and shrubs not only grow up, they also

Princess flower makes a wonderful specimen (above)

Birds and squirrels are frequent garden visitors (middle & bottom photos)

grow out. Within a few years what started as a small plant may become a large, spreading tree. Redwoods, often sold as cute seedlings, are an example of fast-growing, potentially huge trees not suitable for many gardens.

Another consideration that relates to size is placement. Don't plant trees and shrubs too close to houses, walkways, entryways or driveways. A tree planted right next to a house may hit the overhang of the roof, and trying to fix the problem by pruning will only spoil the natural appearance of the tree. Plants placed too close to paths, doors and driveways may eventually block access to them completely. Trees and shrubs planted near sidewalks or driveways increase the potential for root damage to those structures.

Consider, too, the various features of tree and shrub species. A feature is an outstanding element, such as

Coast redwood (above)

Mass planting of bearberry (below)

flowers, bark or shape, which attracts you to the plant. Decide which of the following features are most important to you and which will best enhance your garden. Many plants have more than one feature, providing interest for a longer period of time. Whether you are looking for showy flowers, fall color, fast growth or a beautiful fragrance, you can find trees or shrubs with features to suit your design; consult the individual accounts in this book and the Quick Reference Chart on p. 342.

Form is the general shape and growth habit of the plant. From tall and columnar to wide and gracefully weeping, trees come in a wide variety of shapes. Similarly, shrubs may be rounded and bushy or low and ground hugging. Form can also vary as the year progresses. Often, an interesting winter habit makes a tree or shrub truly outstanding.

You should be familiar with some growth form terminology when considering a purchase. A 'shade tree' commonly refers to a large, deciduous tree but can be any tree that provides shade. An 'upright,' 'fastigiate' or 'columnar' plant has the main branches and stems pointing upward and is often quite narrow. 'Dwarf' properly refers to any variety, cultivar or hybrid that is smaller than the species, but the term is sometimes mistakenly used to mean a small, slow-growing plant. If a species grows to 100', a 50' variety of that species would be a dwarf, but it might still be too big for your garden. 'Prostrate' and 'procumbent' plants are low growing, with branches and stems that spread horizontally over

Columnar or fastigiate plant (above)

Well-planted shrub bed (below)

Ginkgo (above)

I have a lot of friends who miss the fall colors of their native states. Many trees and shrubs can treat us to fall color in Northern California; the trick to knowing which you'll like best is to shop in fall when local trees are turning color.

Holly (below)

the ground. These forms are sometimes grafted onto upright stems to create interesting, often weeping, plant forms, as is often done with weeping Japanese maples.

Foliage is one of the most enduring and important features a plant will provide in the garden. Leaves come in myriad colors, shapes, sizes, textures and arrangements. You can find shades of green, blue, red, purple, yellow, white or silver; variegated types have two or more colors combined on a single leaf. The variety of shapes is even more astounding, from short, sharply pointed needles to wide, rounded leaves the size of dinner plates. Leaf margins can be smooth, like those of many rhododendrons, or so finely divided the foliage appears fern-like, as with some Japanese maple cultivars. Foliage often varies seasonally, progressing from tiny, pale green spring buds to the vibrant colors of fall. Evergreen trees provide welcome greenery even when winter is at its wettest and coldest.

An entire garden can be designed based on varied foliage. Whether it forms a neutral backdrop or stands out in sharp contrast with the plants around it, foliage is a vital consideration. Variegated leaves can add an interesting note to the garden, especially in the evening.

Flowers are often more than enough reason to grow trees or shrubs that are dull or even unattractive the rest of the year, such as the goldenchain tree. Flowering of a species generally takes place over a few weeks or occasionally a month; very few woody plants flower for the entire summer.

Keep this limitation in mind when selecting woody plants. If you choose species with staggered flowering periods, you will always have something in bloom. You can achieve different but equally striking effects by grouping plants that flower at the same time or by spreading them out around the garden.

Fruit comes in many forms, including winged maple samaras, dangling birch catkins, spiny horsechestnut capsules and the more obviously 'fruity' Oregon grape berries and quince pomes. Fruit is often very attractive and provides interest in the garden in late summer and fall, when most plants are past their prime. When the fruit drops, however, it can create quite a mess and even a bad odor if it is allowed to rot on the ground. Choose the location of your fruiting tree carefully. If you know the fruit can be messy, don't plant near a patio or sidewalk. Most fruit isn't very troublesome, but keep in mind that there may be some clean-up required during and after the fruiting season. Olives, female ginkgo plants and even camellias can be a clean-up problem.

Bark is one of the most overlooked features of trees and shrubs. Species with interesting bark will greatly enhance your landscape, particularly in winter when the exposed bark on a deciduous tree may be one of the most interesting features of your garden. Bark can be smooth, ridged, furrowed, papery, scaly, exfoliating or colorful. A few trees valued for their interesting bark are birches, tulip trees, crape myrtles, Japanese maples and paperbark maples.

Crape myrtle has attractive flowers and bark (above)

Trident maple trunk (below)

Fragrance, though usually associated with flowers, is also a potential feature of the leaves, fruit and even wood of trees and shrubs. The flowering quinces, cedars, sweetboxes and lilacs are examples of plants with appealing scents. Try to plant a species whose fragrance you enjoy where the scent will waft into an open window. Make sure you check out the plant's growth habit prior to planting.

Branches fall somewhere between form and bark as a feature, and, like those two features, they can be an important winter attribute for the garden. Branches may have an unusual gnarled or twisted shape, or they may bear protective spines or thorns.

Growth rate and **life span**, though not really aesthetic features of woody plants, are nonetheless important aspects to consider. A fast-growing

Butterfly bush is a fast grower (above), lilac (below)

Flowering quince (below)

tree or shrub that grows 24" or more a year will mature quickly and can be used to fill in space in a new garden. A slow-growing tree or shrub that grows less than 12" a year may be more suitable in a space-limited garden. A short-lived plant appeals to some people because they enjoy changing their garden design or aren't sure exactly what they want in their garden. Short-lived plants usually mature quickly and therefore reach flowering age quickly as well. A long-lived tree is an investment in time. Some trees can take a human lifetime to reach their mature size, and some may not flower for 10 years after you plant them. You can enjoy a long-lived tree as it develops, and you will also leave a legacy for future generations, because the tree may very well outlive you.

Dwarf Alberta spruce is a slow grower (above)

GETTING STARTED

Before you fall in love with the idea of having a certain tree or shrub in your garden, it's important to consider the type of environment the species needs and whether any areas of your garden are appropriate for it. The best bet is to put your planting areas on what we call a plot plan. It doesn't have to be fancy or precisely measured. Some things to include are compass points, fences and structures in relation to the sun. The north side of the house certainly doesn't need a large shade tree. This tree belongs on the hot side of the house that faces south. The next step is to list plants you love and see if they are appropriate for your landscape needs. Keep in mind, it is easier to change an idea with an eraser than a shovel.

All plants are adapted to certain growing conditions in which they do best. Choosing plants to match your garden conditions is far more practical than trying to alter your garden to match the plants. On the other hand, it is through the use of trees and shrubs that we can best alter the conditions in a garden. Over time, a tree can change a sunny, exposed garden into a shaded one, and a hedge can turn a windswept area into a sheltered one. The woody plants you choose must be able to thrive in the garden as it exists now, or they may not live long enough to produce these changes in your garden. Light, soil conditions and exposure are all factors that will guide your selection.

As you plan, look at your garden as it exists now, but keep in mind the

changes trees and shrubs will bring. There are landscape CDs for your computer that can give you pictures of how your garden will look in 10 years or more, and some consultants specialize in doing 'virtual landscapes.' However, pen and paper may still be your best bet.

Light

Buildings, trees, fences, the time of day and the time of year influence the amount of light that reaches your garden. There are four basic levels of light in the garden: full sun, partial shade (partial sun), light shade and full shade. Some plants are adapted to a variety of light levels, but most have a preference for a narrower range.

Full sun locations receive direct sunlight all or most of the day. An example would be a location along a south-facing wall. *Partial shade* locations receive direct sun for part of the day and shade for the rest. An east- or west-facing wall gets only partial shade. *Light shade* locations receive shade most or all of the day, but with some sun getting through to ground level. The ground under a small-leaved tree is often lightly shaded, with dappled light visible on the ground beneath the tree. *Full shade* locations receive no direct sunlight. The north wall of a house is considered to be in full shade.

It is important to remember that exposure to sun may mean more intense heat in some regions than in others. On the coast, where the heat is generally more moderate, many trees and shrubs thrive in full sun, but inland the same plants may need partial or light shade to protect them

Aucuba grows well in full shade (above)

Birch provides light, dappled shade (below)

Camellia prefers acidic to neutral soil

from the summer heat. Additionally, the shady side of a building may shelter plants in the heat of summer but can cause a longer, colder winter than some plants can tolerate. You can use this situation to your advantage if, for example, you live on the coast and are trying to grow shrubs (such as lilacs) that need a good freeze in order to flower the following summer. In Northern California, there are shrubs selected for their ability to bloom regardless of the winter chill factor. Check with a local expert if you are unsure.

Soil

Plants have a unique relationship with the soil they grow in. Many important plant functions take place underground. Soil holds air, water, nutrients and organic matter. Plant roots depend upon these resources for growth, while using the soil to hold the plant body upright.

Soil particles are called either sand, silt or clay, depending on their size. The large particles of sandy soil do not compact easily and leave air pockets between them. As a result, water drains quickly from sandy soil, and nutrients tend to get washed away. Clay particles are so small they can be seen only through a microscope. Clay holds the most nutrients, but it also compacts easily and has little air space. Clay is slow to absorb water and equally slow to let it drain. Silt particles are intermediate in size—smaller than sand but larger than clay. Most soils are composed of a combination of sand, silt and clay and are called 'loams.' Along the Northern California coastal plain, you may also encounter serpentine—a combination of impenetrable rock with layers of clay—that requires the addition of organic matter. A 50-50 serpentine/planting mix is recommended.

Particle size is one factor in the drainage and moisture-holding properties of your soil; slope is another. Knowing how quickly the water drains out of your soil will help you decide whether you should plant moisture-loving or drought-tolerant plants. Doing a drainage test will give you the best idea of how the soil drains. Rocky soil on a hillside may drain very quickly, but don't confuse this with run-off. Water the hillside, then dig into the area. If it is at all dry, it will need the addition of organic matter until moisture absorbs into the planting location. Low-lying areas tend to retain water longer, and some areas may rarely drain at all. Moist areas suit plants that require a consistent water supply; constantly wet areas suit plants adapted to boggy conditions. Drainage can be improved in very wet areas by adding gravel to the soil, by installing some form of drainage tile or by building raised beds. We advise against adding sand to clay soils because it can easily make your soil as hard as concrete. Water retention in sandy or rocky soil can be improved by adding organic matter.

Another aspect of soil that is important to consider is the pH, a measure of acidity or alkalinity. Soil pH influences the availability of nutrients for plants. A pH of 7 is neutral; values lower than 7 are acidic and values higher than 7 are alkaline. Many soils in coastal areas tend to be acidic, whereas in other areas soils may be more alkaline. You can test your soil if you plan to amend it. Soil can be made more alkaline with the addition of horticultural lime. It is more difficult to acidify soil, but you can try adding horticultural sulfur or composted bark, leaves or needles. It is much easier to amend soil in a small area rather than in an entire garden. The soil in a raised bed or planter can easily be adjusted to suit a few plants whose soil requirements vary greatly from the conditions in your garden. Most plants prefer a neutral soil pH, between 6.5 and 7.5.

Drainage Test

If you are unsure that the spot you picked will drain well enough to prevent standing water, try this simple method of checking how quickly water drains from the soil. Dig a test hole 1' in diameter and 1' deep. Fill the hole to the top with water and let it drain completely. Fill the hole with water again and note the time. Note the time again when the water has completely drained from the hole. A drainage rate of ½" or less per hour is considered poor and will limit plant selection or may require expensive drainage work to alleviate the problem. Another option is to import soil to make mounds or use in raised planter beds.

Checking soil drainage rate (above & below)

Bigleaf hydrangea (above)

Aluminum sulfate can be added to many soils to acidify them. Aluminum is the element that turns hydrangeas blue when it is present in low pH (acidic) soils.

Exposure

Exposure is a very important consideration in gardens that include woody plants. Wind, heat, cold, rain and rarely snow are the elements to which your garden may be exposed, and some plants are more tolerant than others of the potential damage these forces can cause. Buildings, walls, fences, hills and existing hedges or other shrubs and trees can all influence your garden's exposure.

Wind can cause extensive damage to woody plants, particularly to evergreens in winter. Plants can become dehydrated in windy locations because they may not be able to draw water out of the soil fast enough to replace that lost through the leaves. Broad-leaved evergreens, such as rhododendrons and azaleas, are most at risk from winter dehydration, so a sheltered site is often recommended for them. Woody plants often make excellent windbreaks that will shelter other plants in the garden, but strong, gusting winds can cause even bigger problems if large trees are

Hedges provide excellent shelter (below)

blown over. Windbreaks should be made up of trees that are flexible in the wind or that are planted far enough from any buildings to avoid extensive damage should they blow over. Hedges and trees temper the effect of the wind without the turbulence that is created on the leeward side of a more solid structure like a wall or fence.

Hardiness zones should be used only as guidelines. Rose daphne, for example, is listed as a Zone 4 plant but can thrive in Zone 3. Don't be afraid to try species that are not listed as hardy for your area. Plants are incredibly adaptable and just might surprise you.

Here are some tips for growing out-of-zone plants.

- Before planting, observe your garden on a frosty morning. Are there areas that escape frost? Are you in a frost-free area? These are potential sites for tender plants.
- Shelter tender plants from the prevailing wind.
- Mulch young plants in fall with a thick layer of clean organic mulch, such as bark chips, bark dust, composted leaves or compost mixed with peat moss, or with special insulating blankets you can find at garden centers. Ensure organic mulches have a minimum depth of 12" for good winter protection. Mulch for at least the first couple of winters.
- In regions with snow, cover an entire frost-tender shrub with salt-free snow for winter. You can also cover or wrap it with burlap or horticultural cloth, or if it is in a container or planter, place it under shelter or against a house for protection.

Full sun exposure (above)

Shelter hollies from drying winds (below)

PURCHASING WOODY PLANTS

Now that you have thought about what sorts of features you like and what range of growing conditions your garden offers, you can select the plants. Any reputable garden center should have a good selection of popular woody plants. Finding more unusual specimens may require a few phone calls and a trip to a more specialized nursery.

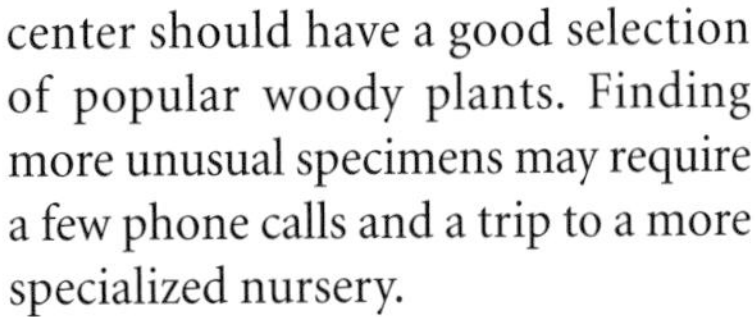

Many garden centers and nurseries offer a one-year warranty on trees and shrubs, but because trees take a long time to mature, it is always in your best interest to choose the healthiest plants. Never purchase weak, damaged or diseased plants, even if they cost less. Avoid the 'I want to take it home and make it well' syndrome. Examine the bark and avoid any plants with visible damage. Observe the leaf and flower buds. If they are dry and fall off easily, the plant has been deprived of moisture. The stem or stems should be strong, supple and unbroken. The rootball should be soft and moist when touched. Do not buy a plant with a dry rootball. The growth should be even and appropriate for the species. Shrubs should be bushy and branched to the ground. Trees should have a strong leader. Selecting a healthy tree or shrub will give it the best chance in your garden.

Woody plants are available in three forms.

Bare-root stock has roots surrounded by nothing but moist sawdust or peat moss, with or without a plastic bag. Non-packaged materials are usually a better choice, because they have a larger root system. The roots must be kept moist and cool, and planting should take place as soon as possible. Bare-root stock is the least expensive way to purchase plants of the three forms, and it is available in Northern California from mid-December to mid-March. Shrubs from mail-order companies usually come this way.

Balled-and-burlapped (B & B) stock comes with the roots surrounded by soil and wrapped in burlap, often secured with a wire cage for larger plants. The plants are usually field grown and then balled and burlapped the year they are sold. It is essential that the rootball remain moist. Large trees are available in this form as are rhododendrons and Japanese maples. Be aware that the soil and rootball are often very heavy, and there may be an extra expense for delivery and planting. Balled-and-burlapped stock is usually less expensive to purchase than container-grown stock. The B & B season is very short in Northern California, so it is advisable to shop in December or January for the best quality.

Container plants are grown in pots filled with potting soil and have established root systems. This form is the most common at garden centers and nurseries. It is the most expensive way to buy plants because the plants have been nurtured for months or years in the container. Container stock establishes very quickly after planting and can be planted almost any time during the growing season. It is also easy to transplant. When choosing a container-grown plant, make sure it hasn't been in the container too long. If the roots are encircling the

Temporary winter storage (above)

Fall selection is sometimes limited (below)

inside of the pot, then the plant has become root-bound. A root-bound tree or shrub will not establish well, and as the roots mature and thicken, they can choke and kill the plant. Be aware that some field-grown stock may be placed in plastic or other containers instead of burlap; ask if you are not sure. Such plants must be treated like balled-and-burlapped stock.

Bigger is not always better when it comes to choosing woody plants for your garden. Both research and observation have shown that smaller plants establish better, grow up healthier and are more robust than larger plants.

Plants can be damaged by improper transportation and handling. You can lift bare-root stock by the stem, but do not lift any other trees or shrubs by the trunk or branches. Rather, lift by the rootball or container, or if the plant is too large to lift, place it on a tarp or mat and drag it. Remember, too, that the heat produced inside a car can quickly dehydrate a plant. If you are using a truck for transport, lay the plant down or cover it to shield it from the wind. Many growers cover plants with shade cloth to protect them from the wind. Even a short trip through the city can be traumatic for a plant. Going down the freeway at 80 miles an hour in an open truck isn't very healthy for any plant. Avoid mechanical damage, such as rubbing or breakage of the plant, during transport.

At home, water the plant if it is dry and keep it in a sheltered location until you plant it. Remove damaged growth and any broken branches, but do no other pruning. Plant your tree or shrub as soon as possible. A bare-root tree or shrub should be planted in a large container of potting soil if it will not be planted outdoors immediately.

Root-bound plant

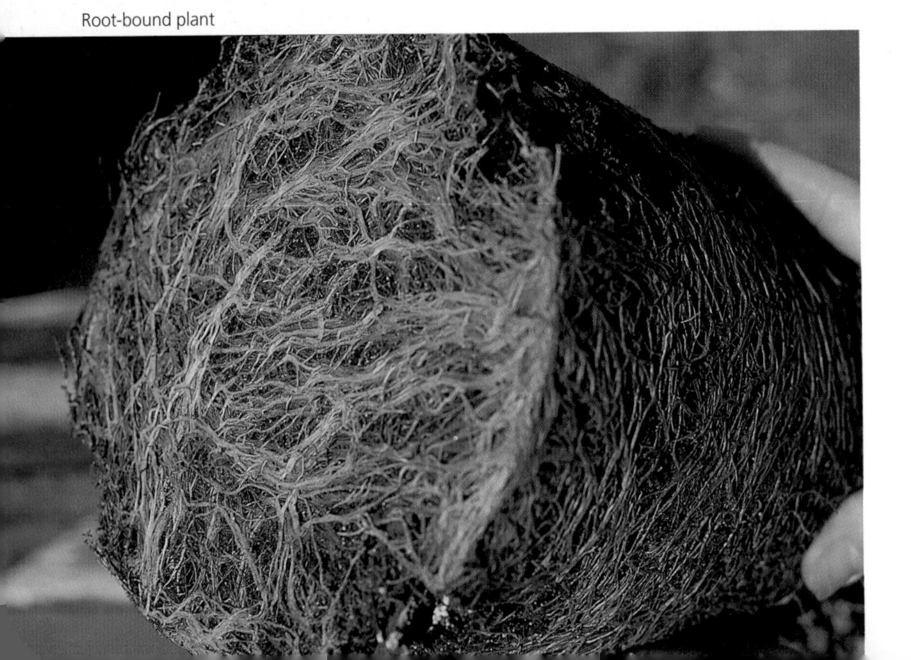

PLANTING TREES & SHRUBS

Before you pick up a shovel and start digging, step back for a moment and make sure the site you're considering is appropriate. The most important thing to check is the location of any underground wires or pipes. Even if you don't damage anything by digging, the tree roots may cause trouble in the future, or if there is a problem with the pipes or wires you may have to cut down the tree in order to service them. Most utility companies will, at no charge, come to your house and locate any underground lines. Prevent injury and save time and money by locating utilities before you dig.

Check also the mature plant size. The plant you have in front of you is probably pretty small. Once it reaches its mature height and spread, will it still fit in the space you have chosen? Is it far enough away from the house, the driveway and the sidewalk? Will it hit the overhang of the house? Are there any overhead power lines? If you are planting several shrubs, make sure they won't grow too close together once they are mature. The rule of thumb for spacing: add the mature spreads together and divide by two. For example, when planting a shrub with an expected spread of 4' and another with an expected spread of 6', you would plant them 5' apart. For hedges and windbreaks, the spacing should be one-half to two-thirds the spread of the mature plant to ensure there is no observable space between plants when they are fully grown.

When to Plant

For the most part, trees and shrubs can be planted any time of year, though some seasons are better for the plants and more convenient than others. Fall is the best time to plant trees and shrubs in Northern California. The root system continues to grow in through winter and will be more established before the heat of summer. Bare-root stock must be planted in winter because it

Well-planted shrub beds

I've often been asked 'How many plants do I need to cover a hillside with plants that grow 5' in each direction?' Let's say you have 800 sq. ft to plant, and your plants cover a 5' x 5' area. That is 25 sq. ft per plant. Divide 25 into 800 and you get 32 plants that are needed to cover the area. Finally, double-check the conditions. Will the soil drainage be adequate? Will the plant get the right amount of light? Is the site very windy? Remember, it's easier to start with the plant in the right spot and in the best conditions you can give it. Planning ahead saves time and money in the long run.

is available only at that time, and it must be planted as soon as possible to avoid moisture loss. B & B is only available in winter, from December to February. If the plant comes in a heavy soil, we recommend that this soil be washed off before planting, especially for such plants as rhododendrons and Japanese maples. Container stock can be planted at any time of year, with the exception of frost-sensitive plants, such as cape plumbago and princess flower, which are typically planted in the spring after all danger of frost has passed.

Many gardeners avoid planting during the hottest and driest part of summer, mainly because of the extra work that may be involved with supplemental watering. Because irrigation is a way of life here, avoiding summer may not be an issue. Not many gardeners enjoy planting in the winter rains. In our colder winter regions in the northeast and east, planting in spring is recommended because it gives the plants a chance to become established before the next winter sets in.

The time of day to plant is also a consideration. Avoid planting during the heat of the day. Planting in the morning, in the evening or on cloudy days will be easier on both you and the plant. It is a good idea to plant as soon as possible after you bring your specimen home. If you have to store the tree or shrub for a short time before planting, keep it out of the direct sun and ensure the rootball remains moist. Keep in mind that most nurseries water their plants every other day, (every day for 4" pots).

Sizing up the hole (above), digging the hole (below)

Adding organic matter to backfill (below)

Preparing the Hole

Trees and shrubs should always be planted at the depth at which they were growing—just above the roots if you are unsure what the depth was for bare-root stock. You should notice a different color at the base of the trunk noting the soil line in the field. The depth in the center of the hole should be equal to the depth of the rootball or container, whereas the depth around the edges of the hole should be twice the depth of the rootball or container. Making the center higher will prevent the plant from sinking as the soil settles and will encourage excess water to drain away from the plant.

Be sure that the plants are not set too deep, particularly in a moist climate, because roots can't breath properly and the bark and crown are likely to rot if they are even a few

Rhododendron should be planted so the top of the root mass is slightly above the soil line

inches too deep. Most potted field-grown trees are planted too deep in the pot to help keep the freshly dug tree from tipping over, and there may be mulch on top of the soil as well. Planting such a tree to the same depth as the level in the pot is not a good idea. Scrape off the soil until you find the root mass, and then plant so that the top of the root mass is slightly above soil level.

The diameter of the hole for balled-and-burlapped and container stock should be two to three times the width of the rootball or container. It is also a good idea to loosen the top layer of soil around the edges of the hole with a garden fork or similar tool. In heavy clay soils or serpentine, you may have to enlarge the initial excavation.

The soil in the rootball or container is not likely to be the same as the soil you just removed from the hole. In such cases, you will have to create a transition zone from the rootball soil to the undisturbed soil by adding compost and/or planting mix to the backfill soil. Heavy clay soils can be mixed half-and-half with compost and/or planting mix. Light sandy soils can have up to one-third compost and/or planting mix added. If the soil of the rootball is the same as the soil you just dug up, then no soil amendment is necessary.

When the plant roots grow into the amended backfill soil, they are generally introduced to and can acclimatize to the existing, on-site soil. The roots then have no problem growing into the undisturbed soil. What you don't want is to have two different soil types in direct contact with each other, which creates an interface that water and roots have difficulty penetrating. It is also good practice to roughen up the sides and bottom of the hole to aid in root transition. The organic matter in the amended backfill soil that is adjacent to the existing soil will leach into the existing soil, which allows for further root development beyond the hole. Earthworms will also transport organic matter into the existing soil.

If the roots do not venture beyond the immediate area of the hole, the tree or shrub will be weaker and more susceptible to problems, and the encircling roots could eventually choke the plant. A tree will also be more vulnerable to blowdown in a strong wind. Do not backfill with straight planting mix either, which also creates a soil interface.

Planting Balled-and-Burlapped Stock

Burlap was originally made of natural fibers. It could be left wrapped around the rootball and would eventually decompose. Modern burlap may or may not be made of natural fibers, and it can be very difficult to tell the difference. Synthetic fibers will not decompose and will eventually choke the roots. To be sure your new plant has a healthy future, it is always best to remove the burlap from around the rootball. If there is a wire basket holding the burlap in place, it should be removed as well. Strong wire cutters may be needed to get the basket off.

With the basket removed, sit the still-burlapped plant on the center mound in the hole. Lean the plant to one side and roll the burlap down to the ground. When you lean the plant in the opposite direction, you should be able to pull the burlap out from under the roots. If you know the burlap is natural and decide to leave it in place, be sure to cut back the top so none of it shows above ground level. Exposed burlap can wick moisture out of the soil and prevent your new plant from getting enough water.

If possible, plants should be oriented so that they face the same direction that they have always grown in. Don't worry if you aren't sure—the plant will just take a little longer to get established. As a general rule, the leafiest side was probably facing south.

Past horticultural wisdom suggested removing some of the top branches when planting to make up for the roots lost when the plant was dug out of the field. The theory was that the roots could not provide enough water to the leaves, so top growth should be removed to achieve 'balance.' We now know that top growth—where photosynthesis occurs

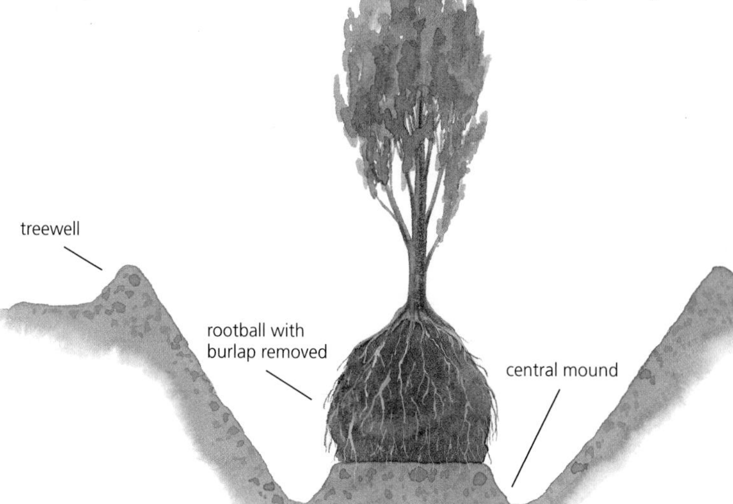

Planting balled-and-burlapped stock

and thus where energy is produced—is necessary for root development. The new tree or shrub might drop some leaves, but don't be alarmed; the plant is doing its own balancing. A very light pruning will not adversely affect the plant, but remove only those branches that have been damaged during transportation and planting. Leave the new plant to settle in for a year or two before you start any formative pruning.

Planting Container Stock

Containers are usually made of plastic or pressed fiber. All types of containers should be removed before planting. Although some containers appear to be made of peat moss, they do not decompose well. The roots will be unable to penetrate the pot sides, and the fiber will wick moisture away from the roots.

Container stock is very easy to plant. Gently remove or cut off the container and observe the root mass to see if the plant is root-bound. If roots are circling around the inside of the container, they should be loosened or sliced. Any large roots encircling the soil or growing into the center of the root mass instead of outward should be removed before planting. A sharp pair of hand pruners or a pocketknife will work well for this task.

Place the plant on the central mound. Orientation is less important with container-grown stock than with balled-and-burlapped stock because container plants have been moved around during their development.

Planting Bare-root Stock

Remove the plastic and sawdust from the roots. Fan out the roots and center the plant over the central mound in the hole. The central mound for bare-root stock should be cone-shaped and larger than the mound for other types of plant stock. Use the cone to help spread out and support the roots. The hole for bare-root stock should be a little deeper than the fully extended roots and wide enough to work comfortably in. Amend the backfill soil as mentioned above.

Backfill

When the plant is standing in the hole straight up, now is the time to replace the soil. Backfill should reach the same depth the plant was grown at previously, or just above the rootball. If planting into a heavier soil, raise the plant about 1" to improve surface drainage, allowing water to move away from the crown and roots. Keep graft unions aboveground if your plant is grafted stock. If you have amended the backfill soil, ensure it is well mixed before putting it into the hole.

When backfilling, it is important to have good root-to-soil contact for initial stability and good establishment. Large air pockets remaining after backfilling could cause unwanted settling. The old method was to tamp or step down the backfilled soil, but the risk of soil compaction and root damage has caused this practice to fall out of favor. Use water to settle the soil gently around the roots and in the hole, taking care not to drown the plant. It is a good idea

1. Gently remove container

2. Ensure proper planting depth

3. Backfill with amended soil

4. Settle backfilled soil with water

5. Ensure newly planted shrub is well watered

6. Add mulch

Russian olive in its new home

to backfill in small amounts rather than all at once. Add some soil, then water it down, repeating until the hole is full. Stockpile any remaining soil after backfilling and use it to top up the soil level around the plant after the backfill settles. Do not put any stockpiled soil directly over the rootball. Ensure good surface drainage away from the new transplant. Do not allow the plant to sit in a puddle.

It is a good idea to mulch around all new plantings with either cedar bark or shredded redwood bark. These products will stay put, unlike pebble bark or peat moss. They also contain a natural fungicide so that there is no danger to the base of the plant.

Staking

Staking provides support to a plant while the roots establish. It is not recommended, however, unless absolutely necessary, because unstaked trees develop more roots and stronger trunks. Generally, newly planted trees will be able to stand on their own

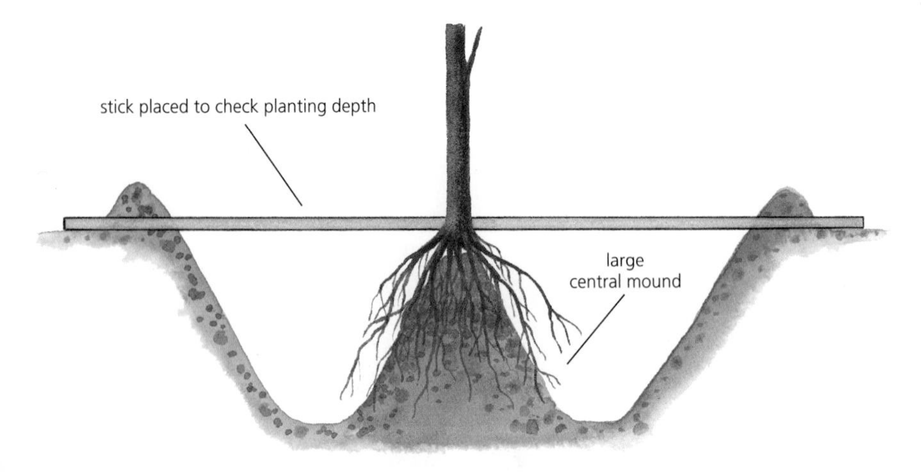

Planting bare-root stock

without staking. Some weak-stemmed trees will require staking, but the stakes should be removed as soon as the tree can stand on its own. The exceptions to this rule are when training standards and woody vines. In windy locations, trees over 5' tall may need some support until the roots establish, to prevent them from blowing over.

There are two common methods for staking newly planted trees. For both methods you can use either wood or metal stakes.

The **two-stake** method is used for small trees, about 5–6' tall. Drive stakes into the undisturbed soil just outside the planting hole on opposite sides of the tree, 180° apart. Driving stakes in right beside the newly planted tree can damage the roots and will not provide adequate support. Tie string, rope, cable or wire to the stakes. The end that goes around the trunk of the tree should be wide, belt-like strapping that will not injure the trunk. Your local nursery should have ties designed for this purpose. Attach at a height of about 3–4' above the ground.

The **three-stake** method is used for larger trees and trees in areas subject to strong or shifting winds. The technique is similar to the two-stake method, but with three stakes evenly spaced around the tree.

Here are a few points to keep in mind, regardless of the staking method used:

- Don't wrap rope, wire or cable directly around a tree trunk—always use non-damaging materials.

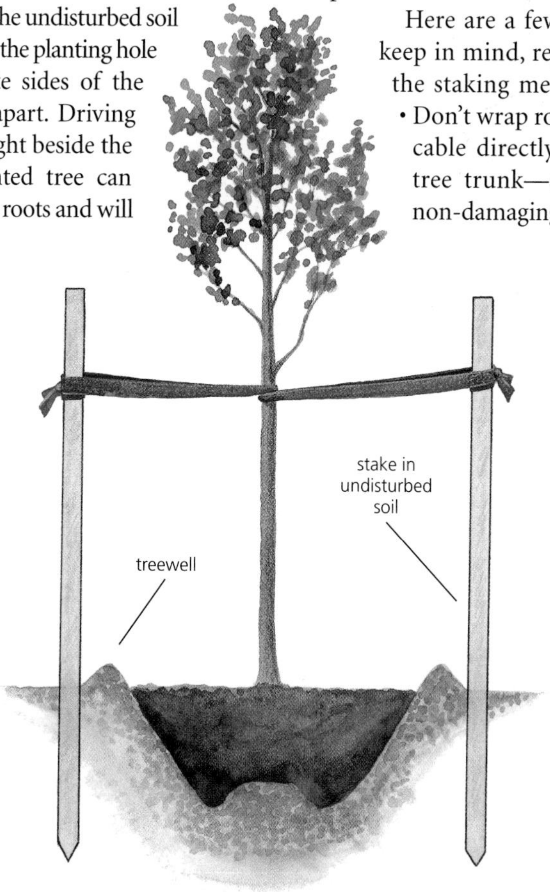

Two-stake method

- Readjust the strapping every two to three months to prevent any rubbing or girdling injury.
- Never tie trees so firmly that they can't move. Young trees need to be able to move in the wind so that the trunk strengthens and so that roots develop more thickly in appropriate places to compensate for the prevailing wind.
- Don't leave the stakes in place too long. One year is sufficient for almost all trees. The stake should be there only long enough to allow the roots some time to fill in. The tree will actually be weaker if the stake is left for too long, and over time the ties can damage the trunk and weaken or kill the tree.
- With deciduous trees, the best time to remove the stakes is in winter when the tree has gone dormant.

Treewells

A treewell is created by building up a low mound of soil in a ring around the outer edge of the filled-in planting hole. When you water your tree, this ring will keep the water from running away before it soaks down to the roots. Although a treewell is not necessary, it can make it easier to keep your new plant well watered until it becomes established. The treewell will be most useful during dry periods and should be removed during rainy periods to prevent the roots from becoming waterlogged. Remove after one to two years.

Transplanting

If you plan your garden carefully, you should rarely need to move trees or shrubs. Some woody plants (indicated as such under their individual descriptions) resent being moved once established, and for these species transplanting should be avoided wherever possible. For all species, the younger the tree or shrub, the more likely it is to re-establish successfully when moved to a new location.

Woody plants inevitably lose most of their root mass when they are transplanted from one location to another. The size of the tree or shrub will determine the minimum size of the rootball that must be dug out in order for the plant to survive. A general guideline is that for every 1" of main stem width, measured 6–12" above the ground, you need to excavate a rootball a *minimum* of 12" wide, and preferably larger. Trees with a trunk diameter of 2" or greater should be moved by professionals with heavy equipment. The moving of established natives, such as strawberry tree, should never be attempted by non-professional tree movers. Smaller plants should only be moved if absolutely necessary and only in winter months.

Some older sources recommend pruning the roots of a tree or shrub a year or so before transplanting. We strongly discourage this practice. It adds an additional, unnecessary stress before the major trauma of transplanting, making the plant more vulnerable to pests and diseases and reducing the likelihood that it will re-establish successfully. The only time roots need to be pruned is just before you plant them into your garden, and only if the roots are broken, shredded or damaged in some way.

CARING FOR WOODY PLANTS

The care you give your new tree or shrub in the first year or two after planting is the most important. During this period of establishment, it is critical to keep the plant well watered and fed, to remove competing weeds and to avoid all mechanical damage. Be careful with lawn mowers and string trimmers, which can quickly girdle the base of the tree and cut off the flow of food and water between roots and branches. Remember that whatever you do to the top of the plant affects the roots, and vice versa.

Once trees and shrubs are established, they generally require minimal care. A few basic maintenance tasks, performed on a regular basis, will save time and trouble in the long run.

Weeding

Weeding is a consideration for trees and shrubs in a garden bed. Weeds compete with plants for space, light and nutrients, so keep them under control and give your garden ornamentals the upper hand. When pulling weeds or scuffing the soil with a hoe, avoid damaging the delicate feeder roots of shallow-rooted shrubs and trees. Weed killers will probably not kill your woody plants but can weaken them, leaving them susceptible to attack by pests and diseases. A layer of mulch is the best way to suppress weeds.

I have found that a fall application of weed seed inhibitor, such as Surflan™, can prevent weeds before they start to grow and save several hours of unproductive gardening. Weed suppression is especially important around groundcovers and close-growing shrubs.

Mulching

Mulch is an important gardening tool. It helps soil retain moisture, it buffers soil temperatures and it prevents soil erosion during heavy rains or strong winds. Mulch prevents weed seeds from germinating by blocking out the light, and it can deter pests and help prevent diseases. It keeps lawn mowers and line trimmers away from plants, reducing the chance of damage. Mulch can also add aesthetic value to a planting.

Organic mulches can consist of compost, bark chips, shredded leaves, cedar bark, redwood bark and grass clippings. These mulches are desirable—they add nutrients to the soil as they break down. Because they break down, however, they must be replenished on a regular basis. Inorganic mulches consist of materials such as stones, gravel or plastic, which do not break down and so do not have to be topped up regularly. When using stones or gravel, soil filling will always be in the spaces. You may wind up with a major maintenance challenge in that weed seeds will find haven among the rocks in successive years as soil fills the spaces. An application of weed seed inhibitor in early fall will prevent the weeds in the first place. Inorganic mulches can disrupt the microbial balance by preventing worms and other microorganisms from moving freely to the surface.

For good weed suppression, the mulch layer should be at least 3" thick and be placed on top of a layer of newspaper. Avoid piling mulch up

Organic shredded bark mulch

around the trunk or stems at the base of the plant because doing so can encourage fungal decay and rot. Try to maintain a mulch-free zone immediately around the trunk or stems.

Watering

The weather, type of plant, type of soil and time of year all influence the amount of watering that will be required. Pay attention to the wind, because it can dry out soil and plants quickly. Different plants require different amounts of water; some, such as birches, will grow in waterlogged soil, while others, like many pine species, prefer a dry, gravelly soil. Heavy, clay soils retain water for a longer period than light, sandy soils. Plants will need more water when they are on slopes, when they are flowering, during windy days and when they are producing fruit. The rule of thumb for newly transplanted materials is to water every other day for at least three weeks. After that period, the roots of the plant should have entered the prepared soil. Twice a week for a month is sufficient unless you see the plant wilt. You should then be able to go to a once-a-week watering schedule. After the first couple of years, most plants in Northern California will need little or no water during the summer. The exception would be the shade-loving plants, such as camellias and azaleas.

Plants are good at letting us know when they are thirsty. Look for wilted, flagging leaves and twigs as a sign of water deprivation. Make sure your trees and shrubs are well watered in fall until the winter rains start to take over. Be aware that we may get rain early in fall and then a dry spell of several weeks. During this time it may be necessary to apply water, especially for plants under the eaves of houses, which traditionally receive little or no watering during the rainy season.

Once trees and shrubs are established, they will likely need watering only during periods of excessive drought. To keep water use to a minimum, avoid watering in the heat of the day because much will be lost to evaporation. Instead, water in the morning or evening when it is cooler. Also, use lots of organic matter in the soil to help the soil absorb and retain water. Mulch also helps prevent water loss. Finally, collect and use rainwater whenever possible.

Many gardeners and homeowners like to have both trees and grass on their properties, and very often they are grown in the same location. Trees and turfgrass have different water and nutrient needs, and our management practices in these situations tend to benefit either the lawn or the trees, but not both. Lawns often get watered frequently and lightly. When trees and lawns get this type of watering, tree roots tend to be right at the surface. This situation causes all kinds of problems, such as uneven lawn surfaces and cracked sidewalks. Nutritional differences can cause problems for trees because turfgrass is often fertilized throughout summer, which can promote tree problems.

We advise not to grow turfgrass right up to the base of trees and shrubs. Have a mulched, grass-free area under the tree or shrub at least out to the dripline. If you have turfgrass growing up to the tree, wait until the grass is starting to show signs of wilt; then deeply water the whole area. Note that many trees and shrubs should not be planted in lawns nor near driveways because of the potential for root damage to the hardscape.

FERTILIZING

Most garden soils provide all the nutrients plants need, particularly if you mix compost or other organic fertilizers into the soil each year. Not all plants have the same nutritional requirements, however. Some plants are heavy feeders, while others thrive in poor soils. Be aware of the feeding requirements of the tree or shrub you choose. Be sure to use the recommended quantity of fertilizer, because too much does more harm than good. Fertilizer applied in too high a concentration can easily burn roots. Chemical fertilizers are more concentrated and therefore can cause more problems than organic fertilizers. Make sure to check out the new organic fertilizers on the market that contain soil microbes that help the soil come into balance.

Granular fertilizers consist of small, dry particles that can be spread with a fertilizer spreader or by hand. Slow-release types reduce the risk of over application because the nutrients are released gradually over the growing season. One application per year is normally sufficient; applying the fertilizer in early spring will provide nutrients for spring growth. In garden beds they can be mixed into the soil.

Tree spikes are slow-release fertilizers that are quick and easy to use. Pound the spikes into the ground around the dripline of the tree or

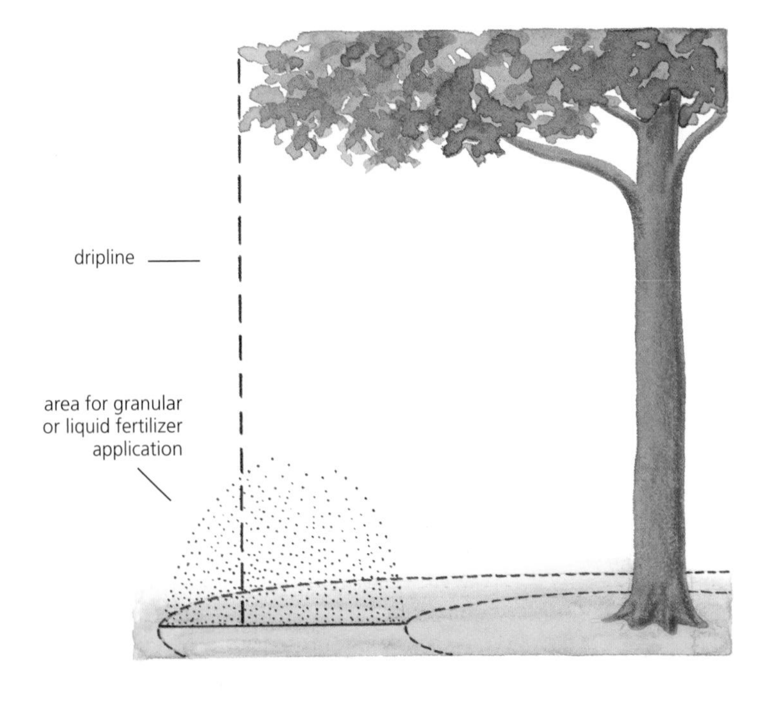

shrub, avoiding any roots. These spikes work very well for fertilizing trees in lawns, because grass tends to consume most of the nutrients released from surface applications.

Fertilizing is done to correct a visible nutrient deficiency, correct a deficiency identified by a soil and tissue test, increase vegetative, flower or fruit growth and increase the vigor of the plant.

If fertilizer is not applied correctly or not needed, your tree may not benefit. In fact, it may increase the susceptibility to some pests and may accelerate decline of the tree.

If you are unsure if your trees and shrubs need fertilizing, consult your local qualified nursery professional for advice. They are trained to spot plant problems, including nutrient deficiencies, by observation. You can take a leaf sample to the nursery professional, but note to always seal the sample in a clear plastic envelope or bag.

For trees and shrubs, a soil test or a foliar tissue test alone may give false readings. Leaves may show a nutrient deficiency; the soil may show an abundance but the nutrient is tied up by pH. Getting both tests done gives an excellent idea of fertility needs or problems.

Soil tests should include salt index, especially for arid areas. Use fertilizers with a low-salt index, such as bonemeal, bloodmeal or well-rotted manure. High-salt fertilizers increase the risk of root burn (desiccation). Avoid using fast-acting fertilizers.

If you do not wish to encourage fast growth, do not fertilize. Remember that most trees and shrubs do not need fertilizer. Fall fertilizing with some chemical fertilizers is not recommended because they may encourage tender growth that is easily damaged in winter. Allowing leaf litter to remain on the ground after the leaves fall in autumn promotes natural nutrient cycling of nitrogen and other elements in the soil. Do not fertilize trees during times of drought because roots do not absorb nutrients during drought.

Princess flower benefits from once-a-month feedings

Late-fall application of organic fertilizers is recommended because the winter rains will allow what I call seepage of the material deep into the root zone. Organic fertilizer depends on the action of the soil microbes to break down the fertilizer into nutrients the plant can use. Because microbial action decreases as the soil temperature decreases in late fall and through winter, the plant won't have any frost-sensitive growth.

PRUNING

Pruning maintains the health and attractive shape of a plant; increases the quality and yield of fruit; controls and directs growth; and creates interesting plant forms and shapes, such as espalier, topiary and bonsai. Pruning is possibly the most important maintenance task—and the easiest to mess up. Fortunately for new gardeners, it is not difficult to learn and is quite enjoyable if done correctly from the beginning.

Proper pruning combines knowledge and skill. General knowledge about how woody plants grow and specific knowledge about the growth habits of your particular plant can help you avoid pruning mistakes that can ruin a plant's shape or make it susceptible to disease and insect damage.

If you are unsure about pruning, take a pruning course or hire a professional, such as a certified ISA (International Society of Arborists) member. Pruning courses are offered by local garden centers, botanical gardens, adult education courses and master gardeners. Certified professionals understand the plants and have the specialty pruning equipment to do a proper job. They might even be willing to show you some pruning basics. You should always call a professional to prune a tree growing near a power line or other hazardous area, or to prune a large branch that could damage a building, fence, car or pedestrian when it falls.

Plants are genetically programmed to grow to a certain size, and they will always try to reach that potential. If

you are spending a lot of time pruning to keep a tree or shrub in check, the plant is probably wrong for that location. It cannot be emphasized enough how important it is to consider the mature size of a plant before you put it into the ground.

When to Prune

Many gardeners are unsure about what time of year they should prune. Knowing when a plant flowers is the easiest way to know when to prune. Trees and shrubs that flower in the early part of the year, before about July, such as boxleaf azaras and forsythias, should be pruned after they are finished flowering. These plants form flower buds for the following year over summer and fall. Pruning just after the current year's flowers fade allows plenty of time for the next year's flowers to develop, without removing any of the current season's blooms. Trees and shrubs that flower in about July or later, such as hardy hibiscus, can be pruned early in the year. These plants form flower buds on new wood as the season progresses, and pruning in the late dormant season just before the new growth begins will encourage the best growth and flowering.

In Northern California, the most dormant time for trees and shrubs is a six- to eight-week window from the last week in December to mid-February. This period is the best time to prune most trees, with the exception of frost-sensitive plants, such as cape plumbago and rhododendron, which are pruned after all danger of frost has passed.

Pineapple-shaped shrubs (above)

Pom-pom topiary (above)

Bonsai mini-topiary at Filoli (below)

Trees and shrubs vary greatly in their pruning needs. Some plants, such as boxwoods, can handle heavy pruning and shearing, while other plants, such as flowering cherries, may be killed if given the same treatment. The amount of pruning also depends on your reasons for doing it; much less work is involved in simply tidying the growth, for example, than in creating an elaborate topiary specimen. Inspect trees and shrubs annually for any dead, diseased or awkwardly growing branches and to determine what pruning, if any, is needed.

Some plants, such as maples, have a heavy flow of sap in spring. The best time to prune these plants is in January and early February. Pruning at this time lessens the incidence of insects and disease. Take care when pruning any trees in the late dormant season because many canker-causing organisms are active at this time.

Pruning trees in fall is not recommended because a number of wood-rotting fungi species release spores at that time.

Always prune out any dead, diseased, damaged, rubbing and crossing branches as soon as you discover them, at any time of year.

When Not to Prune

Do not prune trees or shrubs when their buds have started swelling and the new growth is emerging. Wait until the leaves have fully formed and flowers are spent before pruning. This caution is particularly important for the heavy bleeding trees such as birch.

Professional tree service

The Kindest Cut

Making proper pruning cuts cannot be emphasized enough. Proper cuts minimize the area where insects and disease can attack. They are also made where the plant is most efficient at taking care of the wound. **Do not make flush cuts and do not leave stubs—they will cause a number of tree problems.**

Using the right tools makes pruning easier and more effective. The size of the branch being cut determines the tool to use. **Hand pruners** are used for cutting branches up to 3/4" in diameter. Using hand pruners for cutting larger stems increases the risk of damage and can be physically strenuous. **Loppers** are long-handled pruners used for branches up to 1 1/2" in diameter. Loppers are good for removing old stems. Hand pruners and loppers must be properly oriented when making a cut. The blade of the hand pruners or loppers should be to the plant side of the cut and the hook to the side being removed. If the cut is made with the hook toward the plant, the cut will be ragged and slow to heal.

Pruning saws have teeth specially designed to cut through green wood. They can be used to cut branches up to 6" in diameter and sometimes larger. Pruning saws are easier to use and much safer than chainsaws. **Hedge clippers** or **shears** are good for shearing and shaping hedges.

Make sure your tools are sharp and clean before you begin any pruning task. If the branch you are cutting is diseased, you will need to sterilize the tool before using it again. A solution of bleach and water (1 part

Proper hand pruner orientation (above)

Pom-pom topiary (below)

Heading back cuts

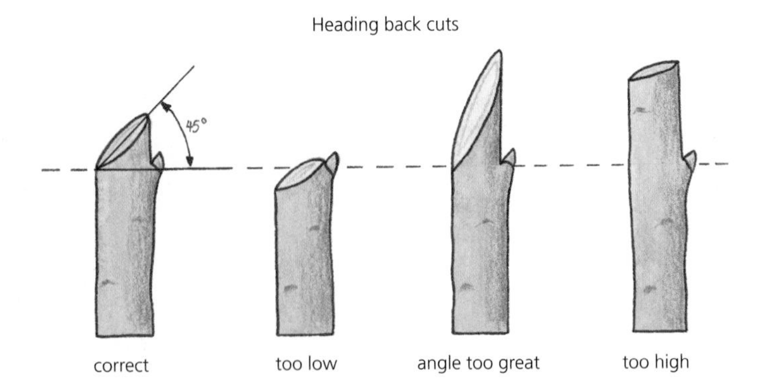

bleach to 10 parts water) is effective for cleaning and sterilizing. Sterilizing is a must when controlling blight and other systemic diseases.

You should have a basic familiarity with the following types of pruning cuts.

Cutting back to a bud is used for shortening a branch, redirecting growth or maintaining the size of a tree or shrub. The cut should be made slightly less than ¼" above a bud. If the cut is too far away from or too close to the bud, the wound will not heal properly. Make sure to cut back to buds that are pointing in the direction you want the new growth to grow in. For any plants with oppositely arranged leaves, cut straight across the stem about ¼" above a pair of buds. This type of cut should only be done on one- to two-year-old wood. Otherwise, it is a topping cut and unhealthy for the tree.

Cutting to a lateral branch is used to shorten limbs and redirect growth. This cut is similar to cutting back to a bud. The diameter of the branch you are cutting back to must be at least one-third and preferably half of the diameter of the branch you are cutting off, otherwise it is a topping cut. The cut should be made slightly less than ¼" above the lateral branch and should line up with the angle of the branch. Make cuts at an

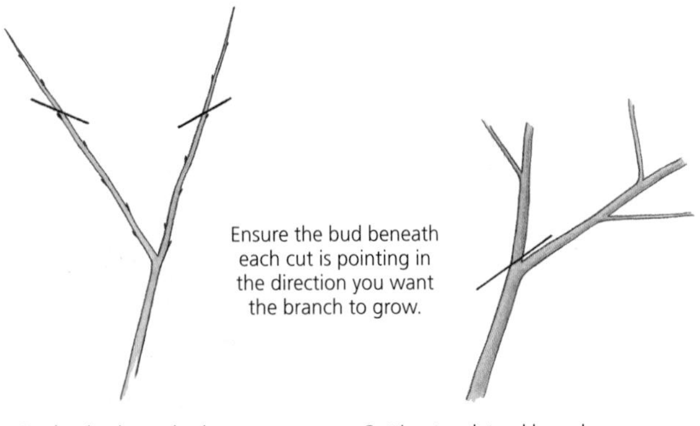

Cutting back to a bud

Cutting to a lateral branch

angle whenever possible so that rain doesn't sit on the open wound.

Removing limbs can be a complicated operation for large branches. Because of the large size of the wound, it is critical to cut in the correct place—at the branch collar—to ensure quick healing. The cut must be done in steps to avoid damaging the bark. The first cut is on the underside of the branch a short distance from the trunk of the tree. The purpose of this cut is to prevent bark from peeling down the tree when the second cut causes the main part of the branch to fall. The first cut should be 4–6" up from the crotch and should extend one-third of the way through the branch. The second cut is made about 2–4" further up the branch from the first cut and is made from the top of the branch. This cut removes the majority of the branch. The final cut should be made just above the branch collar. The plant tissues at the branch collar quickly create a barrier to disease and insects.

The use of pruning paint or paste has been much debated. The current

Pruning can create interesting forms

consensus is that these substances do more harm than good. Trees and shrubs have a natural ability to create a barrier between living wood and dead and decaying sections. An unpainted cut will eventually heal over, but a cut treated with paint or paste may never heal properly.

To prune or cut down large trees, it is best to hire a certified arborist. These professionals are trained for the task and have the necessary equipment and insurance. Many fences, cars and even houses have been damaged by people who simply

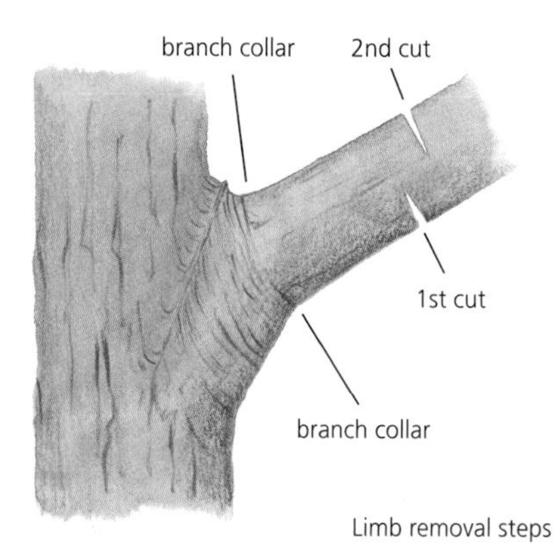

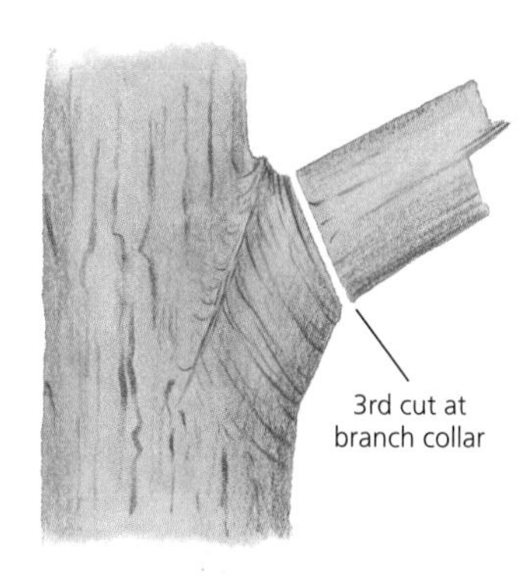

Limb removal steps

didn't have the equipment or the know-how when they tried to remove a large branch or tree.

Shearing is used to trim and shape hedges. Only plants that can withstand heavy pruning should be sheared because some of the normal pruning rules (such as being careful where you cut in relation to buds) are disregarded here. Informal hedges take advantage of the natural shape of the plant and require only minimal trimming. These hedges generally take up more room than formal hedges, which are trimmed more severely to assume a neat, even appearance. Formal hedges are generally sheared a minimum of twice per growing season. Make sure all sides of the hedge are trimmed to promote even growth. The base of the hedge should always be wider than the top to allow light to reach the entire hedge and to prevent it from thinning out at the base. Remember that a hedge will gradually increase in size despite shearing, so allow room for this expansion when planting your hedge.

Thinning is a rejuvenation process that maintains the shape, health and productivity of shrubs and some trees (see below). It opens up space for air and light to penetrate and provides room for younger, healthier branches and selected suckers to grow. Thinning often combines the first three cuts discussed above, and it is the most frequently performed pruning practice. Plants that produce new growth from ground level (suckers) should be pruned using this method.

A shrub that is thinned annually should have one-quarter to one-third of the growth removed. Cutting the oldest stems encourages new growth without causing excess stress from loss of top growth. Although some plants can be cut back completely to the ground and seem to suffer no ill effects, it is generally better to remove only up to one-third of the growth.

The latest research has shown that trees, for the most part, should not be thinned. The small inner branches break up the wind so it doesn't catch and potentially crack large branches or the main stem. Unless you are growing a tree specifically for fruit production, we don't recommend

incorrect

correct

Hedge shape

thinning trees. One exception we note is a process called windowing, where selected branches are carefully removed to enhance a view. This process should only be done by certified ISA professionals.

The following steps can be followed to thin most multi-stemmed shrubs.

1) Remove all dead, diseased, damaged, rubbing and crossing branches to branch junctions, buds or ground level.
2) Remove about one-third of the growth each year, leaving a mix of old and new growth in the remaining crown and cutting unwanted stems at or close to the ground. Avoid cutting stems below ground level because many disease organisms are present in soil.
3) Thin the top of the shrub to allow air and light penetration and to balance the growth. This step is not always necessary because removing one-third of the oldest stems generally thins out the top as well.
4) Repeat the process each year on established, mature shrubs. Regular pruning of shrubs will keep them healthy and productive for many years.

Thinning cuts

New growth (candles) of Norway spruce (above)

Tree sheared to perfect cone shape (below)

Coniferous Trees & Shrubs

These are plants that produce cones, such as spruce, pine and juniper. Most of these trees and shrubs need little to no pruning other than to fix damage or to correct wayward growth. Conifers can be pruned in our dormant season. Summer and fall pruning should be avoided because of the possibility of infestation by bark beetles.

When removing a branch, cut it back to the point of origin. Ensure you are cutting the branch at the branch collar, which is often difficult to see on coniferous plants. Never cut the tips off branches of spruce, fir and pine, where all the new growth is generated.

Many coniferous species, including cypress, false cypress, pine, spruce and fir, do not regenerate new growth from old wood. It is especially important to select plants to fit the space available—excess pruning may result in an ugly tree or shrub. Junipers can rejuvenate from old wood, but it is a slow process.

Most conifers have a central leader that should be maintained for as long as possible. If the leader is damaged or broken, it will need to be replaced as soon as possible. Remove the damaged leader, cutting back to a strong, preferably upright shoot. Ensure you have cut below the damaged portion. Gently insert a straight stake next to the main trunk. Do not insert the stake into the ground. Tie the stake to the main trunk. Bend the new leader as upright as possible and tie it to the stake. Remove the stake when the new leader is growing strongly upright. If a young tree has two leaders, remove the weaker one.

The new growth of pine, spruce and fir are known as candles. Growth of these plants can be controlled and directed by pinching the fully extended candles by up to half of their length. If you want more upright growth, select the longest, strongest candle and remove all other candles at each branch tip. For bushiness, shorten all candles by half. Always pinch the candles with your fingers; do not use hand pruners or shears.

Some coniferous plants are selected for unusual growth, such as dwarf and fastigiate (narrowly upright) forms, and are usually propagated vegetatively. Sometimes the growth will revert back to the usual growth exhibited by the species and will need to be removed.

Cedar and juniper can both be lightly sheared for hedging. Begin the training when the plants are very young.

Tree Topping (or What Not to Do)

One pruning practice that should never be used is tree topping. Trees have been topped to control their height or size, to prevent them from growing into overhead power lines, to allow more light onto a property or to prevent a tall tree from toppling onto a building. Topped trees are ugly and can create a hazard. A tree may be killed by the stress of losing half its live growth, or by the gaping, slow-to-heal wound that makes the tree vulnerable to insects and wood-rotting fungi. The heartwood of topped trees rots out

Well-pruned conifer planting (above)

Large cones as entrance sentries (above)

Topping stresses and disfigures trees (below)

Topiary bunny at Gamble Gardens

quickly, resulting in a weak trunk. The crotches on new growth that sprouts from the area of the cut also tend to be weak. Topped trees, therefore, are very susceptible to storm damage and blowdown. Hazards aside, topped trees can ruin the aesthetic value of a landscape.

It is much better to completely remove a tree and start again with one that will grow to a more appropriate size, than to attempt to control the growth of a mature specimen that is too large.

Pollarded trees are the ones that look like tootsie pops. Pollarding is a high-maintenance practice that must begin when the plants are very young, and there are very few plant species that lend themselves to this practice. Some people top mature trees to get a pollarding effect, which is highly detrimental to the health of the tree (see previous column).

Specialty Pruning

Custom pruning methods, such as topiary, espalier and bonsai, are used to create interesting plant shapes.

Topiary is the shaping of plant material into animal, abstract and geometric forms. True topiary uses species of hedge plants sheared into their desired shape. Species that can handle heavy pruning, such as boxwoods, are chosen. A simpler form of topiary involves growing vines or other trailing plants over a wire frame to achieve the desired form. Small-leaved ivies and other flexible, climbing or trailing plants work well for this kind of topiary.

Espalier involves training a tree or shrub to grow in two dimensions instead of three, with the aid of a solid wire framework. The plant is often trained against a wall or fence, but it can also be free standing. This method is popularly applied to fruit trees, such as apples, when space is at a premium. Many gardeners consider the forms attractive and unusual, and you may wish to try your hand at it even if you have lots of space.

Bonsai is the art of creating miniature versions of large trees and landscapes. A gardener prunes the top growth and roots and uses wire to train the plant to the desired form. The severe pruning creates a dwarfed form of the species.

PESTS & DISEASES

Tree and shrub plantings can be both assets and liabilities when it comes to pests and diseases. Many insects and diseases attack only one plant species. Mixed plantings can make it difficult for pests and diseases to find their preferred hosts and establish a population. At the same time, because woody plants are in the same spot for many years, problems can become permanent. The advantage is that beneficial insects, birds and other pest-devouring organisms can also develop permanent populations.

For many years, pest control meant spraying or dusting, with the goal to eliminate every pest in the landscape. A more moderate approach advocated today is known as IPM (Integrated Pest Management or Integrated Plant Management). The goal of IPM is to reduce pest problems to levels at which only negligible damage is done.

Of course, you, the gardener, must determine what degree of damage is acceptable to you. Consider whether a pest's damage is localized or covers the entire plant. Will the damage being done kill the plant, or is it affecting only the outward appearance? Are there methods of controlling the pest without chemicals?

Chemicals should be the last resort, because they do more harm than good. They can endanger the gardener and his or her family and pets, and they kill as many good organisms as bad, leaving the whole garden vulnerable to even worse attacks.

A good IPM program includes learning about your plants and the conditions they need for healthy growth: what pests might affect your plants; where and when to look for those pests; and how to control them. Keep records of pest damage

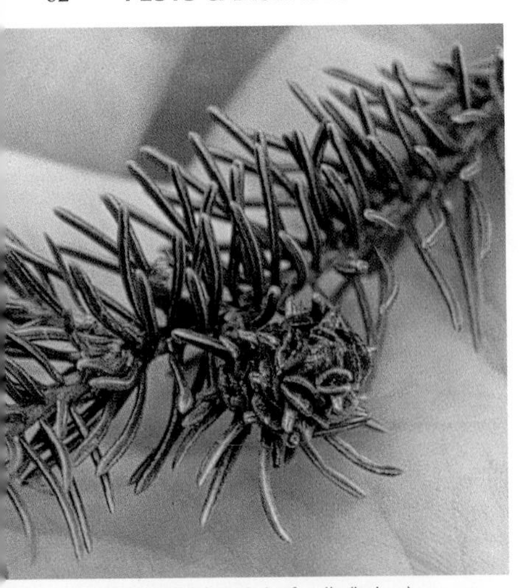

Adelgid gall (above), leaf galls (below)

Ladybird beetle (below)

because your observations can reveal patterns useful in spotting recurring problems and in planning your maintenance regime.

It is important to properly and quickly identify what is affecting your plants so that the right corrective measures are taken. It could be insects, disease, nutrient deficiency, adverse weather or poor management practices. If you are unsure what is happening, contact your local garden center or nursery for advice. Local botanic gardens, garden clubs, some post-secondary schools and the internet are other good sources for information.

There are four steps in effective and responsible pest management. Cultural controls are the most important. Physical controls should be attempted next, followed by biological controls. Resort to chemical controls only when the first three possibilities have been exhausted. Consulting local resources, such as Ag Commissioners and certified nursery staff, is advisable.

Cultural controls are the gardening techniques you use in the day-to-day care of your garden. Keeping your plants as healthy as possible is the best defense against pests. Growing trees and shrubs in the conditions they prefer and keeping your soil healthy, with plenty of organic matter, are just two of the cultural controls you can use to keep pests manageable. Choose resistant varieties of trees and shrubs that are not prone to problems. Space the plants so that they have good air circulation around them and are not stressed from competing for light, nutrients and space. Remove diseased foliage and branches, and either burn the material or take it to a permitted dumpsite. Prevent the spread of disease by keeping your gardening tools clean and by raking fallen leaves and dead plant matter at the end of every growing season. Remove plants from the landscape if the same pests decimate them every year.

Physical controls are generally used to combat insect problems. An example of such a control is picking insects off shrubs by hand, which is not as daunting as it may seem if you catch the problem when it is just beginning. Other physical controls include barriers that stop insects from getting to the plant, and traps that catch or confuse insects. Physical control of diseases often necessitates removing the infected plant part or parts to prevent the spread of the problem.

Biological controls make use of populations of predators that prey on pests. Animals such as birds, snakes, frogs, spiders, ladybird beetles (lady bugs) and certain bacteria can play an important role in keeping pest populations at a manageable level. Encourage these creatures to take up permanent residence in your garden. A birdbath and birdfeeder will encourage birds to enjoy your yard and feed on a wide variety of insect pests. Beneficial insects are probably already living in your landscape, and you can encourage them to stay by planting appropriate food sources. Many beneficial insects eat nectar from flowers such as the perennial yarrow. Certain beneficial insects are attracted to gardens when rotted fruit is placed in a container under shrubs.

A handy method to kill diseased or insect infested materials is to place the material in a black plastic garbage bag and leave it in full sun for at least three weeks. Once the material is sterilized, it can safely be placed in your garbage can.

Chemical controls should rarely be necessary, but if you must use them there are some 'organic' options available. Organic sprays are no less dangerous than chemical ones, but they will break down into harmless compounds. The main drawback to using any chemicals is that they may also kill the beneficial insects you have been trying to attract to your garden. Organic chemicals are available at most garden centers. You should follow the manufacturer's instructions carefully. A large amount of insecticide is not going to be any more effective in controlling pests than the recommended amount.

Sticky trap

To invite toads into the garden, place a cracked clay pot on its side and place in a moist, shady spot. They will come.

Frogs eat many insect pests (above)

I'm discovering a whole new world of benefits from certain composts where the organisms they contain create conditions on plants that prevent diseases and insects. Universities, because of their connection to the chemical industries, are reticent to even admit that this may well be the cure for many of the problems in modern-day gardens and farms. I'm currently working with Strybing Arboretum and Golden Gate Park in researching these possibilities. I know my compost tea prevents mildew and black spot on my roses.

Please note that if a particular pest is not listed on the manufacturer's package, that product will not control it. Proper and early identification of pests is vital to finding a quick solution.

There is an awakening in the pesticide industry caused by consumer demand for effective pest products that do not harm the environment. Biopesticides are made from plants, animals, bacteria and minerals. Microbial pesticides contain microbes such as bacteria, fungi, viruses and other microbes as the active ingredient. Plant pesticides are derived from naturally occurring plant compounds. Biochemical pesticides come from other naturally occurring substances that control pests by nontoxic means. They are much less harmful than conventional pesticides and for the most part target only the pest. They are effective in small quantities, and they decompose quickly in the environment. Hopefully, these products will reduce the reliance on chemical pesticides.

Whereas cultural, physical, biological and chemical controls are all possible defenses against insects, diseases can only be controlled culturally. It is most often weakened plants that succumb to diseases. Healthy plants can often fight off illness, although some diseases can infect plants regardless of their level of health. Prevention is often the only hope: once a plant has been infected, it should probably be destroyed to prevent the disease from spreading.

Glossary of Pests and Diseases

ANTHRACNOSE

Fungus. Yellow or brown spots on leaves; sunken lesions and blisters on stems; sunken lesions drop out; edge of lesions maroon-tinged; can kill plant.

What to Do. Choose resistant varieties and cultivars; keep soil well drained; thin out stems to improve air circulation; avoid handling wet foliage. Remove and destroy infected plant parts; clean up and destroy debris from infected plants at end of growing season; application of liquid copper will minimize damage.

APHIDS

Tiny, pear-shaped insects, winged or wingless; green, black, brown, red or gray. Cluster along stems, on buds and on leaves. Example: woolly adelgids. Suck sap from plants; cause distorted or stunted growth. Sticky honeydew forms on surfaces and encourages sooty mold growth.

What to Do. Squish small colonies by hand; brisk water spray dislodges them; many predatory insects and birds feed on them; spray serious infestations with insecticidal soap.

BEETLES

Many types and sizes; usually rounded in shape with hard, shell-like outer wings covering membranous inner wings. Some are beneficial, e.g., ladybird beetles ('ladybugs'); others, e.g., June beetles, leaf skeletonizers and weevils, eat plants. Larvae: see Borers, Grubs. Leave wide range of chewing damage: make small or large holes in or around margins of leaves; consume entire leaves or areas between leaf veins ('skeletonize'); may also chew holes in flowers. Some bark beetle species carry deadly plant diseases.

What to Do. On shrubs, pick beetles off at night and drop them into an old coffee can half filled with soapy water (soap prevents them from floating); spread an old sheet under small trees and shrubs and shake off beetles to collect and dispose of them; use a broom to reach tall branches. A product called Hot Pepper Wax Insect Repellant™ is an insect repellant that will discourage

Aphids (above), predatory ladybird beetle larva (below)

Leaf skeletonizer damage

beetle damage. Hot Pepper Wax Insect Repellant™ is also known to discourage rabbits and deer.

BLIGHT

Fungal diseases, many types; e.g., leaf blight, needle blight, snow blight. Leaves, stems and flowers blacken, rot and die.

What to Do. Thin stems to improve air circulation; keep mulch away from base of plant; remove debris from garden at end of growing season. Remove and destroy infected plant parts. Sterilize your equipment after each cut, or you could further spread the blight.

BORERS

Larvae of some moths, wasps, beetles; among the most damaging plant pests. Worm-like; vary in size and get bigger as they bore under bark and sometimes into heartwood. Burrow into plant stems, branches, leaves and/or roots; destroy vascular tissue (plant veins and arteries) and structural strength. Tunnels left by borers create sites for infection and decomposition to begin.

What to Do. Keep tree or shrub as healthy as possible with proper fertilizing and watering; may be able to squish borers within leaves. Remove and destroy bored parts; may need to remove entire plant.

BUGS (TRUE BUGS)

Small insects, up to ½" long; green, brown, black or brightly colored and patterned. Many beneficial; a few pests, such as lace bugs, pierce plants to suck out sap. Toxins may be injected that deform plants; sunken areas left where pierced; leaves rip as they grow; leaves, buds and new growth may be dwarfed and deformed.

What to Do. Remove debris and weeds from around plants in fall to destroy overwintering sites. Spray plants with insecticidal soap.

CANKER

Swollen or sunken lesion on stem or branch, surrounded by living tissue. Caused by many different bacterial and fungal diseases. Most canker-causing diseases enter through wounded wood. Woodpeckers drilling for insects may unwittingly infect plants.

What to Do. Maintain plant vigor; avoid wounds on trees; control borers and other bark-dwelling insects. Prune out and destroy infected material. Sterilize pruning tools before, during and after use on infected plants.

CATERPILLARS

Larvae of butterflies, moths, sawflies, including budworms, cutworms, leaf rollers, leaf tiers, loopers. Chew foliage and buds. Can completely defoliate a plant if infestation severe.
What to Do. Removal from plant is best control. Use high-pressure water and soap or pick caterpillars off by hand if plant is small enough. Cut off and burn large tents or webs of larvae. Control biologically using the naturally occurring soil bacterium *Bacillus thuringiensis* var. *kurstaki*, or B.t. for short (commercially available), which breaks down gut lining of caterpillars. Dormant oil can be applied in spring. Tree trunks can be wrapped or banded to prevent caterpillars from climbing tree to access leaves.

Caterpillar on fir (above)
Fuzzy galls on leaf underside (below)

FIRE BLIGHT

Highly destructive bacterial disease of the rose family, whose members include apples, cotoneasters, hawthorns, cherries and firethorns. Infected areas appear to have been burned. Look for bent-over twigs, branches that retain leaves over winter and cankers forming on lower parts of plant.
What to Do. Choose resistant plant varieties. Remove and burn infected material, making cuts a minimum of 24" below infected area. Sterilize tools after each cut on infected plant. Re-infection is possible because fire blight is often carried by pollinating birds and insects and enters plant through flowers. If whole plant is infected it must be removed and burned. There have been substantive reports that the use of fish emulsion as a foliar spray on infected trees will prevent further damage.

GALLS

Unusual swellings of plant tissues. Can affect leaves, buds, stems, flowers, fruit or trunks. May be caused by insects or diseases. Often a specific gall affects a single genus or species.

Leaf miner damage

What to Do. Cut galls out of plant and destroy them. Galls caused by insects usually contain the insect's eggs and juvenile forms. Prevent these galls by controlling insect before it lays eggs; otherwise, try to remove and destroy infected tissue before young insects emerge. Generally, insect galls are more unsightly than damaging to plant. Galls caused by diseases often require destruction of plant. Avoid placing other plants susceptible to same disease in that location.

GRUBS

Larvae of different beetles, commonly found below soil level; usually curled in C-shape. Body white or gray; head may be white, gray, brown or reddish. Problematic in lawns; may feed on roots of shallow-rooted trees and shrubs. Plant wilts despite regular watering; may pull easily out of ground in severe cases.

What to Do. Toss any grubs found while digging onto a stone path or patio for birds to devour; apply parasitic nematodes or milky disease spore to infested soil (ask at your local garden center).

LEAFHOPPERS & TREEHOPPERS

Small, wedge-shaped insects; can be green, brown, gray or multi-colored. Jump around frantically when disturbed. Suck juice from plant leaves. Cause distorted growth. Carry diseases such as aster yellows. Treehoppers also damage tree bark when they slit it to lay eggs.

What to Do. Encourage predators by planting nectar-producing species like yarrow. Wash insects off with strong spray of water; spray with insecticidal soap.

LEAF MINERS

Tiny, stubby larvae of some butterflies and moths; may be yellow or green. Tunnel within leaves, leaving winding trails; tunneled areas lighter in color than rest of leaf. Unsightly rather than health risk to plant.

What to Do. Remove debris from area in fall to destroy overwintering sites; attract parasitic wasps with nectar plants. Remove and destroy infected foliage; can sometimes squish by hand within leaf. Traps of blue sticky cards will prevent re-infection if placed in the garden in early spring.

LEAF CUTTER BEE

Cut neat, smooth circles from the edges of leaves.

What to Do. Nothing. It is a beneficial insect as a pollinator. Damage is only aesthetic. They are among the major pollinators in Northern California.

LEAF ROLLERS

see Caterpillars

LEAF SKELETONIZERS

see Beetles

LEAF SPOT

Two common types: one caused by bacteria and the other by fungi. *Bacterial:* small speckled spots grow to encompass entire leaves; brown or purple in color; leaves may drop. *Fungal:* black, brown or yellow spots; leaves wither; e.g., scab, tar spot.

What to Do. Bacterial infection more severe; must remove entire plant. For fungal infection, remove and destroy infected plant parts. Sterilize removal tools; avoid wetting foliage or touching wet foliage; remove and destroy debris at end of growing season. Compost tea also works in most instances.

MEALYBUGS

Tiny crawling insects related to aphids; appear to be covered with white fuzz or flour. Sucking damage stunts and stresses plant. Mealybugs excrete honeydew that promotes growth of sooty mold.

What to Do. Remove by hand on smaller plants; wash plant off with soap and warm water; wipe off with alcohol-soaked swabs; remove leaves with heavy infestations; encourage or introduce natural predators such as mealybug destroyer beetle and parasitic wasps; spray with insecticidal soap. Keep in mind larvae of mealybug destroyer beetles look like very large mealybugs.

Powdery mildew

MILDEW

Two types, both caused by fungus, but with slightly different symptoms. *Downy mildew:* yellow spots on upper sides of leaves and downy fuzz on undersides; fuzz may be yellow, white or gray. *Powdery mildew:* white or gray powdery coating on leaf surfaces that doesn't brush off.

What to Do. Choose resistant cultivars; space plants well; thin stems to encourage air circulation; remove any debris in fall. Remove and destroy infected leaves or other parts. Spray compost tea or highly diluted fish emulsion (1 teaspoon per quart of water) to control powdery mildew. Control downy mildew by spraying foliage with a mixture of 5 tablespoons of horticultural oil and

Snail eating leaf

2 teaspoons of baking soda per gallon of water. Three applications one week apart will be needed.

MITES

Tiny, eight-legged relatives of spiders; do not eat insects, but may spin webs. Almost invisible to naked eye; red, yellow or green; usually found on undersides of plant leaves. Examples: bud mites, spider mites, spruce mites. Suck juice out of leaves. May see fine webbing on leaves and stems; may see mites moving on leaf undersides; leaves become discolored and speckled, then turn brown and shrivel up.

What to Do. Wash off with strong spray of water daily until all signs of infestation are gone; predatory mites available through garden centers; mist plants to raise humidity to suppress reproduction; spray plants with insecticidal soap or apply horticultural oil at 5 tbs. per gallon of water. Spray may have to be repeated in 30 to 40 days.

MOSAIC

see Viruses

NEMATODES

Tiny worms that give plants disease symptoms. One type infects foliage and stems; the other infects roots. *Foliar:* yellow spots that turn brown on leaves; leaves shrivel and wither; problem starts on lowest leaves and works up plant. *Root-knot:* plant is stunted; may wilt; yellow spots on leaves; roots have tiny bumps or knots.

What to Do. Mulch soil, add organic matter, clean up debris in fall. Don't touch wet foliage of infected plants; can add parasitic nematodes to soil. Remove infected plants in extreme cases.

ROT

Several different fungi that affect different parts of the plant and can kill plant. *Crown rot:* affects base of plant, causing stems to blacken and fall over and leaves to yellow and wilt. *Root rot:* leaves yellow and plant wilts; digging up plant will show roots rotted away.

What to Do. Keep soil well drained; don't damage plant if you are digging around it; keep mulches away from plant base. Destroy infected plant if whole plant affected. When replanting in area make sure plant is resistant to rot. Do not replace with same variety of plant material.

Wood-rotting fungi and other decay organisms

RUST

Fungi. Pale spots on upper leaf surfaces; orange, fuzzy or dusty spots on leaf undersides. Examples: blister rust, cedar-apple rust.

What to Do. Choose rust-resistant varieties and cultivars; avoid handling wet leaves; provide plant with good air circulation; clear up garden debris at end of season. Remove and destroy infected plant parts. A winter spray with lime-sulfur will delay infection the following year.

SAWFLIES

see Caterpillars

SCAB

see Leaf Spot

SCALE INSECTS

Tiny, shelled insects that suck sap, weakening and possibly killing plant or making it vulnerable to other problems. Once female scale insect has pierced plant with mouthpart it is there for life. Juvenile scale insects are called crawlers.

What to Do. Wipe off with alcohol-soaked swabs; spray with water to dislodge crawlers; prune out heavily infested branches; encourage natural predators and parasites; spray dormant oil in spring before bud break.

SLUGS & SNAILS

Common pests in gardens. Both are mollusks; slugs lack shells whereas snails have spiral shells. Slimy, smooth skin; can be up to 8" long, many are smaller; gray, green, black, beige, yellow or spotted. Leave large, ragged holes in leaves and silvery slime trails on and around plants.

What to Do. Attach strips of copper to wood around raised beds or to smaller boards inserted around susceptible groups of plants; slugs and snails will get shocked if they touch copper surfaces. Pick off by hand in the evening and squish with boot or drop in can of soapy water. Spread wood ash or diatomaceous earth (available in garden centers) on ground around plants; it will pierce their soft bodies and cause them to dehydrate. CAUTION: do not use the diatomaceous earth that is used for swimming pool filters. Beer in a shallow dish may be effective. Sluggo™ is a bait product that is animal friendly and will control most infestations.

SOOTY MOLD

Fungus. Thin black film forms on leaf and reduces amount of light getting to leaf surface.

Mosaic virus (above)

What to Do. Wipe mold off leaf surfaces; control insects like aphids, mealybugs, whiteflies (honeydew left on leaves encourages mold).

TAR SPOT

see Leaf Spot

THRIPS

Difficult to see; may be visible if you disturb them by blowing gently on an infested flower. Yellow, black or brown; tiny, slender; narrow fringed wings. Suck juice out of plant cells, particularly in flowers and buds, causing mottled petals and leaves, dying buds and distorted and stunted growth.

What to Do. Remove and destroy infected plant parts; encourage native predatory insects with nectar plants like yarrow; spray severe infestations with insecticidal soap. Use blue sticky cards to prevent re-infection. Horticultural oil will kill the adults.

VIRUSES

Plant may be stunted and leaves and flowers distorted, streaked or discolored. Viral diseases in plants cannot be treated. Examples: mosaic virus, ringspot virus.

What to Do. Control insects like aphids, leafhoppers and whiteflies that spread disease. Destroy infected plants.

WEEVILS

see Beetles

WHITEFLIES

Tiny flying insects that flutter up into the air when plant is disturbed. Tiny, moth-like, white; live on undersides of plant leaves. Suck juice out of leaves, causing yellowed leaves and weakened plants; leave behind sticky honeydew on leaves, encouraging sooty mold growth.

What to Do. Destroy weeds where insects may live. Attract native predatory beetles and parasitic wasps with nectar plants like yarrow; spray severe cases with insecticidal soap. Can make a sticky flypaper-like trap by mounting tin can on stake; wrap can with yellow paper and cover with clear baggie smeared with petroleum jelly; replace baggie when full of flies. Plant sweet alyssum near plants. Apply horticultural oil.

WILT

If watering hasn't helped a wilted plant, one of two wilt fungi may be at fault. *Fusarium wilt:* plant wilts, leaves turn yellow then die; symptoms generally appear first on one part of plant before spreading to other parts. *Verticillium wilt:* plant wilts; leaves

curl up at edges; leaves turn yellow then drop off; plant may die.
What to Do. Both wilts difficult to control. Choose resistant plant varieties and cultivars; clean up debris at end of growing season. Destroy infected plants; solarize (sterilize) soil before replanting (this may help if you've lost an entire bed of plants to these fungi)—contact local garden center for assistance.

WOOLLY ADELGIDS

see Aphids

WORMS

see Caterpillars, Nematodes

RECIPES

RECIPES FOR ANT CONTROL

Mix 3 cups of water, 1 cup of white sugar and 4 teaspoons of boric acid in a pot. (Boric acid is available in powdered or crystal form.) Bring this mix just to a boil and remove it from the heat source. Let the mix cool. Pour small amounts of this cooled mix into bottlecaps or other similar small containers and place them around the area you want to get rid of ants. Another variation of this recipe is to mix equal parts of borax and icing sugar and apply in the same manner as above.

RECIPES FOR PEST CONTROL

Coffee Grounds Spray Recipe

Boil 2 pounds coffee grounds in 3 gallons water for about 10 minutes. Allow to cool; strain the grounds out of the mixture. Apply as a spray.

Insecticidal Soap

You can make your own insecticidal soap at home. Mix 1 teaspoon of mild dish detergent or pure soap (biodegradable options are available) with 1 quart of water in a clean spray bottle. Spray the surface areas of your plants, and rinse them off well about an hour after spraying.

Compost Tea

Mix 1 to 2 pounds of compost in 5 gallons of water. Let sit for 4–7 days. For use, dilute the mix until it resembles weak tea. Apply as a foliar spray or use during normal watering.

Horticultural Oil

Rule of thumb for mixing horticultural oil: 5 tablespoons oil per 1 gallon of water.

ABOUT THIS GUIDE

The trees and shrubs in this book are organized alphabetically by common name. You can also locate plants by looking in the index for alternative common names and Latin names. The Quick Reference Chart at the back of the book (pp. 342–47) acts as a detailed table of contents to the plants; this handy guide will help you plan your garden with a diversity of forms, features, foliage types and blooming times.

Our favorite species, hybrids and cultivars are listed in the 'Recommended' section of each account, but keep in mind many more types are often available, and new forms are developed all the time. Check with your local nursery or garden center.

Because our region has such a tremendous geographical and climatic diversity, we can only refer to seasons in a general sense throughout the book. Remember the timing and duration of the seasons for your particular area when planning flowering and fruiting times in your garden.

The Trees & Shrubs

Abelia

Abelia

Features: flowers, foliage, stems **Habit:** large, rounded, evergreen or semi-evergreen shrub **Height:** 3–8' **Spread:** up to 10' **Planting:** B & B, container; spring, fall **Zones:** 5–9

THESE SHRUBS ARE IDEAL for growing around native oaks and other existing native species. Abelias naturalize after two years in the ground, requiring only minimal maintenance after that time. The cultivar 'Edward Goucher' makes a great addition to gardens in the Bay Area. It can also tolerate the heat in the hot interior valleys, but it requires additional watering there. Deer seem to avoid abelias that have been in the ground for two to three years.

Abelia is named for Dr. Clarke Abel (1780–1826), who discovered and introduced Abelia chinensis *while working as a physician at Lord Amherst's embassy in China.* Abelia chinensis *is a parent of* A. *x* grandiflora*, the most popular abelia.*

Growing

Abelias prefer **full sun** but tolerate partial shade. The soil should be **moist, fertile, slightly acidic to slightly alkaline** and **well drained.** To prevent desiccation of the leaves, plant abelias in a spot that is sheltered from cold, drying winds.

Pruning is best done in late winter or early spring. When pruning, think of giving this plant the shape of a graceful water fountain. At the very least, remove winter-damaged growth and trim stems that are growing in undesired directions. Trimming or shearing the ends off the branches will create distorted growth, so branches to be removed should be cut right back to the ground. An old abelia can be rejuvenated by cutting the entire plant back to within a few inches of the ground.

A. x *grandiflora* (all photos this page)

A. x *grandiflora* (all photos both pages)

Tips

Abelias are valued for their glossy, dark green leaves and their funnel-shaped, white or pink flowers, which are produced sporadically all summer. Abelias are good plants for both formal and informal gardens and hedges, and they are attractive individually or in groups. They can be used in shrub and mixed borders and combine well with oleanders and photinias.

In mild areas, these plants are evergreen; in cool areas, they are semi-evergreen. The roots are mostly cold hardy. Any leaves and stems that are severely damaged in cold winters will grow back from root level.

Recommended

A.* x *grandiflora (Glossy Abelia) has white or pale pink flowers. The foliage turns red or bronze in fall, and this color will persist through

These striking shrubs can attract butterflies and hummingbirds to your yard.

the winter in mild areas. In colder areas the leaves will drop, revealing the attractive exfoliating stems. The shrub grows up to 8' tall and spreads 5–10'. **'Sherwood'** ('Nana') is more compact, growing 3–4' tall and spreading up to 5'. It makes a useful groundcover on banks too steep to mow. (Zones 5–9; will survive but may suffer damage in Zone 5)

A. **'Edward Goucher'** has larger, showier, dark pink flowers and is a smaller plant, growing to about 5' tall. This hybrid is not quite as hardy as *A.* x *grandiflora* and is likely to drop its leaves in winter. (Zones 7–9)

Problems & Pests

Infrequent problems with fungal leaf spot, root rot or mildew are possible.

Acacia

Acacia

Features: flowers, foliage, fast growth **Habit:** small, large-crowned tree or shrub **Height:** 1–30' **Spread:** 12–40' **Planting:** container; fall, early spring **Zones:** 8–11

I THINK ACACIAS HAVE BEEN GETTING A BAD RAP. THEY ARE BLAMED for all sorts of allergies, but they bloom at the same time as most pine trees pollinate. Pine trees produce 10 times the irritants. Acacias have some historical significance—the Ark of the Covenant is said to have been made from one of these trees, although there do not seem to be acacias indigenous to that part of the Middle East. Most acacias come from South Africa, Tasmania and Australia.

Growing

Acacias prefer to grow in **full sun** in **moderately fertile, neutral to slightly acidic, well-drained** soil. Plant in a location that is protected from high wind and from sustained temperatures below 20° F. Acacia plants need deep,

infrequent watering when establishing but little or no watering once established. Plant fernleaf acacia away from structures.

Prune in spring after blooming. Remove dead or diseased branches and any wayward branches that affect the appearance. When removing a branch, make sure you cut it back to the main stem. Acacias benefit from having the center of the plant thinned to allow light to reach the inner branches. Thinning the center also helps prevent wind damage.

Tips

Acacias are relatively short-lived, usually living about 20 years. An acacia may live up to 30 years if the tree is healthy and enjoys optimal growing conditions. The advantage to acacias is that they grow fast.

Fernleaf acacia is a perfect shade tree for dry, hot spots in the landscape. It also works well as a feature

A. baileyana (all photos this page)

Acacia baileyana *is named after the Australian botanist F.M. Bailey (1827–1915).*

tree or as a background. Make sure you give enough room for the crown when growing it as a feature tree.

You can train fernleaf acacia to grow as a single-stemmed tree or as a multi-stemmed large shrub. For a single-stemmed tree, prune away the lower branches. To train it as a multi-stemmed shrub, remove the main, central shoot when the plant is young. As a multi-stemmed shrub, fernleaf acacia makes a great bank planting, as does prostrate acacia.

Prostrate acacia is one of the longest-lived acacias. It tolerates heat on hillsides and is an ideal groundcover around established oaks. Deer and rabbits find it quite distasteful.

A. baileyana (all photos both pages)

Acacias attract a variety of creatures to your garden. Bees enjoy the flowers, and birds and other forest creatures enjoy the ripened fruit.

The fragrant flowers of acacias are good for cutting. Fernleaf acacia is especially attractive as a floral arrangement filler, and it lasts several days longer than cut ferns. The gray foliage makes a lovely accent in rose arrangements.

Recommended

A. baileyana (Fernleaf Acacia, Bailey Acacia) is a commonly grown evergreen species that grows 15–30' tall and 20–40' wide. It produces a wide, round crown of pendulous branches with blue to silver gray, fern-like foliage. Clusters of spherical, bright yellow flowers are produced in early to mid-winter, sometimes blooming into spring. **'Purpurea'** has deep maroon new growth that fades as the foliage ages. (Zones 8–10)

A. redolens (Prostrate Acacia) is a fast-growing, prostrate to mound-forming, evergreen shrub that is 1–6' tall and up to 15' wide. In spring, it produces puffy, yellow, ball-like flowers. This acacia is heat and drought tolerant, making it a good choice for low- or no-maintenance plantings. **'Desert Carpet'** grows 24" tall, spreads 12' and can be planted in partial shade. (Zones 9–11)

Problems & Pests

Acacias have infrequent problems with scale insects, mimosa webworm and leaf spot.

Angel's Trumpet

Trumpet Flower

Brugmansia (Datura)

Features: flowers, foliage, fragrance **Habit:** large shrub or small tree
Height: 10–12' **Spread:** 10–12' **Planting:** container; spring, fall **Zones:** 10–12

WHEN I FIRST SAW THIS PLANT, I WAS IN BERKELEY VISITING MY cousin, Bob. The large, trumpet-shaped flowers were white and had a wonderful fragrance. I took a cutting from the plant and brought it home to my grandmother in Willits, where I lived at the time. She was totally delighted. Like most angel's trumpets, it rooted easily, but unfortunately the winter cold that year killed it.

Climatic conditions can affect the color of the flowers. What is yellow on one plant in one climate can be orange on the same plant in a different climate. The climate can also affect flower form; double flowers can be produced in one climate, and the same plant can produce single flowers in another climate.

Growing

Angel's trumpets grow in **full sun** to **partial shade**. The soil should be **fertile, moist** and **well drained**. Don't allow the plants to completely dry out, particularly during hot, dry weather. Wilting plants will recover quickly when watered. Plant in a sheltered place out of the wind, where the leaves will not be torn. Frost will damage these plants.

Prune before any new growth appears in spring. Cut out any branches that are weak or crowding and any that are affecting the shape. If necessary, angel's trumpets can be cut back hard to 6–12" above the soil.

Tips

Angel's trumpets tend to flower at night. Grow these plants where you will be able to enjoy their intoxicating perfume in the evening—near a patio or in a large container on a deck. If angel's trumpets are planted under an open window, the scent will carry into the room. They are attractive when used as specimen plants or planted in groups.

The genus in which these plants are classified varies. They may be attributed to either *Brugmansia* or *Datura*, which are closely related genera. In general, the herbaceous annuals and perennials are classified as *Datura* while the woody plants are classified as *Brugmansia*. Another source says *Datura* flowers are erect, and *Brugmansia* flowers are hanging. Don't worry too much about the names; if you find a plant you like, go ahead and try it.

'Charles Grimaldi' (below)

B. x *insignis* (above)

Recommended

The following selections are all large shrubs or small trees with fragrant, pendulous flowers that bloom from summer to frost.

B. candida has fragrant, white, trumpet-shaped flowers that may open only at night. The scent is strongest in the evening and at night. **'Double White'** bears double, white flowers. **'Grand Marnier'** has apricot yellow flowers. (Zones 10–12)

B. **'Charles Grimaldi'** has large, funnel-shaped, lemon yellow flowers. It is an excellent container plant for a patio or deck. (Zones 10–12)

B. x ***insignis*** has large flowers in shades of pink and white. **'Jamaica Yellow'** has light yellow flowers. (Zones 10–12)

Problems & Pests

Problems with whiteflies, spider mites and mealybugs are possible. These problems are more likely on plants grown indoors.

Angel's trumpets are in the family Solanaceae, *the same family as tomatoes, potatoes, peppers and nightshade plants. As with many other plants in this family, angel's trumpets are poisonous and should be kept away from any children or pets that might eat the flowers.*

'Charles Grimaldi' (below)

Arbutus
Strawberry Tree, Madrone
Arbutus

Features: flowers, fruit, bark, habit **Habit:** spreading or shrubby, broad-leaved, evergreen tree **Height:** 5–100' **Spread:** 5–70' **Planting:** B & B, container; spring, fall **Zones:** 7–9

IN MY YOUTH, WE HAD A TREE IN OUR YARD THAT WAS OVER 80' tall. It was an *A. menziesii,* and it took four people with hands clasped to reach around the base. My cousin and I used it for a treehouse. My father did not like the tree because it was constantly dropping fruit, leaves and bark, although he might have liked it better if leaf blowers had been invented. This species is a California native found along coastal areas as far south as Carmel and in the Sierras where winter rains are adequate.

Both arbutus *(Latin) and* madroño *(Spanish) mean 'strawberry tree,' in reference to the bright red fruits of this magnificent evergreen tree.*

Growing

Arbutus prefers a **sheltered** spot in **full sun.** The soil should be **fertile, humus rich** and **well drained.** It can be difficult to grow because it hates the heavy clay soil of most Northern California gardens. Perfect drainage is necessary, and planting in a raised bed helps. Avoid overwatering—arbutus is drought and salt tolerant. Pruning is not usually required.

Arbutus does not like having its roots disturbed. Plant young stock, and make sure the location is a permanent one.

Tips

Use arbutus in a woodland garden or as a specimen tree. Include the smaller cultivars in a shrub or mixed border.

A. *unedo* (above)

Birds love arbutus fruits, but humans can suffer stomachaches if they eat too many.

A. *unedo* 'Compacta' (below)

A. menziesii (above & below)

Recommended

A. **'Marina'** has large, green leaves, rosy pink flowers and red and yellow fruit. It grows 30–40' tall and wide. This cultivar was the boulevard tree used in the Pan Pacific Exposition in San Francisco in 1915. It fell out of use until it was 'rediscovered' in 1993, when it was cloned to produce most of the trees we see in gardens and nurseries today. This tree is a wonderful substitute for *A. menziesii*, which can be temperamental in many gardens. (Zones 7–9)

A. menziesii (Pacific Madrone, Arbutus) is a spreading or shrubby tree that is native to western North America. It grows 50–100' tall and 50–80' wide. White flowers appear in erect clusters in early summer, followed by the warty red fruits, borne in equally striking clusters. The fruits may stay on the tree until December. A particularly attractive feature is the distinctive reddish bark that continuously peels off to reveal the perfectly smooth, greenish young bark underneath. (Zones 7–9)

A. unedo (below)

A. unedo (Mediterranean Strawberry Tree) is a spreading, shrubby tree with shredding, exfoliating, red-brown bark. It grows 15–30' tall, with an equal spread. White flowers appear in fall, followed by warty red fruits. **'Compacta'** is a slow-growing tree with slightly contorted branches. It grows to about 10' tall. **'Elfin King'** is a compact, bushy form that flowers and fruits profusely. It grows 5–10' high and wide. (Zones 7–9)

Problems & Pests

Fungal leaf spot, tent caterpillars and scale insects can cause some trouble.

A. menziesii *is native along the Pacific coast, where it can be found on rocky cliffs overlooking the water.*

A. menziesii (below)

A. menziesii (above)

The fruit of A. unedo *makes excellent jam.*

A. unedo (below)

Aucuba

Japanese Aucuba, Spotted Laurel

Aucuba

Features: foliage, fruit, adaptability **Habit:** bushy, rounded, evergreen shrub **Height:** 3–10' **Spread:** 3–10' **Planting:** container; spring, fall **Zones:** 6–9

THIS LARGE-LEAVED, HARDY, TROPICAL-LOOKING PLANT HAS many landscape uses in shade, partial shade or morning sun areas. The foliage and berries are a dynamic addition to any garden. The variegated forms can add a large splash of yellow to otherwise dull landscapes. Aucubas can make excellent houseplants and perform well as container specimens in shade. If you have a problem with root competition in any shaded area, aucuba is the plant to choose because it will compete with established plantings.

Growing

Aucuba grows well in **partial to full shade** in **moderately fertile, humus-rich, moist, well-drained** soil. It will tolerate full sun in coastal areas. It requires water on a regular basis and may suffer sunburn on a hot day if it dries out. Sunburn will appear as large, circular, black spots on the foliage. If spots appear, wait until fall to eliminate the unsightly leaves, thereby allowing them to protect the rest of the plant from damage during subsequent heat spells in summer. Plants with variegated foliage show the best leaf color in partial shade. This plant adapts to most soil conditions as long as the soil is not waterlogged, and it tolerates urban pollution and salty, windy coastal conditions.

Aucuba shrubs generally require no pruning, but they can be pruned to control their height. Hedges can be trimmed in spring.

Tips

Aucuba can be used in deeply shaded locations where no other plants will grow. It can also be used as a specimen, in a large planter and as a hedge or screen. Under the canopy of larger trees, this shrub will compete well for moisture and nutrients. It is also effective as a houseplant.

Generally, both a male and female plant must be present for the female to set fruit. The fruits are not edible.

'Crotonifolia' (above)

Florists use this plant in many of their arrangements. The cuttings root easily in water, and when the flowers of the bouquet have faded, you can plant the rooted cuttings to create new shrubs.

A. japonica (below)

A. japonica (above)

Recommended

A. japonica has a neatly rounded habit and glossy green leaves. It grows 6–10' tall and wide. Female plants develop red berries in fall. Many cultivars are available, usually developed for their variegated foliage. **'Crotonifolia'** is a male plant with white-and-gold-blotched leaves. **'Rozannie'** is a compact plant with dark green leaves. It grows 36" tall, with an equal spread. This cultivar has male and female parts in the same flower rather than on separate plants, so only one plant is needed in order to have fruit. **'Variegata'** (Gold Dust Plant) is a female plant with yellow-spotted leaves. (Zones 6–9)

The leaves and fruit of Aucuba contain aucubin, a mildly toxic substance which, when eaten, can cause nausea, vomiting and sometimes fever.

Use a variegated cultivar to add brightness to foundation plantings on the north and east sides of buildings and in dark corners in your home.

Problems & Pests

Blight can kill off parts of the plant. Remove these damaged parts. Aucuba is also prone to attacks by mealybugs and mites. Root rot and leaf spot are other possible problems.

This tough plant is tolerant of frost, deep shade, pollution and neglect.

'Crotonifolia' (above & below)

Beautyberry

Callicarpa

Features: fruit **Habit:** bushy, deciduous shrub with arching stems **Height:** 3–10' **Spread:** 3–8' **Planting:** container; spring, fall **Zones:** 6–10

IN CALIFORNIA, WHEN A NURSERY SALESPERSON TELLS A POTENTIAL client that a tree or shrub goes dormant, it becomes a tough sale. I think beautyberry is definitely worth planting, even though it goes dormant. I absolutely fell in love with its wonderful berries when I first saw them at Swarthmore College in Pennsylvania. Years later I added a couple of these plants to the perennial shrub garden in San Rafael, and I was delighted with their arching growth and the berries that seemed as bright as traffic lights. Beautyberry tolerates the rugged weather of the Sierras as well as the heat of the Sacramento Valley. Its water requirements are moderate, so it is a natural choice for summer vacation homes where it may get neglected. Because the berries last a long time, beautyberry shrubs make an interesting addition to any garden, especially after their leaves are gone.

Growing

Beautyberries grow well in **full sun** or **light shade**. The soil should be **well drained** and of **average fertility**.

Pruning can be done in spring. Flowers and fruit are formed on the current year's growth. Cut the plant back to within 12" of the ground once the buds start to swell in spring, which will encourage new growth and lots of fruit later in summer. Annual trimming will also keep the plant looking neat.

In colder areas the branches may be damaged over winter. Cut off any damaged growth in spring. Even plants that die back completely in winter will revive with new growth in spring.

If the growth is getting out of hand, or if you have missed pruning for a couple of years, one option is to cut back hard to within 4" of the ground in spring.

C. bodinieri (above)

The genus name of beautyberry, Callicarpa, *is derived from the Greek words* kallos, *meaning beauty, and* karpos, *meaning fruit.*

To add interest to floral arrangements, use cut stems of fruiting branches.

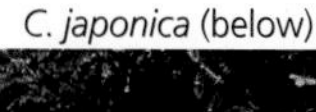

C. japonica (below)

C. *bodinieri* (all photos both pages)

Tips

Beautyberries can be used in naturalistic gardens and in shrub and mixed borders. These shrubs can be treated as herbaceous perennials if the plants regularly die back in winter because the flowers are produced on new wood.

Recommended

C. bodinieri (Bodinier Beautyberry) grows up to 6–10' tall and spreads 5–8'. This species produces many pinkish purple berries and has a loose, relaxed habit. Fall foliage may be orange, purple or pinkish. **'Profusion'** is aptly named. It bears the colorful fruit in abundance. (Zones 6–10)

The spectacular violet to metallic purple fruiting of the beautyberry makes the best show as a group planting.

C. dichotoma (Purple Beautyberry) grows about 3–4' tall, with an equal or slightly greater spread. The purple fruits are borne in dense clusters at the base of each leaf, surrounding the arching branches. (Zones 6–10)

C. japonica (Japanese Beautyberry) can grow to 10' tall but usually grows 4–6' tall and wide. It is an open shrub with arching branches and purple fruit. The foliage turns reddish purple in fall. **'Leucocarpa'** is a white-fruited cultivar. (Zones 6–10)

Problems & Pests

Scale insects, leaf spot, mildew and dieback are possible problems, but they are not serious and do not occur frequently.

To encourage vigorous new growth each spring, feed plants that suffer winter dieback.

Beech

Fagus

Features: foliage, bark, habit, fall color, fruit
Habit: large, conical to oval, deciduous tree
Height: 30–90'
Spread: 12–70'
Planting: B & B, container; spring **Zones:** 4–9

BEECH IS ONE OF THE BEST TREES to cast shade where shade is wanted. The denseness of the shade and the fibrous roots prevent any serious planting underneath, but these drawbacks are the trade-off for a dependable cool spot in the garden. At Filoli, copper beeches were planted 36" apart and shaped into a hedge to surround the extraordinary cut-flower beds. The hedge is maintained at 8' tall and has two arched gates set into it at either end. The dense shade created by beech trees is perfect for a birdbath and bench, providing quiet and coolness on a hot day.

Growing

Beech grows equally well in **full sun** or **partial shade.** The soil should be of **average fertility, loamy** and **well drained**, though this tree tolerates almost all well-drained soils. Beeches are sensitive to salt and will suffer when planted right on the coast and near roadways where salt is used in winter.

Very little pruning is required. Pruning should be done only to raise the crown so that it can be walked under. Remove dead or damaged branches in spring or any time after the damage occurs. *F. sylvatica* is a popular hedging plant that responds well to severe pruning.

Tips

Beeches make excellent specimen trees. They are also used as street trees and shade trees or in woodland gardens. These trees need a lot of space. The European beech's adaptability to pruning makes it a better choice in a small garden.

The nuts are edible when roasted.

Recommended

F. sylvatica (European Beech) is a spectacular tree that can grow 90' tall and 60–70' wide in ideal conditions. It is usually smaller in gardens, growing 60' tall and 40' wide, but as a tree it is still too massive for most settings. The species is best used for hedges in smaller gardens. It transplants easily and is tolerant of varied soil conditions. You can find a number of interesting cultivars of this tree, and several are small enough to use in the home garden. **'Atropunicea'** (Copper Beech) ('Purpurea')

F. sylvatica (above)

Beeches retain their very smooth and elastic bark long into maturity.

Weeping form of 'Atropunicea' (below)

is a deep red to purple-leaved form with the same habit as the species. Purple-leaved weeping forms are also available. **'Fastigiata'** ('Dawyck') is a narrow, upright tree. It can grow to 80' but spreads only about 12'. Yellow or purple-leaved forms are available. **'Pendula'** (Weeping Beech) is a dramatic tree whose pendulous branches reach down to the ground. It varies in form: some specimens spread widely, resulting in a cascade effect, while others are rather upright with branches drooping from the central trunk. This cultivar can grow as tall as the species, but a specimen with the branches drooping from the central trunk may be narrow enough for a home garden. **'Tricolor'** ('Roseo-Marginata') has striking foliage with pink-and-white variegation that develops best in partial shade. The foliage can burn in the hot sun. This slow-growing tree matures to about 30'. It can be grown as a smaller tree in a large planter. 'Tricolor' is a favored tree for training as a bonsai specimen. (Zones 4–9)

Beech nuts provide food for a wide variety of animals, including squirrels and birds, and they were once a favorite food of the passenger pigeon, now extinct.

'Tricolor' (below)

'Pendula' (below)

Problems & Pests

Canker, powdery mildew, leaf spot, bark disease, borers, scale insects and aphids can afflict beech trees. None of these pests causes serious problems.

Young lovers' initials carved into a beech will remain visible for the life of the tree—an effect that outlasts many teenage relationships.

'Tricolor' (above)

Birch

Betula

Features: foliage, fall color, habit, bark, winter and early-spring catkins **Habit:** open, deciduous tree **Height:** 30–100' **Spread:** 15–40' **Planting:** container (spring, fall), sometimes available as bare-root (January and February) **Zones:** 2–10

IN THE EASTERN PART OF NORTH America, the conventional wisdom has been to plant birches in groups of three or more. Besides esthetics, the intention is to offset the effects of birch blight. The theory was that at least one would survive if more than one was planted, so it became common practice to plant three or more birches in a landscape. Luckily, Northern California does not have birch blight problems. Because birches tend to become surface rooted when used as lawn trees, plant flowerbeds under them or mulch the area around the trunk. Do not plant these trees under power lines, and absolutely never top them.

The bark of B. papyrifera *has been used to make canoes, shelters, utensils and—as both the Latin and common names imply—paper.*

B. *papyrifera* (above)

Growing

Birches grow well in **full sun, partial shade** or **light shade**. The soil should be of **average to rich fertility, moist** and fairly **well drained.** Many birch species naturally grow in wet areas, such as along streams. They don't, however, like to grow in permanently soggy conditions. Provide adequate water during hot, dry weather because the foliage will dry out and appear scorched.

Minimal pruning is required. Remove any dead or damaged branches as well as those that are growing awkwardly. Any pruning of live wood should be done in late summer or fall to prevent the excessive bleeding of sap that occurs in spring.

Tips

Often used as specimen trees, birches' small leaves and open crowns provide light shade that allows perennials and annuals to flourish beneath them. Birch trees are also attractive when grown in groups near natural or artificial water features. They need quite

Some people make birch syrup from the heavy flow of sap in spring, in the same way maple syrup is made.

B. *albosinensis* (below)

B. papyrifera (above), B. pendula (below)

a bit of room to grow, so they are not the best choice in gardens with limited space.

Recommended

B. albosinensis (Chinese Paper Birch, Chinese Red Birch) is a large tree growing 80–100' tall and 30' wide. It has attractive, peeling, orange, red-orange or orange-brown bark. Freshly exposed bark is a cream color. (Zones 5–10)

B. jacquemontii (*B. utilis* var. *jacquemontii*) (Whitebarked Himalayan Birch) has striking pure white bark. It grows 40–60' tall and spreads about half as wide. This tree is very effective in winter against a dark green background or clear blue sky. It is more upright than other varieties and keeps its form better than most. (Zones 5–10)

B. papyrifera (Paper Birch, Canoe Birch) has creamy white bark that peels off in layers, exposing cinnamon-colored bark beneath. It grows about 70' tall and spreads about 30'. This tree prefers moist soil. Native to most cool climates in North America, the paper birch dislikes hot summer weather. (Zones 2–7)

B. pendula (European White Birch) is a pyramidal to rounded tree with graceful, arching branches growing from upright main stems. It usually grows to a height of 30–40' in gardens, but it can reach up to 80' in ideal conditions. The tree spreads about half of its height. The branches of **'Laciniata'** ('Dalecarlica,' 'Gracilis') are more pendulous than the species, and the foliage is deeply cut. It is a very attractive specimen tree. **'Youngii'** is a dome-forming selection that requires the main stem to be staked to a desired height. The branches then hang down from that height. (Zones 2–10)

Problems & Pests

Aphids are fond of birch trees, and the sticky honeydew these insects secrete may drip off the leaves. Avoid planting birches where drips can fall onto parked cars, patios or decks. Leaf miners and tent caterpillars can be a problem. The bronze birch borer can be a fatal problem, especially for *B. pendula*. Paper birch is resistant to this borer. Trunks of all birches need to be protected from deer, mice and other animals until the trunk reaches 3–4" in diameter.

B. papyrifera (above), *B. jacquemontii* (below)

Bird-of-Paradise Bush

Caesalpinia (Poinciana)

Features: flowers **Habit:** upright, open-branched, roundish shrub **Height:** 6–12' **Spread:** 3–12' **Planting:** container; spring, fall **Zones:** 9–11

THE FIRST TIME I SAW THIS PLANT IN BLOOM WAS AT MY UNCLE ED and Aunt Sadie's home in Sacramento. My parents, my sister and I visited them once a year, and I was relegated to the loft in the attic. Right below in the garden was this most beautiful flowering plant with fern-like leaves. It was next to a water cooler draped in burlap where butter, milk and green vegetables were stored. In the mornings, I was awakened by birds playing in the water and resting on the branches of this shrub.

Growing

Grow these plants in **full sun** in **light, well-drained** soil. Established plants do best with occasional deep watering. Bird-of-paradise bush will benefit from the addition of organic matter to the soil before planting and the use of organic mulch during the growing season.

Prune these shrubs annually before new growth begins in spring. Remove dead, diseased, crossing, rubbing and damaged branches as well as any

growth that spoils the overall shape. These shrubs may be pruned into tree form or trained as espalier plants.

Tips

Caesalpinia spp. enjoy hot conditions and are quick growers. Place the plant where you can enjoy the flowers and the hummingbirds the flowers attract. Use in a shrub or mixed bed. It is a good choice for those hot areas in your garden that might not receive regular water.

Recommended

C. gilliesii (*Poinciana gilliesii*) (Bird-of-Paradise Bush, Yellow Bird of Paradise) is an evergreen to deciduous shrub, growing 6–10' tall and spreading 3–8' wide, with fern-like foliage. In summer it produces clusters of yellow flowers with prominent bright red stamens. (Zones 9–11)

C. pulcherrima (*Poinciana pulcherrima*) (Barbados Pride) is a deciduous shrub that reaches 10–12' in height and spreads 6–12'. It bears clusters of orange to orange-red flowers with red stamens in summer. The growth is somewhat denser than that of *C. gilliesii.* (Zones 9–11)

C. pulcherrima (above)

You can propagate Caesalpinia *spp. by softwood cuttings in spring, by semi-hardwood cuttings in summer or by seed. Scratching the seeds and soaking them in hot water will aid germination.*

C. gilliesii (below)

Bluebeard

Blue Spirea

Caryopteris x *clandonensis*

Features: flowers, foliage, scent **Habit:** rounded, spreading, deciduous shrub **Height:** 24–36" **Spread:** 24–36" **Planting:** container; spring, fall **Zones:** 5–9

I HAVE HAD SOME WONDERFUL EXPERIENCES WITH THIS SHRUB. Its intense blue flowers were an easy sale in the nursery. Many people in warm areas look for blue flowers to add a cooling feeling to any landscape. This effect is particularly needed in areas such as the Sacramento Valley, Central Valley and foothills of the Sierras. Because this shrub goes dormant in winter and pruning it back is a necessity, it always looks good. Bluebeard is a good companion plant around citrus and shade trees, and it works well in other landscapes that do not require excessive water. It is interesting used as a border around groundcovers on hillsides, providing that the roots do not sit in water in winter. It is a knockout when planted with bright-colored perennials, such as coreopsis and black-eyed Susan.

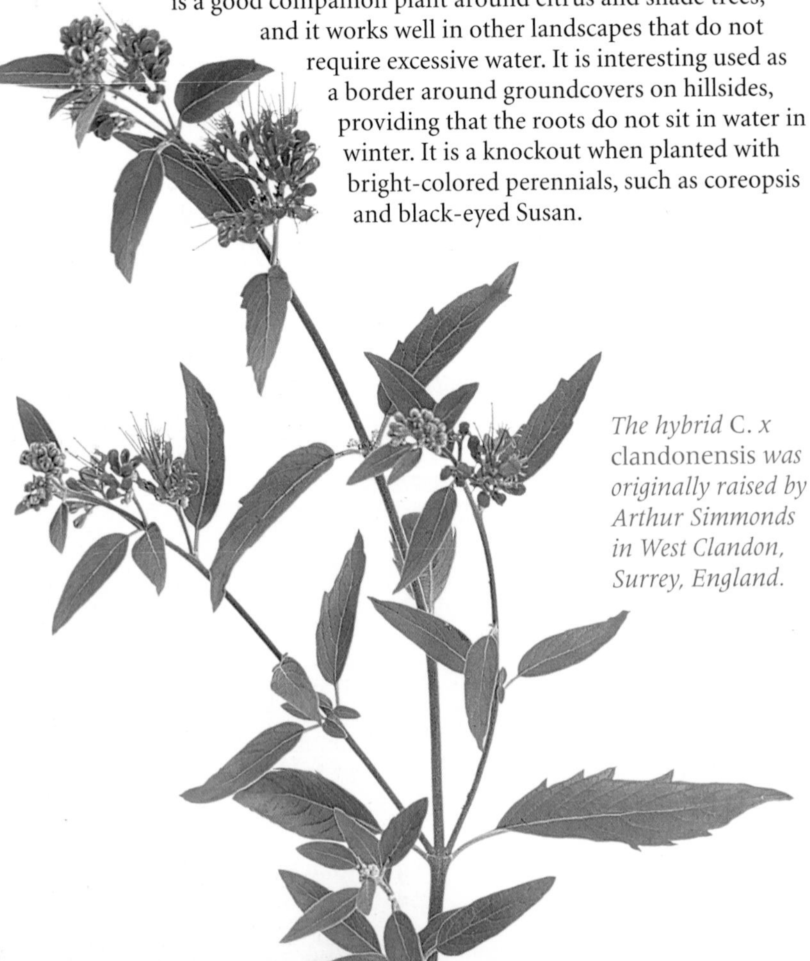

The hybrid C. x clandonensis *was originally raised by Arthur Simmonds in West Clandon, Surrey, England.*

Growing

Bluebeard prefers **full sun** but tolerates light shade. It does best in soil of **average fertility** that is **light** and **well drained.**

Pruning this shrub is easy. It flowers from mid-summer to frost, so cut the plant back to within 2–6" of the ground each spring. Flowers form on the new growth that emerges. Deadheading or light shearing once the flowers begin to fade will encourage more flowering. This plant is treated as a perennial in areas where it dies back each winter. New growth will sprout from the base in spring if this occurs.

The name Caryopteris *is derived from the Greek* karyon *(nut) and* pteron *(wing), referring to the winged fruit.*

Tips

Include bluebeard in your shrub or mixed border. The bright blue, late-season flowers are welcome when many other plants are looking past their flowering best.

'Dark Knight' (all photos this page)

Recommended

C.* x *clandonensis is a low-growing, mound-forming shrub that is 24–36" tall and wide, with aromatic stems, foliage and flowers. **'Blue Mist'** has light blue flowers. It rarely exceeds 24" in height. **'Dark Knight'** has dark blue flowers and silver gray leaves. **'Worcester Gold'** has bright, yellow-green foliage that contrasts vividly with the violet blue flowers. It grows about 36" tall, with an equal spread. This cultivar is often treated like a herbaceous perennial because the growth is often killed back in winter. (Zones 5–9)

Bog Rosemary

Marsh Rosemary

Andromeda

Features: foliage, flowers **Habit:** low-growing, evergreen shrub **Height:** 6–24" **Spread:** 8–36" **Planting:** container; spring, fall **Zones:** 2–6

BOG ROSEMARY IS THE PERFECT PLANT FOR THOSE ROCK GARDEN areas that stay wet during the summer months. Growing much like regular creeping or mounding rosemary, it can be used to accent rather than cover large boulders. Lacecap hydrangeas and bird's-nest ferns, which have wonderful, broad leaves, are perfect companions for bog rosemary. You may have to order this plant from a specialty nursery, but it is currently available.

In Greek mythology, Andromeda was the daughter of Cassiopeia. She angered Poseidon and was chained to a rock in the ocean—as isolated as wild bog rosemary, which grows on moss hummocks in a boggy sea.

Growing

Bog rosemary grows well in **full sun** to **light shade**. The soil should be **moist, well drained** and **acidic**, with lots of **organic matter** worked in. Plant bog rosemary in a cool part of the garden in light shade to protect it from summer heat.

Bog rosemary can be pruned in spring when the flowers have faded and new growth is just beginning. Stems can be cut back to remove almost all of last year's growth. Replace old, scruffy plants.

Tips

Include bog rosemary in a rock garden or woodland garden, by a water feature or as a groundcover underneath other acid-loving shrubs.

Do not make a tea with or otherwise ingest bog rosemary—it contains andromedotoxin, which can lower blood pressure, disrupt breathing and cause cramps and vomiting.

Recommended

A. polifolia is an attractive plant with light pink flowers in spring and early summer. It grows up to 24" tall and spreads up to 36". **'Alba'** has white flowers and is a dwarf plant that grows about 6" tall and 8" wide. **'Blue Ice'** has exceptional grayish blue foliage. **'Compacta'** is a dwarf cultivar with pink flowers. It grow about 12" tall and spreads about 8". (Zones 2–6)

A. polifolia (above), 'Blue Ice' (below)

A. polifolia (below)

Bottlebrush

Callistemon

Features: flowers, habit **Habit:** rounded, evergreen shrub or small tree
Height: 10–30' **Spread:** 10–15' **Planting:** container; spring, fall **Zones:** 9–11

THIS VERSATILE SHRUB CAN BE PLANTED ALMOST ANYWHERE IN the garden. I have seen it planted under Monterey pine, and it thrives without water or any care or any fuss whatsoever. Allow it to grow into its natural shape, which resembles a fountain. It can be made into a hedge, but it will soon form an excess number of woody stems that will not generate new wood. It has been used as a small tree in difficult locations, such as planting strips near sidewalks. The knobby, spent flowering stems make interesting additions to dry flower arrangements. If it has been pruned badly and looks like a branch out of Sleepy Hollow, cut it back drastically to within 12" of the ground and start all over again.

Growing

Bottlebrush prefers to grow in **full sun** in **moist, well-drained, neutral to slightly acidic** soil, though it will tolerate slightly alkaline soil. It requires regular watering for the first two years, after which it requires none. Minimal pruning is required. Remove dead, diseased and damaged branches and any growth that spoils the shape after flowering or in spring, before new growth begins. Do not prune the branches below the lowest leaves or the branches may not generate any new growth.

Tips

Bottlebrush can be used as an informal hedge or screen, in a shrub bed or as a specimen plant. The flowers are rich in nectar and will attract hummingbirds and other birds. If used as a hedge, do not prune into a box form. Remove only those branches that spoil the graceful form of the plant. To train bottlebrush as a tree, you will have to stake it with a solid stake that will support the plant for several years. Once a year, check that the ties are not cutting into the trunk.

C. citrinus is slightly hardier than *C. viminalis*, but both will suffer damage if the temperature drops to 20° F. Keep *C. viminalis* out of any drying winds.

Select varieties can be propagated by tip cuttings in summer. The seed is very difficult to germinate.

C. citrinus (above)

Bottlebrush stems continue to grow from the tips of the flower clusters. The woody seed capsules that remain on the branch may appear to become embedded in the branch as the branch thickens.

Recommended

C. citrinus (Lemon Bottlebrush) grows naturally as a large shrub, 10–15' tall and wide. When trained as a single-stemmed tree, it can reach 25' tall. The erect, spike clusters of scarlet to crimson flowers have protruding stamens. They are borne on the tips of the branches and bloom in late spring to early summer and again in fall. New leaves are tinted pink to red, maturing to dark green. Mature foliage has a lemon aroma when crushed. (Zones 9–11)

C. viminalis (Weeping Bottlebrush) is a large shrub or small tree growing 20–30' tall and spreading 12–15' wide. It produces clusters of bright red flowers in late spring to early summer on arching to pendulous branches. **'Captain Cook'** is a rounded shrub growing 6' tall and wide and bearing bright red flowers from early summer to fall. (Zones 9–11)

Problems & Pests

Aphids and scale insects may be problems. Stem gall, canker and leaf spot are infrequent problems. Check for ants periodically—they are usually a precursor of insect problems.

Boxleaf Azara

Azara

Features: habit, foliage, flowers **Habit:** large shrub or small tree **Height:** 12–18'; may reach 30' **Spread:** 8–12' **Planting:** container; spring **Zones:** 7–9

HERE IS A PERFECT EVERGREEN PLANT THAT CAN ACT AS A SCREEN for an ugly stucco wall that is a problem to cover. I recommend training it as a freestanding espalier instead of tying it to a trellis. It is wonderful for wood-shingled exteriors as well. Because it tolerates complete shade, it serves as a wonderful background for such plants as camellias, fuchsias, rhododendrons, Exbury azaleas and other shrubs that are dormant in winter. One of my favorites of the plants used in the Eichler tract home developments in the Bay Area, boxleaf azara was commonly used to divide driveways and courtyards.

Growing

Boxleaf azara does well in **partial shade**, but it will tolerate full shade. Grow it in **fertile, humus-rich, moist, well-drained** soil. Keep it in a location out of the hot afternoon sun and sheltered from cold winds. Prune after flowering is complete. Lightly cut back any branches that affect the shape, and thin crowded branches. Growth starts off slowly, but after the plant establishes itself for a couple of years, the rate of growth increases to 18" a year.

Tips

Boxleaf azara is a good addition to a shrub bed or border. Try it next to a pond or at the edge of a woodland garden.

Recommended

A. microphylla is an evergreen small tree or large shrub that grows 12–18' tall and 8–12' wide. In ideal conditions, and after many years, this plant may reach 30' tall. In late winter it produces clusters of fragrant, nodding, yellow to yellow-green flowers. The fruits are orange berries. Plants growing in complete shade likely will not bear fruit. (Zones 7–9)

The fragrant flowers have no petals—the stamens provide the show. The fragrance smells like vanilla to some and chocolate to others. It smells like a strawberry milkshake to me.

Butterfly Bush

Summer Lilac

Buddleia (Buddleja)

Features: flowers, habit, foliage **Habit:** large, deciduous shrub with arching branches **Height:** 4–20' **Spread:** 4–20' **Planting:** container; spring, fall **Zones:** 5–10

WHEN I FIRST PLANTED THIS BUSH IN MY PERENNIAL BED I WAITED with baited breath for the butterflies it would attract when it bloomed. There were only two types of insects I called butterflies: the monarch and the yellow swallowtail. When all I saw were these peculiar little orange-and-yellow nothings all over the flowers, I thought that I had been misinformed of the wonders of this plant. On my radio show *Bob Tanem in the Garden*, I interviewed Rick Mikula, the author of *The Family Butterfly Book*. I learned about the mourning cloak, the great spangled fritillary, the American painted lady and my favorite, the buckeye. Butterfly bush plants attract hummingbirds as well.

Growing

Butterfly bushes prefer to grow in **full sun**. Plants grown in shady conditions will produce few, if any, flowers. Ideally, the soil should be **fertile** and **well drained**, but it will tolerate most average well-drained soils as well.

Pruning is different for each species. *B. alternifolia* and *B. globosa* form flowers on the previous year's growth.

Each year, once the flowers have faded, cut the flowering shoots back to within a couple of buds of the main plant framework. *B. alternifolia* will also benefit from some formative pruning. It can be trained as a shrub or into a tree form.

B. davidii forms flowers on the current year's growth, so cut the shrub back to within 6–12" of the ground early each spring to encourage new growth and plenty of flowers. Removing spent flowerheads will encourage new shoots and extend the blooming period.

Tips

Butterfly bushes make beautiful additions to shrub and mixed borders. The graceful, arching branches make them excellent specimen plants. *B. alternifolia* is a particularly beautiful specimen when trained to form a small weeping tree. The dwarf forms that stay under 5' are suitable for small gardens.

B. globosa (above)

Butterfly bushes are among the best shrubs for attracting butterflies and bees to your garden. Don't spray your bush for pests—you will harm the beautiful and beneficial insects that make their homes there.

B. davidii (below)

Recommended

B. alternifolia (Alternate-Leaved Butterfly Bush) grows 10–20' tall, with an equal or slightly narrower spread. It can be trained to form a tree, leaving the branches lots of room to arch down around the trunk. In late spring or early summer, panicles of light purple flowers form at the ends of the branches, flopping around in a wonderful state of disarray. **'Argentea'** has silvery gray leaves. (Zones 5–10)

B. davidii (Orange-Eye Butterfly Bush, Summer Lilac) is the most commonly grown species. It grows 4–10' tall, with an equal spread. It has a long blooming period, bearing flowers in bright and pastel shades of purple, white, pink or blue from mid-summer to fall. The following popular cultivars are a few of the many available: **'Black Knight'** has dark purple flowers; **'Dubonnet'** has large spikes of pinky purple flowers; **'Pink Delight'** has pink flowers; and **'White Bouquet'** has white flowers. (Zones 5–9)

B. globosa (Orange Butterfly Bush, Orange Ball Tree) is a semi-evergreen

Butterfly bushes have a habit of self-seeding, and you may find tiny bushes popping up in unlikely places in the garden.

to evergreen shrub that reaches 8–15' in height and spread. In spring it bears distinctive balls of fragrant, yellow to deep orange flowers. The dark green, strikingly veined leaves may be up to 8" long. (Zones 6–9)

B. *davidii* (all photos both pages)

Problems & Pests

Many insects are attracted to butterfly bushes. Most just come for the pollen, and any others aren't likely to be a big problem. Good air circulation will help prevent fungal problems that might otherwise afflict these plants.

California Lilac

Ceanothus

Features: flowers, habit, foliage **Habit:** bushy, evergreen shrub **Height:** 1–15' **Spread:** 6–16' **Planting:** container; spring **Zones:** 7–10

GROWING UP IN WILLITS, I HAD THE WONDERFUL OPPORTUNITY to play in a nearby vacant lot, which is now a school. My cousin Bob and I decided that gold was everywhere in California. It was only logical to start digging in this vacant lot. The area in which we dug our mine was loaded with an evergreen shrub with white, very fragrant flowers. I now know that it was a form of California lilac. The lot was also loaded with quail. Bob and I would set traps and start digging for gold while we waited for the unsuspecting quail to trip the traps. We deserted our claim after only digging a 1' deep, 4' by 4' excavation. The quail never did discover our traps, and we never came close to finding gold, but the memory is brought back every time I see a California lilac in bloom.

Growing

California lilacs prefer to grow in **full sun**. The soil should be **well drained** and can range from slightly acidic to slightly alkaline. These lilacs are heat and drought resistant and generally undemanding in Northern California gardens. They require little or no water after the second year in the ground.

Pruning should take place in late spring after the blooming cycle is complete. Evergreen species and cultivars flower on the previous year's growth and need very little pruning. The flowering shoots can be cut back after they are finished flowering. Remove any growth that is damaged over winter. To maintain low growth on groundcover plants, prune back shoots that are growing upright at any time of the year.

'Concha' (above & below)

These shrubs are considered short-lived, lasting about 5–10 years. Full sun and a protected site will prolong their lives.

'Julia Phelps' (above), *C. griseus* var. *horizontalis* (below)

Tips

California lilacs can be included in a shrub or mixed border. The low-growing cultivars can be used as groundcovers or trained to grow up walls or over rocks. Ensure there is enough space for these plants to reach their full size. Pruning to keep them inbounds can shorten their lifespan. Pinching the tips early in the season can help control plant size.

These shrubs can tolerate some frost and will often recover from winter damage. Coastal gardeners will have the best luck with California lilacs. Gardeners in the hot interior valleys should choose plants that are from locally grown sources for the best results.

Recommended

C. **'Concha'** has arching branches and dense, dark green foliage. It grows 6–10' tall and wide and bears a bounty of dark blue blooms in spring. This plant tolerates summer water provided it has proper drainage. (Zones 8–10)

C. gloriosus (Point Reyes Ceanothus, Point Reyes Creeper) is a low-growing, spreading shrub with tough, leathery, spiny, dark green leaves. It grows to 12–18" in height and spreads 12–16'. The blue or purple flowers are borne from spring to early summer. **'Anchor Bay'** has denser growth and darker blue flowers than the species but only spreads half as wide. **'Emily Brown'** grows to 36" tall and 12' wide and bears dark, violet blue to indigo flowers. Its dark green leaves are prominently toothed. (Zones 7–10)

C. griseus (Carmel Ceanothus) is a spreading shrub growing 8–10' tall and 8–12' wide. It produces pale violet-blue flowers in spring. More often used are the low-growing plants of this species. ***C. g.* var. *horizontalis*** (Carmel Creeper) grows 18–30" tall and spreads 8–15', bearing light blue flowers. **'Yankee Point'** grows to 36" tall and 8–10' wide. Its flowers are bright blue and are produced abundantly. (Zones 8–10)

C. **'Julia Phelps'** is a rounded shrub growing 4–6' tall and 7–9' wide. Violet to dark indigo flowers are produced from late spring to early summer. This *Ceanothus* is deer resistant (Zones 8–10)

'Anchor Bay' (above), 'Yankee Point' (below)

Problems & Pests

Borers can wipe out a plant, although they usually only infest weakened plants. Aphids, gall moths, mealybugs, psyllids, tent caterpillars and whiteflies can be problems. Canker and root rot can occasionally afflict California lilacs. They are prone to oak root fungus and other root rots if exposed to summer moisture.

*Many species of California lilac are native to our state. They mainly inhabit the dry, scrubby chaparral along the coast and in the foothills. You will often find California lilac growing along with manzanita (*Arctostaphylos *spp.) and* Yucca whipplei.

California Pepper Tree

Pepper Tree, Peruvian Mastic Tree

Schinus

Features: flowers, foliage, habit **Habit:** evergreen tree with spreading crown **Height:** 20–40' **Spread:** 20–40' **Planting:** container, B & B; spring (after frost danger has passed) **Zones:** 9–11

THIS TREE WAS ORIGINALLY BROUGHT TO CALIFORNIA FROM PERU by missionaries. The oldest living California specimen is found in Mission San Luis Rey de Francia in Southern California. It was planted around 1805. Another very old specimen of this tree is found at the Presidio in San Francisco. These magnificent trees are alive today more than likely because they were ignored and never cared for or watered all those years.

Growing

California pepper trees grow well in **full sun** in **well-drained, moderately fertile** soil. They need some water when they are establishing, but take care not to overwater them. California pepper trees tolerate poorer soils and drought once established. In the hottest areas, it might be necessary to protect young trunks from sunburn until the leaf coverage is sufficient.

Tips

A California pepper tree can make a handsome shade tree for an outdoor living area or play yard. It is suitable as a specimen tree and can be trained to make an informal hedge. California pepper trees have aggressive surface roots, so avoid planting them near sewer, water or drainage lines or paved surfaces. Use organic mulch out to the dripline.

Contact with the foliage can aggravate dermatitis, hay fever and asthma.

Recommended

S. molle is a broad-headed tree with fine-textured, mid- to bright green, drooping foliage on weeping branchlets. The trunk and main branches become heavy and gnarled with age. It produces drooping clusters of tiny, yellowish white flowers from late spring to summer, with male and female flowers on the same or separate trees. Attractive, rose pink, berry-like fruits are produced from the female flowers in fall and winter. (Zones 9–11)

Problems & Pests

Scale insects, spider mites and root rots, including Texas root rot, can all cause problems.

Oldest specimen at San Luis Rey de Francia (above)

The seed is sometimes sold as pink pepper, but in large quantities it can be very toxic. The seed is also used as a decoration when making wreaths.

Camellia

Camellia

Features: flowers, foliage, habit **Habit:** upright to spreading shrub or small tree **Height:** 18"–20', sometimes to 50' **Spread:** 3–12' **Planting:** container, B & B; fall to spring **Zones:** 7–9

'YULETIDE' IS ONE OF MY FAVORITE CAMELLIA CULTIVARS BECAUSE it can take more sun than many of the others. I have used it as a hedge in full sun along the coast and in Belvedere with spectacular results. One of the major problems with camellias happens in winter during the rainy season. We forget to water plants under the eaves of houses, which can cause a major stress on camellias, as well as on other plants in the same situation.

Growing

Camellias prefer to grow in **light to partial shade** in **well-drained** soil with lots of organic matter mixed in. They prefer **acidic to neutral** soil. *C. japonica* prefers the more acid end of the scale. Protect camellias from strong, hot sun and drying winds. They may also suffer damage if temperatures drop below 15° F. Propagate them in summer and fall by seed or by stem cuttings of the current season's growth. It takes around seven years from seed to bloom. Find a true yellow-flowering seedling and you can retire.

When planting, ensure that the base of the tree is slightly above grade and that the soil is not covering the base. Never bury the rootball and do not use a treewell. Add a 2" layer of loose and airy organic mulch, such as cedar bark or shredded redwood bark, to help keep the roots cool for the first two to three years. Older, vigorous plants will shade their own roots. They should be fed monthly with an acidic, organic fertilizer, beginning after blooming is complete and until the flower buds form in fall. Do not overfertilize. Camellias can take regular watering provided the soil is very well drained. Older plants do very well without regular watering.

Camellias can be pruned as much or as little as desired. Pruning while they are in bloom is best because that is when they are most dormant. They can be trained to be large, erect shrubs, hedges, small

C. sasanqua cultivar (above)

C. japonica *cultivars are classified by the size and form of the flowers. The flower sizes are miniature (less than $2\frac{1}{2}$" across), small ($2\frac{1}{2}$–3"), medium (3–$3\frac{1}{2}$"), medium large ($3\frac{1}{2}$–4"), large (4–5") and very large (over 5" across). The flower forms are single, semi-double, anemone, peony, rose-form double and formal double.*

C. reticulata cultivar (below)

C. *sasanqua* cultivar (above), *C. japonica* cultivar (below)

trees or low, sprawling shrubs. After flowering, remove dead, diseased and damaged branches and any dead blooms from around the base. To stimulate more branching, cut branches just above where the lighter-colored, new growth meets the darker-colored, older growth. Cut back any growth that is spreading out of bounds. Camellias should only be pruned with hand pruners. Never use shears. To help control and prevent disease and pests, thin out dead, weak or spindly growth prior to the first growth cycle after the dormant season.

Tips

Camellias are evergreen plants suitable for mixed beds, borders and woodland gardens, as specimens or as container plants. The soil for container plantings should be 50% organic matter and 50% potting mix.

Some camellias produce a plethora of flower buds, often more than they can open. Selective debudding will allow the remaining buds to form larger, stronger and more prominent flowers. If you don't have time to thin the buds or you forget, don't fret, the plants will be quite happy regardless. Naturally occurring bud drop may be caused by overwatering or underwatering, or by a period of very low humidity.

Recommended

There are almost 300 species and thousands of cultivars of camellias. The following selections are a small sample of the most popular garden camellias. Check with your local nursery or garden center to see what is available. The best time to shop is from December through March.

C. japonica is the most commonly available species and is the parent of most of the garden camellias. It is variable in size and form, usually growing 6–12' tall, with an equal spread. Older specimens can reach 20' or more in height. *C. japonica* produces shiny green leaves and has flowers that come in shades of white, pink or red. The flowers can be solid or bicolored, with striped, blotched or picotee patterns. They have golden yellow stamens that may or may not be visible depending on the flower form. Flowering time varies depending on which cultivar is selected. Early-flowering camellias bloom from October to January, mid-season is from January to March and late bloomers flower from March to May. Selecting plants

C. reticulata cultivar (above)

The first C. reticulata *to come out of Asia was taken to England by the East India Company's Captain Rawes in 1820. This species has sterile blooms borne on trees that have attained 60' in height in their native Canton.*

C. japonica cultivar (below)

with different flowering times can assure colorful blooms from fall to spring. **Higo** camellias have been developed over the last 400 years on the Japanese island of Kyushu. They are more compact than the species. The single flowers come in the same colors as other *C. japonica* selections, but the cluster of golden stamens is quite prominent, often up to half the diameter of the flower. **'Asahi No Minato,' 'Jitsu Getsu Sei'** and **'Tenju'** are some of the more available varieties. The single flowers are not in and of themselves spectacular, but the overall effect is very striking, especially as container plants. These plants lend themselves to the creation of perfect bonsai. (Zones 7–9)

C. reticulata produces dull green, well-veined, leathery leaves and some of the largest and showiest flowers of all the camellias. The flowers are present from January to May. The plants are more upright and open than *C. japonica,* growing to 10–15' tall and 8–10' wide in gardens, with the potential to reach heights of 40–50'. *C. reticulata* dislikes having its roots disturbed and does not tolerate heavy pruning. **'Buddha'** produces very large, rosy pink flowers with inner petals that are unusually erect and wavy. This sparse and open cultivar has a very rapid growth rate. (Zones 7–9)

C. sasanqua (Sasanqua Camellia) is quite variable in size and habit, ranging from 18" tall by 3–6' wide groundcovers to 12' tall by 12' wide large, robust shrubs. Some selections may reach 20' with age. This species tolerates more sunlight, drought and cooler climates than other camellias. It produces many short-lived, single to semi-double, mildly fragrant flowers from October to January in typical camellia colors. The most spectacular cultivars bloom in

C. japonica cultivar (below)

December. This shrub is very useful for many landscape applications, including hedges, groundcovers, street trees and espalier. **'Yuletide'** is a densely foliaged, upright shrub with bright red flowers and bright yellow stamens. (Zones 7–8)

C. sinensis (Tea Camellia) produces dark green, leathery leaves and inconspicuous but very fragrant white flowers on shrubs 6–20' tall and wide. This species is very tolerant of a location composed of full sun and poorer soils. *C. sinensis* is the species that provides all the world's camellia tea. (Zones 7–9)

Problems & Pests

Camellia petal blight can be a major problem. It causes petals to turn brown rapidly. Remove all infected flowers and ensure the area is well cleaned of all plant debris. Remove and replace any mulch. Spray once a month for three months with liquid copper as buds form. Dispose of the refuse in the haul-away garbage. Camellias are sensitive to sunburn and leaf scorch.

Camellias tolerate salt and pollution, making them excellent choices for coastal and urban plantings.

C. japonica (below)

Cape Plumbago

Leadwort

Plumbago

Features: flowers, habit **Habit:** evergreen to semi-evergreen, rounded to mounding shrub with arching branches **Height:** 6–12' **Spread:** 8–10' **Planting:** container; spring (after frost danger has passed) **Zones:** 9–11

THE FOUNTAIN-LIKE GROWTH HABIT OF CAPE PLUMBAGO ADDS A delicate, pea green accent to the most boring of evergreen landscapes. The phlox-like blooms form in early spring and continue until cold weather shuts this shrub down in late fall. It combines well with willowleaf cotoneaster *(Cotoneaster salicifolius)* and other wild-looking plants on hillsides or next to woodland locations and open spaces. Cape plumbago will naturalize after two years and is an ideal shrub to plant under evergreen oak trees.

Growing

Cape plumbago grows in **full sun** to **light shade** in **well-drained** soil that has lots of **organic matter** worked in. A moderate to hard frost will kill the foliage, but the shrub recovers quickly. In frost-free areas cape plumbago remains evergreen all year and can bloom all year. Established plants can tolerate drier conditions. During summer, ensure the soil is moist for the best flowering.

Prune in late winter to early spring before the new growth begins and after the danger of frost has passed. Cape plumbago produces flowers on the current season's growth. Shorten the branches back to a main framework, leaving three to four buds per branch. Cape plumbago suckers readily.

P. auriculata (all photos this page)

Tips

Cape plumbago is suitable for formal or informal hedges, for shrub or mixed borders, for foundation plantings, as filler, as ground or bank covers and in containers. It can be trained to cover walls and fences. It is an ideal shrub to fill in blank spots that are difficult to care for. Cape plumbago will survive even if burned to the ground.

Recommended

P. auriculata (*P. capensis*) (Skyflower, Blue Plumbago, Cape Leadwort) grows 6' tall and 8–10' wide, bearing clusters of white or light blue to sky blue flowers at the branch tips. It can grow 12' tall or more when tied to a support. **'Alba'** bears clusters of white flowers. **'Royal Cape'** produces vivid blue flowers and tolerates more dryness and frost than the species. (Zones 9–11)

Problems & Pests

Cape plumbago could be attacked by aphids and scale insects.

Do not confuse cape plumbago with dwarf plumbago (Ceratostigma plumbaginoides), *which is a 6–12" tall perennial with intense blue flowers.*

Cedar

Cedrus

Features: habit, foliage, cones, bark **Habit:** large, upright, spreading or pendulous, evergreen tree **Height:** 3–100' **Spread:** 3–70' **Planting:** container; spring **Zones:** 7–9

I HAVE SEEN THE CULTIVAR 'GLAUCA PENDULA' TRAINED ON A pergola and used as a background for a garden full of weeping trees, including cherries, mulberries, beech and others. The striking blue needles of the cedar made it a tremendously effective background for those weeping trees. 'Glauca Pendula' also makes a wonderful container plant. I kept one in a barrel for over 35 years, and it was the focal point in over 20 display gardens in which I participated. It probably won 40 blue ribbons for plant specimen and also won 16 Best of Show awards. I sold it to a landscaper who had the perfect location for it—trailing over a 30' granite monolith. I hated to give it up, but I had no choice; I do have visiting rights.

Growing

Cedars grow well in **full sun** or **partial shade.** The soil can be of any type as long as it is **well drained.** A **moist, loamy soil** of **average to high fertility** is preferable. Planting on top of a mounded area to maximize surface drainage will give good results. Very little pruning is required. Remove damaged or dead branches.

These trees tolerate temperatures in the Sierras as well as the warmer valleys in Northern California. They are at their very best along coastal locations and are likely to suffer some damage in colder areas. Daring gardeners who wish to plant these species in colder climates should choose a sheltered location, and be prepared to remove any growth that is damaged by the cold.

Tips

The cedar species are very large trees—much too large for the average home garden—best suited to large properties and parks. Several cultivars are much smaller and can be used as impressive specimen trees in all but the smallest home gardens. If you put the larger cedar species in your front yard, that is all you will have. No lawn, no flowerbeds, no place for dogs and no home.

Recommended

C. atlantica (Atlas Cedar, Blue Atlas Cedar) generally grows 40–60' tall, but it can grow to 100' in good conditions with adequate space. Clusters of needle-like, blue-green leaves are produced on the branches that sweep the ground, spreading to 40' wide. Although this species is a bit too large for the average garden,

C. libani (above)

A portrait of C. libani *graces the national flag of Lebanon. This tree is native to the Middle East, and centuries ago it was one of the only sources of lumber in that region.*

C. atlantica 'Glauca Pendula' (below)

C. *deodara* (all photos this page)

gardeners can consider the cultivar **'Glauca Pendula,'** which is interesting and not as tall. The branches of this cultivar are long and trailing, however, and it can spread just as far as the species. Train it to grow over an arbor, where the branches can trail down. (Zones 7–9)

C. deodara (Deodar Cedar) is an open, graceful tree with nodding branch tips. It grows to 80' tall and 40' wide in large gardens and parks and can reach heights of 150' in the wild. This species has dark bluish green foliage and is the fastest growing of all cedars. Some cultivars are more reasonable in size and more tolerant of winter cold. **'Aurea'** is slow growing, reaching a mature height of about 15'. The foliage is bright yellow and deepens to green as it matures. (Zones 7–9)

C. libani (Cedar of Lebanon) is a slow-growing species that is narrowly pyramidal in youth and stately and irregular in maturity. It grows to 80' tall and spreads almost as wide as tall. It has bright green leaves in youth and dark green leaves in

At one time, C. deodara *was touted as the 'California Christmas Tree.' It was a totally misleading name. The weeping branches do not lend themselves to holding ornaments securely. One Christmas I did use one of these trees. The kids called it the 'Charlie Brown Tree.' The only gifts under that tree were checks and money, given to us by family, that allowed Bev and I to take the kids to Disneyland.*

maturity. Suitable cultivars are available for space-restricted settings. This tree was and is still used for construction in the Middle East. **'Pendula'** is a weeping cultivar that is often grafted to create a small weeping tree, ideal for use as a specimen. **'Sargentii'** is a slow-growing, dwarf cultivar that reaches a height and width of only 3–5'. (Zones 7–9)

Problems & Pests

The biggest problem is top dieback, which can be caused by cold weather, weevils or canker. Root rot can occur in poorly drained soils. *C. libani* is extremely susceptible to root rot in these conditions.

C. deodara (above)

These trees are the 'true cedars'—that is, Cedrus *spp. Confusingly, some 70 different types of trees have been called 'cedar.'*

C. libani (below)

Chinese Pistache

Pistacia

Features: foliage, flowers, fruit **Habit:** erect to spreading, deciduous tree **Height:** 30–60' **Spread:** 30–60' **Planting:** container; spring, fall, any cool weather **Zones:** 7–10

THIS TREE IS ONE OF MY ALL-TIME FAVORITES. NOT ONLY DOES IT grow fairly rapidly from youth to 25', it satisfies the need for fall color in the landscape. It is perfect for transplanted Easterners who feel that fall has deserted them when they don't see any leaves turn color. As a deciduous tree, Chinese pistache has the added value of allowing winter sun to reach your home. It also makes a wonderful lawn or groundcover tree. The ornamental berries have many uses in dry floral arrangements. If berries are not wanted, search for male trees that don't bear fruit.

Growing

Grow Chinese pistache in **full sun** in **moderately fertile, very well-drained** soil. Chinese pistache can tolerate a wide variety of conditions, including drought, pollution, restricted root space and slightly alkaline soil. Younger trees may require staking. Chinese pistache will do well when given occasional deep waterings. (Regular shallow watering may induce *Verticillium* wilt.)

Chinese pistache does not respond well to pruning. Train to form when the plants are young. After that, prune minimally, if needed, in late winter.

Tips

Chinese pistache can be used as a street or shade tree. It is effective planted beside patios and does reasonably well in lawns. It is a good performer in coastal conditions.

The risk of *Verticillium* wilt increases if grass grows inside the dripline. Bumping the trunk with a lawn mower isn't healthy for the tree either.

Male flowers and female flowers are borne on separate plants. For fruit production, both male and female trees are necessary.

Recommended

P. chinensis has leathery, glossy, dark green foliage that turns a vivid orange to red in fall. The fragrant, inconspicuous flowers bloom in mid- to late spring. The spherical, red fruit matures to black on the female trees. (Zones 7–10)

Problems & Pests

Verticillium wilt, dieback, root rot and scale insects might cause problems. Chinese pistache is resistant to oak root fungus.

Chinese pistache often forms a double trunk and does not require cold temperatures to produce good fall color.

Coast Redwood

Giant Sequoia

Sequoia & Sequoiadendron

Features: foliage, bark, cones, habit **Habit:** columnar or conical, evergreen tree
Height: 5–100' **Spread:** 5–50' **Planting:** container; spring, fall **Zones:** 6–10

THE STATE TREE OF CALIFORNIA IS *SEQUOIA SEMPERVIRENS*. *Sempervirens* translates into 'ever living,' which is quite true of this tree's nature. A walk through some of the redwood forests on the coast of Northern California will verify the ability of these trees to survive any disaster. In the Eel River area, you can see areas where the river has deposited 5' of silt around the redwoods and later washed it away. These trees merely set out new root systems to adapt. Fire that burns through a forest of coast redwoods may damage the interior of some of these trees—the trunks can be quite hollow, from the ground up to 20' or so—yet the trees survive and are thriving. Most of this survival is made possible because of the coast redwood's very thick, fibrous bark.

Growing

Coast redwood grows well in **full sun** or **light shade**. The soil should be of **average fertility, moist** and **well drained.** Coast redwood needs regular watering for the first few years of growth and when planted in hot, dry areas. In its native habitat, it is able to get water from the dew on the foliage created by the ocean fog. Coast redwood does not like pollution or urban environments. Pruning is rarely required.

Tips

Coast redwood makes a stunning specimen tree alone or in groups. Never underestimate its potential size—this giant is not for the average garden. Lack of water in summer slows the tree's growth. The smaller cultivars can be used as windbreaks, as hedges and in shrub or mixed borders. Plant coast redwoods while they are small enough to not require staking.

Seedling-grown *Sequoia sempervirens* tends to send up sucker-like growth. If the suckers are not removed, they will slow the growth of the central core. Unlike most coniferous trees, redwood sprouts new shoots from the base if cut down.

Coast redwoods grow best in conditions of high atmospheric pressure and humidity at sea level. Giant sequoias (*Sequoiadendron giganteum*) do best in higher elevations such as Yosemite National Park.

'Adpressa' (above), *Sequoia sempervirens* (below)

Sequoiadendron giganteum (above)

Sequoia sempervirens (above)

Coast redwoods are the tallest conifers in the world; the record-holding specimen is a towering 365' and is found near Ukiah, California.

Recommended

Sequoia sempervirens (Coast Redwood) is a tall, columnar or conical tree, with horizontal branches and drooping branchlets. It is native to the northern coastal regions of California. It grows 50–100' tall and 20–30' wide in gardens but can grow three times as tall in the wild. **'Adpressa'** is a smaller, slower-growing cultivar that is hardier than the species, to Zone 6. It grows 20–30' tall and spreads 10–20'. **'Aptos Blue'** is similar to the species in growth, but it has dense, blue-green foliage. **'Prostrata'** is a dwarf, spreading cultivar. It grows 5' tall and spreads 5–10'. This cultivar has a tendency to revert to the upright form, so watch for and remove any strongly upright growth. **'Woodside'** and **'Filoli'** are thought to be the same. Both have intense blue foliage and irregular growth. (Zones 7–10)

Alternate Species

Sequoiadendron giganteum (*Sequoia gigantea*) (Giant Sequoia, Big Tree) is a large, pyramidal tree that branches to the ground. The foliage is denser and more prickly than coast redwood's. This tree grows 60–100' tall and 30–50' wide in gardens. It prefers moderate watering. It is subject to fungal diseases in humid climates. Giant sequoia is hardier to the cold than coast redwood. Use as a specimen tree in a large setting. It is not tolerant of urban conditions or pollution. The pyramidal shape lends giant sequoia to becoming a living Christmas tree. This tree is very useful as a fire break in the mountains to ward off forest fires. (Zones 6–9; Zone 5, if protected)

Problems & Pests

Redwoods may suffer from iron chlorosis in iron-poor soils. Look for yellowing of the new leaves. Use an iron chelate. The older foliage will naturally turn yellow, then brown and then fall off. Redwood is resistant to oak root fungus.

'Aptos Blue' (above)

Sequoiadendron giganteum (below)

Common Quince

Fruiting Quince

Cydonia

Features: flowers, fruit, habit **Habit:** rounded, deciduous, small tree or large shrub **Height:** 10–25' **Spread:** 10–25' **Planting:** container (spring); bare-root (January and February) **Zones:** 5–9

USUALLY, IF LEFT ALONE BY ITSELF IN THE BACKGROUND OF ignored gardens, common quince will be quite content. I've run across this plant in long-deserted orchards. It was thriving while the rest of the orchard had perished—common quince was the only pectin available in the Mission Gardens. Common quince can live up to 150 or more years, and the trunk becomes quite picturesque with age.

Growing

Common quince prefers **full sun.** The soil should be of **average fertility, well drained** and **moist**. Avoid high-nitrogen fertilizers because they promote lush growth, which is prone to fire blight. Deep cultivation around the base of the plant may damage the shallow roots.

Prune when young to shape the tree and provide a solid, open framework. Remove suckers at the base of the plant and annually open the center of the plant to sunshine and air in winter. Common quince can be trained as a fan espalier against a wall. Training it against a wall is the best treatment in cooler parts of Northern California, where temperatures fall to 5° F.

Tips

C. oblonga is excellent as a specimen. The branches are twisted and contorted, creating an impressive and interesting form that is especially attractive in winter. It can be used in a shrub border or grown strictly for fruit production. Harvest the fruit when ripe or before a hard frost.

Recommended

C. oblonga produces solitary, pale pink to white, shallow, bowl-shaped flowers in spring. The ripe fruit is light golden yellow, aromatic and pear-shaped. The fruit is best when grown in areas with long, hot summers. The dark green leaves have downy undersides and turn rich yellow in fall. **'Orange'** ('Apple') has round, orange-yellow fruit. **'Pineapple'** tastes like its name. (Zones 5–9)

Problems & Pests

Pest possibilities may include scale insects, caterpillars, mealybugs, aphids and Japanese beetles. Other potential problems are fire blight, powdery mildew, brown rot, rust and crown gall.

C. oblonga (all photos this page)

Crape Myrtle

Lagerstroemia

Features: flowers, foliage, bark **Habit:** deciduous, multi-stemmed shrub or small tree **Height:** 20"–25' **Spread:** 26"–25' **Planting:** container, B & B; spring, fall **Zones:** 7–10

UP UNTIL 1940, CRAPE MYRTLE WASN'T RECOMMENDED BECAUSE of its tendency to be infected with powdery mildew. With the advent of horticultural sprays and new hybrids, crape myrtle has become one of my favorite blooming small patio trees. The wonderful flowers come in a rainbow of colors from the middle of June to October. The foliage then turns to many shades of oranges, yellows and pinks. It is advisable to prune crape myrtle every year because the flowers bloom on new wood. Crape myrtles are deer resistant, but the exposed young trunks will need to be protected from male deer that use them to remove the velvet from their antlers. I put corrugated 4" plastic drain hose, split vertically, around the trunk to prevent this damage.

Growing

Crape myrtle performs best in **full sun** but tolerates light shade. It likes **well-drained, neutral to slightly acidic** soil. In alkaline or salty soil, this shrub or small tree may experience burning of the leaf margins and/or chlorosis. Hot winds may also scorch the leaf margins. Ensure regular watering when young. Once established, crape myrtle is quite drought tolerant, but it will do best with an occasional deep watering. Do not water from overhead. Fertilize with organic fertilizer in late winter before the new growth emerges.

'Watermelon' (above), *L. indica* (below)

L. indica needs only minimal pruning in mid- to late winter before the new growth emerges. This species can be trained as a single- or multi-stemmed plant with a rounded crown. Often, the lower branches and any weak stems are removed to show off the attractive bark.

The shrubby hybrids can be sheared for hedges but are best left in a more natural form. They can be treated the same as *L. indica.* Removing the first flush of flowers, once blooming is complete, often promotes new growth and late season blooms. In any case, the seedpods should be removed after flowering.

Tips

Crape myrtles make excellent specimens. *L. indica* can be used for street trees and in lawns. The shrubs can be used for hedging, screening and shrub borders and in mass plantings. Take care when selecting plants for underplanting around crape myrtle—the roots are quite

L. *indica* (all photos this page)

Crape myrtles are planted around commercial orchards for their ability to attract and nourish many different beneficial insects. Avoid pesticides, if possible.

competitive. Long, cool fall seasons yield the best leaf color.

Crape myrtle may produce suckers that should be pruned away once they appear. Crape myrtles self-seed readily, so make sure to pull out all of the newly emerging seedlings. Crape myrtles are easily transplanted from containers into the garden, but they do not like being moved once planted.

Recommended

Indian Tribe Group Hybrids are known for their mildew resistance and improved hardiness. They perform better than *L. indica* in coastal climates. **'Acoma'** (White Crape Myrtle) is a spreading, pendulous shrub that grows 6–10' tall and wide. It produces clusters of white flowers all summer and has exfoliating, light gray-brown bark. The fall color is reddish purple. **'Chickasaw'** is a true dwarf variety. It grows 20" tall and 26" wide and is popular with bonsai enthusiasts. It has lavender flowers. **'Hopi'** produces light to bright pink clusters of blooms over a long period of time. It reaches 8–10' tall and wide, has gray-brown exfoliating bark and orange-red to dark red fall leaf color. **'Tonto'** (Red Crape Myrtle) grows 10–20' tall and wide. It produces abundant clusters of dark fuchsia flowers from mid-summer to early fall. The fall foliage is bright maroon, and the exfoliating bark is a creamy taupe.
(Zones 7–10)

L. indica is a multi-stemmed, small tree growing 15–25' tall and wide. It does best in the hot interior valleys, producing showy clusters of ruffled, crepe-like flowers in white and shades of red, pink and purple all summer. The foliage begins as bronze-tinged light green, aging to dark glossy green in summer and turning yellow, orange or red in fall. The gray-brown bark exfoliates to reveal the pinkish bark beneath. **'Catawba'** grows to 10' tall and wide. It has purple flowers and orange-red fall color. **'Watermelon'** grows as large as the species. It has bright red flowers and yellow fall color. (Zones 7–10)

Problems & Pests

Crape myrtle is prone to powdery mildew, especially in coastal gardens. It may also get aphids, leaf spot, root rot and scale insects.

L. indica (above), *L. indica* cultivar (below)

Cypress

Cupressus

Features: foliage, habit, bark, cones **Habit:** columnar to pyramidal, coniferous tree **Height:** 20–120' **Spread:** 3–40' **Planting:** B & B, container, bare-root; spring, fall **Zones:** 7–10

CYPRESSES ARE WONDERFUL TREES FOR USE AS HEDGES, AND I recommend using seedling-grown plants to make one. The foliage may not be uniform in shape, but the hedge will be far more interesting. Another way to create hedges or screens is by cutting grown cultivars—uniformity and a more formal look is achieved, but the hedge will not be as hardy or sturdy as one created with seedling-grown plants. Whatever method is followed, start with one-gallon plants so the training begins early. Make sure your soil is well prepared and always plant properly.

Growing

Most cypresses prefer **full sun, well-drained soil** and **shelter** from cold wind. *C. arizonica, C. arizonica* var. *glabra* and *C. sempervirens* do well in heat and drier soil. Most of the cypresses require little or no water after the second year.

Cypress doesn't usually require pruning. If you desire a higher crown, *C. macrocarpa* can have some of the lower limbs removed when the plant is young. If you are growing cypress as a hedge, begin training when the plants are young and only trim the young growth. Do not cut into the older wood of any cypress, because cypresses do not regenerate. Most of the time this pencil-shaped conifer is well behaved and contains its lateral growth. Remove shoots of *C. sempervirens* that veer off in the wrong direction.

C. macrocarpa *is native to California's Monterey Peninsula and is very susceptible to* Coryneum *canker fungus. All plants are deer resistant.*

A unique feature of cypress is the mature bark that often breaks off into curling or rounded scales.

C. macrocarpa (all photos this page)

Tips

All cypress are long-lived and make excellent specimen trees. They are also used as screens, windbreaks, hedges and boulevard trees.

C. macrocarpa is used as a specimen along the coast, where it has become a trademark for Carmel. When the trees are planted closely together, the trunks will tend to grow straight and tall. When planted in open sites, the trees develop low, sturdy, spreading branches that produce a broad, dense crown of foliage.

C. macrocarpa (above), 'Stricta' (below)

A strong stream of water once or twice a year will keep the center of the cypress from accumulating dead needles and enhance the health of the tree.

Recommended

C. arizonica (Arizona Cypress, Rough Barked Arizona Cypress) is a densely pyramidal tree that grows 40–50' tall and spreads 20–25' wide. It has green to bluish gray, finely textured, evergreen foliage and roundish, brown-gray female cones that grow to 1" in diameter. The bark is stringy, brown and furrowed. **'Blue Pyramid'** is preferred for specimen planting. **Var. *glabra*** (*C. glabra*) (Smooth Arizona Cypress) is very similar to the species but sheds its bark annually, revealing the smooth cherry red inner bark. The foliage of var. *glabra* has resin glands that appear as white specks. The shedding bark isn't noticeable if these plants are used for hedges. As a specimen, var. *glabra* develops a trunk that will shed. (Zones 7–10)

C. macrocarpa (Monterey Cypress) is narrowly pyramidal when young, spreading as wide as it is tall with age. The species grows 40' tall and wide and can reach 120' tall in ideal conditions. Lemon-scented, dark to bright green foliage forms in erect to spreading sprays. This species grows vigorously to 30–40' within 10 years. **'Aurea'** has golden-colored foliage and is wider spreading than the species. All *C. macrocarpa* trees prefer mild climates and regular winter rainfall. They are not a good choice for the hot interior valleys, preferring coastal conditions. (Zone 9–10)

C. sempervirens (Italian Cypress, Mediterranean Cypress, Funeral Cypress) comes in two basic forms. One form is narrowly columnar, with upright branches and branchlets. The other form is conical, with horizontal branches and drooping branchlets. Both forms grow to 70' tall (with the potential to reach 120' in ideal conditions) and spread to 20' for the horizontal branching form. Both bear dense sprays of gray-green to dark green foliage. **'Stricta'** grows 60–70' tall and spreads 10' and has dark green foliage. **'Swane's Gold'** is compact and upright, growing 20' tall and 36" wide. It bears heavily golden-tipped foliage. (Zones 8–10)

C. torulosa (Himalayan Cypress) is fast growing to 30–50' and is not as susceptible to the problems of other cypresses. *C. torulosa* has pea green foliage and can be trained into many forms. It makes the ideal bonsai specimen. (Zones 8–10)

Problems & Pests

Cypress tip moth (tip miner) is the most common pest. Aphids, bark beetles, mealybugs, scale insects, sawflies, rust and scab are occasional problems. *Coryneum* canker fungus is an incurable disease. The foliage turns yellow, then deep reddish brown and eventually falls off. Remove and destroy any tree that is affected; clean and remove all refuse carefully and immediately.

C. sempervirens (below)

Daphne

Daphne

Features: foliage, fragrant spring flowers **Habit:** upright, rounded or low-growing, evergreen or semi-evergreen shrub **Height:** 6"–6' **Spread:** 3–6' **Planting:** container; early spring, early fall **Zones:** 4–10

WINTER DAPHNE IS EVERYONE'S FAVORITE DAPHNE, EVEN THOUGH it requires exacting conditions and can die unexpectedly for no apparent reason. Its wonderfully fragrant blooms appear in the later part of December and through January. This shrub is native in areas where summer rain is rare, so hold off on the summertime watering as much as reasonably possible. Feeding the shrub can be done twice a year—once after it finishes blooming and again after the new growth stops. If the soil or planting mix drains well, winter daphne can take winter watering. If the draining doesn't go well, protect it from winter rain. It is deer resistant in all areas of Northern California.

Growing

Daphne prefers **full sun** or **partial shade**. The soil should be **moist, very well drained** and of **average to high fertility**. Use a layer of mulch or a living groundcover to help keep the shallow roots cool. Ensure moderate water in summer and very little over the winter.

Winter daphne absolutely needs porous soil. When planting, ensure the crown of the plant is 1–2" above the soil surface. If your soil is too heavy, plant in a raised bed or large container where you can control the watering.

These shrubs have neat, dense growth that needs very little pruning. Remove damaged or diseased branches. Flowerheads can be removed once flowering is finished. Cut flowering stems back to where they join the main branches, which will preserve the natural growth habit of these shrubs.

Tips

Rose daphne makes an attractive groundcover in a rock garden or woodland garden. Burkwood and winter daphnes can be included in shrub or mixed borders; plant them near paths, doors, windows or other places where the wonderful scent can be enjoyed.

Note that *D. laureola* (laurel daphne) is an invasive species in wild areas on the west coast, and it should be avoided.

Daphne, especially winter daphne, has a strange habit of dying suddenly. There are many suggestions as

D. x *burkwoodii* 'Somerset'

to why this sudden death happens and how to avoid it. The best advice is to plant daphne in good, well-drained conditions and then leave it alone. Any disturbance that could stress this shrub should be avoided. Don't move daphnes once they are planted.

All parts of daphne plants are toxic if eaten, and the sap may cause skin irritations. Avoid planting these species where children may be tempted to sample the berries.

Recommended

D.* x *burkwoodii (Burkwood Daphne) is an upright, semi-evergreen shrub. It bears fragrant, white or light pink flowers in late spring and sometimes again in late summer or early fall. It grows 3–5' in height and spread.

D. cneorum 'Variegata' (below & right)

'Carol Mackie' is a common cultivar; its dark green leaves have golden margins. **'Somerset'** has darker pink flowers and grows a little larger than the hybrid species. (Zones 5–10)

D. cneorum (Rose Daphne, Garland Flower) is a low-growing, evergreen shrub. It grows 6–12" tall and can spread to 4'. The fragrant, pale to deep pink or white flowers are borne in spring. Plant in partial shade in the hot interior valleys. **'Alba'** has white flowers, and **'Ruby Glow'** has reddish pink flowers. **'Variegata'** has leaves edged with creamy yellow. (Zones 4–10)

D. odora (Winter Daphne, Fragrant Daphne) is a round, mounding evergreen, which grows 4–6' in

height and spread. The pink to deep red, long-lasting, powerfully fragrant flowers are borne in midwinter. *D. odora* does best when given shade from the hot midday sun. It is also the easiest to transplant. **'Aureo-marginata'** has narrow yellow margins around the leaves. The flowers are a lighter pink than those of the species. (Zones 7–10)

Problems & Pests

Viruses, leaf spot, crown rot, root rot, aphids, scale insects and twig blight can affect daphnes. If there are poor growing conditions, daphnes are more susceptible to these problems. A plant may wilt and die suddenly if diseased.

D. odora (above)

In late winter, cut a few stems and arrange them in a vase indoors—they should bloom in a warm, bright room. Enjoy the sweet scent and the delicate flowers.

Dawn Redwood

Metasequoia glyptostroboides

Features: foliage, bark, cones, buttressed trunk **Habit:** narrow, pyramidal, deciduous conifer **Height:** 70–125' **Spread:** 15–25' **Planting:** container; spring, fall **Zones:** 4–10

IN MY FIRST YEAR AT THE UNIVERSITY OF CALIFORNIA IN 1949, three of the university's botanists discovered fossilized seeds of this plant in China. A front-page story heralded when the botanists were able to sprout three of the seeds they had brought back—a seed from the Jurassic era could be viable! Subsequently, a whole forest of these trees was discovered, and vegetative propagation has made them available. The three trees from the original seeds still exist: two are on the grounds of the University of California, and one is located at the post office in Carmel.

Growing

Dawn redwood grows well in **full sun** or **light shade.** The soil should be **humus rich, slightly acidic, moist** and **well drained.** Wet or dry soils are tolerated, though the rate of growth will be reduced in dry conditions. This tree likes humid conditions and should be mulched and watered regularly until it is established. It does not tolerate salty winds or desert conditions.

Pruning is not necessary. The lower branches must be left in place for the buttressing to develop. Buttressed trunks are flared and deeply grooved, and the branches appear to be growing from deep inside the grooves.

Tips

These large trees need plenty of room to grow. Larger gardens and parks can best accommodate them. These trees are attractive and impressive as single specimens or in group plantings.

Recommended

The cultivars do not differ significantly from *M. glyptostroboides.* Both **'National'** and **'Sheridan Spire'** are narrower than the species. These two have not been in cultivation long enough to have reached their mature heights, but they are expected to be as tall as the species. (Zones 4–10)

Problems & Pests

Dawn redwood is not generally prone to pest problems, though it can be killed by canker infections. Keep ants out of these trees.

M. glyptostroboides (all photos this page)

Don't worry when this tree drops its needles each fall; it's a deciduous conifer.

Dogwood

Cornus

Features: late-spring to early-summer flowers, fall foliage, fruit, habit
Habit: deciduous, large shrub or small tree **Height:** 5–60' **Spread:** 5–60'
Planting: B & B (late winter), container (spring to fall) **Zones:** 2–9

USING DOGWOOD AS THE BASIC FOUNDATION FOR PERENNIAL beds is a good idea. Because most perennials are not at their best in winter, the use of *C. alba* and other dogwoods provides good winter interest. To create more winter interest, the red stems of this shrub combine well with *Acer palmatum* 'Sango Kaku' in the background. A bed of English primroses in front of these trees and shrubs makes an outstanding winter display of color.

Growing

Most dogwoods prefer **full sun** but tolerate light or partial shade. The soil should be of **average to high fertility, moist,** high in **organic matter, neutral** or **slightly acidic** and **well drained.** Avoid the leaf scorch that can happen during the heat spikes in June and September by applying mulch.

Most dogwoods require very little pruning. Simply removing damaged, dead or awkward branches in early spring is sufficient for most species. *C. alba* requires a little more effort because the stem color is best on young growth.

There are two ways to encourage new growth. In early spring you can either cut back about one-third of the old growth to within a couple of buds off the ground, or cut back all stems to within a couple of buds off the ground. Once growth starts, feed drastically cut-back plants.

Tips

Shrub dogwoods can be included in a shrub or mixed border. They look best in groups rather than as single specimens. The tree species make wonderful specimen plants and are small enough to include in most gardens. Use them along the edge of a woodland, alongside a house or near a water feature or patio.

Recommended

C. alba (Red-twig Dogwood, Tatarian Dogwood) is grown for the blood red stems that provide winter interest. The stems are green all summer, turning red as winter approaches. This species reaches

'Cherokee Chief' (all photos this page)

C. kousa *is more dependable and disease resistant than many other dogwood species.*

Use the strong horizontal branching of C. alternifolia *for contrast with vertical lines in the landscape.*

C. alba 'Argenteo-marginata' (above)

5–10' tall and wide. It can develop leaf scorch and canker problems in hot weather. **'Argenteo-marginata'** ('Elegantissima') has gray-green leaves with creamy white margins. **'Sibirica'** has bright red stems that really stand out in winter. (Zones 2–8)

C. alternifolia (Pagoda Dogwood) can be grown as a large, multi-stemmed shrub or as a small, single-stemmed tree. It grows 15–25' tall and spreads 10–25'. The branches grow horizontally, giving the plant an attractive layered appearance. Clusters of small, white flowers appear in early summer. This species prefers light shade. It is a good bet for red fall color. The blue-black fruit is not showy but attracts birds. (Zones 3–8)

C. controversa (Giant Dogwood) is a rounded, spreading tree with tiered branches, and it is the largest of all the dogwood species. It grows quickly to a height and spread of 40–60'. Clusters of creamy white flowers are produced abundantly in spring and are followed by rounded, blue-black fruit that attracts birds. This species needs full sun to make the best show of its creamy white bracts. The fall foliage is bright red. This species is the most heat tolerant of the dogwoods. (Zones 6–9)

C. kousa (above)

C. florida cultivar (below)

C. florida (above)

C. florida (Eastern Dogwood, Flowering Dogwood) is usually grown as a small tree 20–30' tall, with an equal or greater spread. It has horizontally layered branches. The inconspicuous flowers with their showy pink or white bracts appear in mid-spring. **'Cherokee Chief'** has dark pink bracts. **'Cloud Nine'** has large, white bracts. **'Spring Song'** has rose pink bracts. The bracts may be damaged with excessive spring heat. *C. florida* is a companion plant for bulb beds and winter blooming annuals such as pansy and calendula. (Zones 5–9)

C. kousa (above)

C. kousa (Kousa Dogwood) is grown for its flowers, fruit, fall color and interesting bark. It is normally a large, multi-stemmed shrub that grows 20–30' tall and wide. This species is more resistant to leaf blight and the other problems that plague *C. florida*. The white-bracted, late-spring to early-summer flowers are followed by bright red fruit. The foliage turns yellow or red in fall. (Zones 5–9)

C. kousa cultivar (above)

Problems & Pests

Dogwoods are susceptible to a wide variety of problems, including blight, canker, leaf spot, powdery mildew, crown and root rot, cicadas, borers, aphids, leafhoppers, scale insects and whiteflies. *C. florida* and its cultivars are susceptible to anthracnose. Keep *C. florida* as healthy as possible and avoid mechanical damage.

C. kousa (below)

Douglas-Fir

Pseudotsuga menziesii

Features: foliage, cones, habit **Habit:** conical to columnar (with age), evergreen tree **Height:** 6–200' **Spread:** 6–30' **Planting:** container; year-round **Zones:** 4–9

AT MY HOME IN WILLITS, CALIFORNIA, WAS AN 80' TALL DOUGLAS-fir that was my favorite climbing tree. Having a small fear of heights, I never went higher than 20'. My cousin, Bob, went to the top once and drove everyone crazy as he waved the treetop back and forth. When we came down, our bodies, hands and faces were covered with pitch that just wouldn't wash off. Grandpa Conley's solution was to use turpentine on us. Although Bob and I complained that it stung when he hit a scratch, Grandpa just ignored us.

Growing

Douglas-fir prefers **full sun**. The soil should be of **average fertility, moist, acidic** and **well drained,** but Douglas-fir will adapt to most soils with good drainage. Pruning is generally not required.

Tips

The species *P. menziesii* can be grown as a single large specimen tree or in groups of several trees. The smaller cultivars can be grown in smaller gardens as specimens or as part of shrub or mixed borders. When purchasing, select plants grown from local seed sources for the best performance.

Recommended

P. menziesii is native to the Pacific Northwest and as far south as Mexico. It grows 70–200' tall and spreads 20–30'. For those gardeners with small gardens, several cultivars of Douglas-fir are not quite as imposing. **'Fletcheri'** is a dwarf cultivar that grows about 6' tall and can spread 6–8' wide. **'Fretsii'** is a slow-growing cultivar that matures to a height of about 20'. New seedling varieties on the market are a striking blue, much like Colorado blue spruces. (Zones 4–9)

Problems & Pests

Canker, leaf cast (needle version of leaf spot), borers, weevils, spruce budworm and other caterpillars, scale insects, adelgids and aphids can cause occasional problems. Douglas-fir is resistant to oak root fungus.

Pseudotsuga *is Latin for 'false hemlock,' though, as the common name suggests, this tree more closely resembles fir.*

P. menziesii (all photos this page)

Dove Tree

Handkerchief Tree, Ghost Tree

Davidia involucrata

Features: mid- to late-spring flowers, scaly bark **Habit:** rounded, pyramidal, deciduous tree **Height:** 30–65' **Spread:** 15–40' **Planting:** container; year-round **Zones:** 6–10

MY FIRST EXPERIENCE WITH THIS OUTSTANDING TREE WAS AT THE Quarryhill Botanical Gardens in Glen Ellen, California. This specialized botanic garden has the largest collection in the United States of plants indigenous to China, India, Japan and Nepal. Because of the potential for disease, the Quarryhill collection is grown strictly from seeds collected in the area. More than 17,000 plants are in this 40-acre former rock quarry, and entrance is by appointment only. The dove tree I saw was in the landscape in front of some very exotic conifers, which is the best use of this tree.

Growing

Dove tree grows well in **full sun** to **partial shade**. The soil should be **rich, moist, well drained** and have plenty of **organic matter** worked in. Plant in a location that is sheltered from strong winds. In the hot interior valleys, plant in afternoon shade. Keep dove tree away from other trees and shrubs to minimize root competition. Provide regular deep watering.

Very little pruning is required. Remove any branches that are dead or damaged. While the tree is young, encourage a strong main leader and remove any awkward branches.

The orange-brown, scaly bark of the dove tree adds interesting texture to the winter landscape.

Tips

This species makes an excellent medium-sized specimen tree. Don't panic if your young tree doesn't flower after you first plant it. Dove tree rarely flowers before it is 10 years old.

Recommended

D. involucrata is commonly grown. In spring it produces bright green foliage and pairs of large, white, wing-like bracts that curve down around the inconspicuous flowers. The persistent, roundish fruits are purplish brown and about 1" across. **Var. *vilmoriniana*** is often confused with the species, but it is more cold hardy. (Zones 6–10)

Problems & Pests

Dove tree is rarely affected by any serious problems or pests.

D. involucrata (all photos this page)

False Cypress

Chamaecyparis

Features: foliage, habit, cones **Habit:** narrow, pyramidal, evergreen tree **Height:** 6"–100' **Spread:** 10"–65' **Planting:** B & B (December and January), container (year-round) **Zones:** 4–9

FALSE CYPRESSES MAKE GOOD STARTER PLANTS FOR THOSE WHO wish to learn how to bonsai. I usually start with a tree in a one-gallon container. Then I look at the trunks of these plants before purchasing—the more contorted the trunk, the more likely it will make an interesting specimen. I enjoy the intense green of Hinoki false cypress. It is a great addition to an oriental garden or as an accent on a mound surrounded with Irish moss or woolly thyme.

Growing

False cypress prefers **full sun**. The soil should be **fertile, moist, neutral to acidic** and **well drained.** Alkaline soils are tolerated. In hot summer locations, false cypress needs to be mulched. In shaded areas, the growth may be sparse or thin.

No pruning is required on tree specimens. Plants grown as hedges should be trimmed during winter months when they are at their most dormant stage. Avoid severe pruning because new growth will not sprout from old wood. Pinch the new tip growth to control the size and shape.

Dry, brown leaves can be pulled from the base by hand. Plants that are too near fences or house foundations will turn brown on the side that doesn't receive sunlight. Plant so that the mature spread is at least 2' from any solid structure, which allows you to hose down the rear of the tree. Doing so keeps it healthy and helps reduce any infestation of mites.

C. pisifera 'Squarrosa' (above)

In the wild, C. nootkatensis *trees can grow as tall as 165′ and as old as 1800 years.*

C. lawsoniana (below)

C. *pisifera* 'Nana' (above), *C. nootkatensis* (below)

Tips

Tree varieties are used as specimen plants and for hedging. The dwarf and slow-growing cultivars are used in borders and rock gardens and as bonsai. False cypress shrubs can be grown as evergreen specimens in large containers.

As with the related arborvitae and false arborvitae, oils in the foliage of false cypresses may be irritating to sensitive skin.

Recommended

C. lawsoniana (Lawson False Cypress) is native to the western United States. It grows 50–60' tall and spreads 6–15' in the garden. It spreads up to 130' tall in the wild. Over 250 cultivars are available. **'Gnome'** is a loosely rounded cultivar that grows about 36" tall. **'Lutea'** grows to 30' tall and produces golden foliage. **'Pembury Blue'** grows to 50' tall, with pendulous, gray-green sprays of foliage. (Zones 5–9)

C. nootkatensis (Yellow-cedar, Nootka False Cypress) is a west coast native. It grows 30–100' tall, with a spread of about 25'. The growth of this species is quite pendulous. **'Pendula'** grows to 30' tall and has a very open habit and even more pendulous foliage than the species. (Zones 4–8)

C. obtusa (Hinoki False Cypress), a native of Japan, has foliage arranged in fan-like sprays. It grows about 70' tall, with a spread of 20'. **'Minima'** (Golfball Cypress) is a very dwarf, mounding cultivar. It grows about 10" tall and spreads 16". **'Nana'** is a slow-growing cultivar that reaches

3–4' in height, with a slightly greater spread. (Zones 4–9)

C. pisifera (Japanese False Cypress, Sawara Cypress) is another Japanese native. In the wild, it grows 70–150' tall and spreads 15–25'. The cultivars are more commonly grown than the species. **'Filifera Aurea'** (Golden Thread-leaf False Cypress) is a slow-growing cultivar with golden yellow, thread-like foliage. It grows about 8–10' tall. **'Nana'** (Dwarf False Cypress) is a dwarf cultivar with feathery foliage similar to that of the species. It grows into a mound about 12" in height and width. **'Plumosa'** (Plume False Cypress) has very feathery foliage. It grows about 20–25' tall, with an equal or greater spread. **'Squarrosa'** (Moss False Cypress) has less pendulous foliage than the other cultivars. Young plants grow very densely, looking like fuzzy stuffed animals. The growth becomes more relaxed and open with maturity. This cultivar grows about 65' tall, with a spread that is equal or a little narrower. (Zones 4–8)

Problems & Pests

False cypresses are not prone to problems, but they can occasionally be affected by spruce mites, root rot, gall or blight.

C. obtusa 'Nana' (above), *C. nootkatensis* 'Pendula' (below)

Fir

Abies

Features: foliage, cones **Habit:** narrow, pyramidal or columnar, evergreen tree **Height:** 2–75' **Spread:** 3–30' **Planting:** B & B (December and January), container (spring to fall) **Zones:** 3–7

I USED TO SELL CHRISTMAS TREES FOR THE BENEFIT OF BOY SCOUT Troop 61 in San Rafael. We would travel up to Quincy, California, in a large truck to pick up the trees, which we then set up for sale in San Rafael in December. In Quincy, I would join the ground crew and toss the trees up to the truck crew, who would then stack them in the truck. Once I tossed a tree that landed in the middle of my son Bill's forehead. It had the same impact as if I had hit him full force with a lead pipe. I thought I had knocked him out. Bill had no permanent damage, but he never wanted to take the trip again.

Growing

Firs usually prefer **full sun,** but tolerate partial shade. The soil should be **rich, moist, neutral to acidic** and **well drained.** These trees prefer a **sheltered** site, out of the wind, and are generally not tolerant of polluted city conditions. No pruning is required. Dead or damaged growth can be removed as needed.

Tips

Firs make impressive specimen trees in large areas. The species tend to be too large for the average home garden. Several compact or dwarf cultivars can be included in shrub borders or used as specimens, depending on their size. Give these plants plenty of space in which to grow. They do not do well in lawns. Use an organic mulch or plant a groundcover such as low-growing cotoneaster.

A. concolor is far more tolerant of pollution, heat and drought than other *Abies* species, thus it is better adapted for city conditions.

'Violacea' (above)

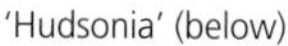

'Hudsonia' (below)

A. balsamea (above), A. concolor (below)

Recommended

A. balsamea (Balsam Fir) is quite pyramidal when young but narrows as it ages. This slow-growing tree can reach 45–75' in height, with a spread of 15–25'. Although balsam fir prefers a well-drained soil, it will tolerate wet soil. This species is native to north-central and northeastern North America and does better in interior regions rather than coastal regions. **'Hudsonia'** grows to only 24" tall, with a spread of 36". It is a natural form of the species, but it is usually sold as a cultivar. It is also sometimes called **'Nana,'** though this cultivar is sometimes sold as a different plant. The two are very similar in size and habit. These dwarf cultivars are more suitable to a small garden than the much larger parent species. (Zones 3–7)

A. concolor (White Fir) is an impressive native of the western United States. The needles have a whitish coating, which gives the tree a hazy blue appearance. It grows 40–70' tall in garden conditions but can grow up to 130' in unrestricted natural conditions. It spreads 15–25'. **'Compacta'** is a dwarf cultivar. It has whiter needles than the species and grows to 10' in height and spread. This cultivar makes an attractive specimen tree. **'Violacea'** has silvery blue needles and is very attractive; it grows as large as the species. (Zones 3–10)

The genus name Abies *comes from the Latin word,* abire, *which means to rise up. The name refers to the lofty height some of the species reach.*

Problems & Pests

Firs are susceptible to quite a few problems, including aphids, bark beetles, spruce budworm, rust, root rot and needle blight.

Firs and spruces resemble each other, but fir needles are soft and flat and spruce needles are sharply pointed. Also, fir cones sit on top of the branches and point up, while spruce cones hang downwards.

*Firs make nice Christmas trees and hold up quite well indoors. Do not confuse these firs with Douglas-fir (*Pseudotsuga menziesii*), which can drop its needles quickly.*

A. concolor (above)

'Hudsonia' (below)

Firethorn

Pyracantha

Features: foliage, flowers, late-summer and fall fruit **Habit:** dense, thorny, evergreen or semi-evergreen shrub **Height:** 2–15' **Spread:** 2–15' **Planting:** container; spring **Zones:** 6–10

IN THE HOUSING BOOM OF THE 1950S, IF YOU DIDN'T COVER YOUR ground with juniper, you covered it with firethorn. Firethorn is a winner, with its ability to be carefree, to become native after the first couple of years and to act as both a groundcover or hedge. As homeowners in Northern California became more sophisticated in their landscape taste, it fell out of favor. It has now made a comeback as the wonderful shrub that it is: relatively disease free, with cascades of white flowers in spring followed by persistent, showy berries for the rest of the year. It also fits into many landscapes as an evergreen background shrub.

Growing

Firethorn prefers **full sun** and tolerates partial shade, but it does not fruit as heavily in partial shade. The soil should be **rich, moist** and **well drained**. Well-established plants will tolerate dry soil, usually requiring no summer water after the second or third year after planting. Shelter plants from strong winds. Firethorn resents being moved once established, and you will resent having to move this prickly plant. Firethorn is cold hardy to 10° F.

P. coccinea (all photos this page)

Some pruning is required in order to keep this plant looking neat and attractive. In a naturalized setting, this shrub can be left much to its own devices. Remove any damaged growth or wayward branches, and trim back new growth to better show off the fruit.

If you are using firethorn in a shrub or mixed border, you will have to prune more severely to prevent it from overgrowing its neighbors. Hedges can be trimmed in early summer to mid-summer. Espalier and other wall-trained specimens can be trimmed in mid-summer. Growth that is used to extend the framework of the specimen can be tied in place as needed.

P. coccinea (above), 'Teton' (below)

Tips

Despite its potential for rampant growth, firethorn has a wide variety of uses. It is often used for formal or informal hedges and barriers because of the abundant prickles. It can be grown as a large informal shrub in naturalized gardens and borders. It can also be used as a climber if tied to a trellis or other supportive framework. Firethorn's responsiveness to pruning and its dense growth habit make it an ideal espalier specimen. The low-growing, spreading types make effective colorful groundcovers, especially for high, full-sun slopes.

Recommended

The following selections produce abundant clusters of creamy white to white flowers in spring to early summer.

P. coccinea is a large, spiny shrub that grows 8–12' tall and wide. It bears bright scarlet fruit. **'Lalandei'** is a vigorous, erect plant growing to 10–15' tall and wide. It is the most popular of this variety and has bright orange-red berries. 'Lalandei' is one of the hardiest against cold. (Zones 6–10)

P. koidzumii (Formosa Firethorn) is a dense, thorny, upright shrub that is 8–12' tall and wide. It bears orange-red fruit. **'Santa Cruz'** is a prostrate to erect shrub that grows to 6' tall and spreads to 10'. It can be kept to 36" tall or lower by removing all upright growth. It bears large, red fruit and is one of the best choices to cover hot, dry slopes. (Zones 6–10)

Firethorn Hybrids are among the most colorful and hardy. *P.* **'Red Elf'** is a compact shrub that grows 24" tall and wide and bears dark green leaves and bright red fruit. It is a great plant for containers and makes a wonderful bonsai. *P.* **'Teton'** is an upright shrub 12–15' in height and 4–8' wide. The leaves are bright green, and the fruit is yellow-orange. *P.* 'Teton' is resistant to fire blight and scab. (Zones 6–10)

The showy fruits of firethorn resemble tiny apples and are attractive to birds. The fruits ferment by January, and when the migrating robins gorge themselves on the fruit, they become a hazard not only to themselves, but the passing traffic as well. Most drivers slow down to avoid the drunk birds.

Problems & Pests

Firethorn is susceptible to fire blight and scab. Fire blight can kill the plant, and scab disfigures the fruit, turning it sooty brown. A few less serious or less frequent problems are root rot, woolly apple aphid, aphids, spider mites, scale insects and lace bugs.

Firethorn obeys the version of Murphy's Law that states the more prickly a plant is, the more pruning it will need.

P. coccinea (below)

Flannel Bush
Fremontia, California Beauty
Fremontodendron

Features: flowers, foliage **Habit:** irregular to rounded, evergreen shrub or tree **Height:** 4–20' **Spread:** 10–20' **Planting:** container; spring (after frost danger has passed) **Zones:** 8–10

MY FIRST EXPERIENCE WITH THIS PLANT WAS ON A VERY HOT DAY at the Alameda County Fair in Pleasanton. My male staff was working without shirts. I forgot to warn them that the 'fuzzy' covering on the leaves of flannel bush is quite abrasive, and they shouldn't let their backs come in contact with them. Fortunately, the carnival people had showers that my people used gratefully. It has always amazed me that deer eat this plant, along with roses, but leave most sages alone. Combine flannel bush with other California natives, such as manzanita *(Arctostaphylos)* and California lilac *(Ceanothus)*.

Growing

Flannel bush requires **full sun** in **well-drained, neutral to slightly alkaline soil** of **moderate to poor** fertility. Don't water this plant after the first season because it is very drought tolerant. If the plant shows signs of water stress, minimal water can be applied in summer as long as there is excellent drainage. Excess water in summer may lead to root rot. Shelter from the cold, drying winds of coastal regions.

Flannel bush flowers on the current season's growth. Prune in midsummer, after the first flush of flowers. Long, unsightly shoots should be removed. The lower branches can be removed to create a small 'tree.' Flannel bush can be trained as an espalier but does not respond to heavy pruning.

Tips

Flannel bush has been used extensively in California for planting along roadsides, in residential landscapes and for watershed protection in wildland settings. After a fire, flannel bush is a resilient shrub—it resprouts abundantly. The new shoots are a valuable forage for deer and domestic livestock. Use at the back of a shrub or mixed border, in containers or as hillside plantings. Protect the trunk from deer, which want to use it as a scratching post.

Contact with the leaves and shoots may irritate the skin.

'California Glory' (all photos this page)

F. 'California Glory' is the oldest known flannel bush hybrid.

Recommended

Three of the following selections are hybrids of *F. californicum*, which produces lemon yellow flowers that all open at the same time, and the slightly smaller *F. mexicanum*, which sporadically produces orange-yellow flowers from spring to fall. The young stems and the underside of the foliage are covered with felt-like hairs. All flannel bushes are relatively short-lived.

F. **'California Glory'** is an upright, spreading shrub 15–20' tall and 10–15' wide, bearing deep yellow, saucer-shaped flowers with red-tinged bracts from spring to fall. Wind, hail or physical disturbances can distribute large amounts of dull black seeds that fall from the capsules. This cultivar is the toughest of all the flannel bushes. (Zones 8–10)

'California Glory' (all photos this page)

F. **'Ken Taylor'** is a hybrid of *F. decumbens,* a low-growing species, and *F.* 'California Glory'. 'Ken Taylor' grows 4–6' tall and spreads 10–12'. Orange-yellow flowers are produced all year on the coast and from spring to fall inland. (Zones 8–10)

F. **'Pacific Sunset'** grows 12–20' tall and wide and bears large, deep orange-yellow flowers for an extended period with maximum blooming in spring. The flower petals have narrowly pointed tips. (Zones 9–10)

F. **'San Gabriel'** is very similar to 'California Glory' but has three to five deeply lobed, dark green leaves. (Zones 9–10)

Problems & Pests

Flannel bush is susceptible to root rot and stem rot in poorly drained soil. Scale insects can be an occasional problem.

The striking yellow flowers are produced in early spring and followed by hairy seed capsules in mid-summer to fall. Use gloves when handling them.

Fremontodendron *was named after the American explorer and amateur botanist, Major-General John Charles Fremont (1813–90).*

'Pacific Sunset' (below)

Flowering Quince

Chaenomeles

Features: spring flowers, fruit, spines **Habit:** spreading, deciduous shrub with spiny branches **Height:** 2–10' **Spread:** up to 15' **Planting:** container; spring, fall **Zones:** 4–9

FLOWERING QUINCE IS A PLANT THAT lends itself to becoming a bonsai specimen. The trunk develops interesting shapes, and it can be made to look very old even when young. Because flowering quince goes dormant in winter, it is best to locate this shrub near evergreen shrubs. When flowering quince blooms early, taking the gloom of winter away, it is easy to forgive its defoliation in spring. The stems can be cut and brought into the house while in bud, and they will open over a couple of weeks. 'Cameo' has a soft apricot color that makes it the perfect backdrop for spring-blooming bulbs. Flowering quince combines well with juniper *(Juniperus)* and pine *(Pinus)*.

Growing

Flowering quinces grow equally well in **full sun** or **partial shade** but bear fewer flowers and fruit in shaded locations. The soil should be of **average fertility, moist** and **well drained**, and **slightly acidic** soil is preferred. They require little or no water after the second year. These shrubs tolerate urban pollution.

On established plants, prune back about one-third of the old growth to the ground each year. Tidy shrubs and promote flowering by cutting back flowering shoots, leaving four to six leaves per shoot. Many plants can get out of hand if not properly pruned.

Flowering quinces are deer resistant in most landscapes.

C. *speciosa* 'Texas Scarlet' (all photos this page)

Tips

Flowering quinces can be included in a shrub or mixed border. They are very attractive grown against a wall. The spiny habit also makes them useful for barriers. Put them along the edge of a woodland or in a naturalistic garden. The dark bark stands out well in winter. They are the first picking flower in spring.

Leaf drop in mid- to late summer is usually caused by leaf spot. Try hiding the plant with later-flowering perennials. Remove the plant if it gets infected with leaf spot every year.

The early-spring flowers and fall fruit will attract birds to your garden.

The fruits of flowering quinces are edible when cooked, and they combine well with apples. The fruit is often used as pectin in several varieties of jellies.

C. speciosa cultivar (below)

Recommended

C. japonica (Japanese Flowering Quince) is a spreading shrub that grows 24–36" tall and spreads up to 6'. Orange or red flowers appear in early to mid-spring, followed by small, fragrant, greenish yellow fruit. This species is not as common as *C. speciosa* and its cultivars. (Zones 4–9)

C. speciosa (Common Flowering Quince) is a large, tangled, spreading shrub. It grows 6–10' tall and spreads 6–15'. Red flowers emerge in spring and are followed by fragrant, greenish yellow fruit. Many cultivars are available. **'Cameo'** is a compact

'Texas Scarlet' (below)

shrub with large, apricot to peach pink, double flowers. **'Texas Scarlet'** bears many red flowers over a fairly long period on plants about half the size of the species. **'Toyo-Nishiki'** is more upright than the species, and a mixture of white, pink and red flowers all appear on the same shrub. (Zones 5–8)

Problems & Pests

In addition to leaf spot (see p. 188), possible but not often serious problems for flowering quince include aphids, canker, fire blight, mites, rust and viruses. Over-fertilization during the growing season increases the risk of these problems.

'Cameo' (above)

Forsythia

Forsythia

Features: early- to mid-spring flowers **Habit:** spreading, deciduous shrub with upright or arching branches **Height:** 18"–10' **Spread:** 4–10' **Planting:** B & B (spring, fall), container (spring, fall), bare-root (spring) **Zones:** 4–10

I CAN'T IMAGINE ANY BETTER PLANT THAN FORSYTHIA TO JUMP-start your garden into the growing season. The yellow bursts of blooms make the perfect backdrop for bulb beds such as tulips and multi-colored narcissus. From the California coast to the high Sierras, this hardy plant can take any temperature. *F.* x *intermedia* performs well in most areas in Northern California. The cultivars 'Beatrix Farrand,' 'Goldtide' and 'Spring Glory' perform well in coastal climates as well as in the interior valleys of California. *F. suspensa* makes a wonderfully dense and spreading groundcover for hillsides that are hard to tame.

Growing

Forsythias grow best in **full sun** but tolerate light shade. The soil should be of **average fertility, moist** and **well drained.**

Correct pruning is essential to keep forsythias attractive. Flowers emerge on growth that is at least two years old. Prune after flowering is finished. On mature plants, one-third of the oldest growth can be cut right back to the ground.

Some gardeners trim these shrubs into a formal hedge, but this practice often results in uneven flowering. An informal hedge allows the plants to grow more naturally. Size can be restricted by cutting shoots back to a strong junction.

Tips

These shrubs are gorgeous while in flower, but they aren't very exciting the rest of the year. Include one in a shrub or mixed border where other flowering plants will take over once the forsythia's early-season glory has passed.

Allow a clematis to twine through your forsythia for a wonderful display of flowers and color.

F. x *intermedia* (all photos this page)

F. x *intermedia* (all photos this page)

Recommended

F.* x *intermedia is a large shrub with upright stems that arch as they mature. It grows 5–10' tall and wide. Yellow flowers emerge in early to mid-spring before the leaves. Many cultivars have been developed from this hybrid. **'Beatrix Farrand'** grows 8–10' tall and 6–8' wide, bearing large, deep yellow flowers on arching branches. **'Goldtide'** bears abundant yellow flowers on shrubs 18–24" tall and 4' wide. **'Lynwood'** ('Lynwood Gold') grows to 7–10' tall and 5–8' wide. The tough, light yellow flowers open widely and are distributed evenly along the branches. **'Spectabilis'** grows to 10' tall and 6–10' wide. It bears bright yellow flowers that are more cold tolerant than those of the species. **'Spring Glory'** is an upright shrub that grows 6' tall and 5–7' wide. It produces a plethora of pale yellow flowers. (Zones 6–9)

F. ovata (Korean Forsythia) is one of the most dependable in our area. It is a bushy, spreading shrub growing 4–6' tall and spreading 10' wide. It is the earliest forsythia to bloom, bearing bright yellow flowers. (Zones 5–8)

***F.* 'Northern Sun'** is a hardy, upright shrub that develops a more arching habit as it matures. It grows 8–10' tall and spreads up to 9'. The yellow flowers are very cold hardy. (Zones 4–8)

F. suspensa (Weeping Forsythia) is a large, dense shrub with weeping branches. It grows 10' tall and wide and bears clusters of golden flowers. It can grow taller if it is given support. (Zones 6–9)

Problems & Pests

Most problems are not serious but may include root-knot nematodes, stem gall and leaf spot.

Cut a few branches before they flower and arrange them in a vase. You won't wait long for the cheerful yellow blooms to appear.

Forsythias can be used as hedging plants, but they look most attractive when grown informally.

F. x *intermedia* (above)

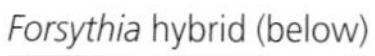

Forsythia hybrid (below)

Fringe Tree

Chionanthus

Features: early-summer flowers, bark, habit **Habit:** rounded or spreading, deciduous, large shrub or small tree **Height:** 10–25' **Spread:** 10–25' **Planting:** container; spring **Zones:** 4–9

ONE OF THE MOST MATURE FRINGE TREES IN CALIFORNIA CAN BE found at Filoli, an estate south of San Francisco that is open to the public. This tree was planted in 1922. The estate, which was built from 1915–17, has a nursery that sells to the public. It is now the property of the National Trust for Historic Preservation. Fringe tree blooms in August, and the blooms last well into September.

Growing

Fringe trees prefer **full sun**. They do best in soil that is **fertile** and **well drained,** but they will adapt to most soil conditions. In the wild, they are often found growing alongside stream banks. Ensure you provide adequate water in your garden.

Little pruning is required on mature plants. To encourage an attractive habit, the stems can be thinned out when the plant is young. Prune after flowering or prune in spring for young plants that aren't yet flowering. To train as a tree, wait until the tree is three to four years old. You can then start pruning off unwanted limbs until you form a single- or multi-trunk small tree.

C. *virginicus* (all photos this page)

C. virginicus (above)

Tips

Fringe trees work well as specimen plants, as part of borders, as large accent shrubs in lawns or beside water features. Plants begin flowering at a very early age.

These trees may not produce fruit because not all trees of a given species bear both female and male flowers. Male flowers produce no fruit, and if only a female tree is present, a male may not be close enough to pollinate it. When fruit is produced, it attracts birds.

Fringe trees can be very difficult to find in nurseries. Home gardeners can propagate these trees at home. Seeds planted outdoors in early or mid-summer will germinate after about two years. Scoring the seed will speed germination. Semi-ripe cuttings or layerings can be started from Chinese fringe tree in mid- or late summer. White fringe tree does not root well from cuttings.

Recommended

C. retusus (Chinese Fringe Tree) is a rounded, spreading shrub or small tree. It grows 15–25' tall, with an equal spread. In late spring to early summer, it bears erect, fragrant, white flowers followed in late summer by dark blue fruit. The bark is deeply furrowed and peeling. This species is a better choice for the hot interior valleys. (Zones 5–9)

The fall color of fringe trees is a bright yellow, even in areas where winters are mild.

C. virginicus (White Fringe Tree) is a spreading, small tree or large shrub. It grows 10–20' tall and has an equal or greater spread. In early summer it bears drooping, fragrant, white flowers, followed only occasionally by dark blue fruit. (Zones 4–9)

Problems & Pests

Fringe trees rarely have any serious problems but can be affected by borers, leaf spot, powdery mildew or canker.

Fringe tree is also known as Old Man's Beard because the flowers resemble the gray whiskers old men often sport.

These small, pollution-tolerant trees are good choices for city gardens. If the tree bears fruit, it is a favorite of birds.

C. retusus (above), *C. virginicus* (below)

Ginkgo

Ginko, Maidenhair Tree

Ginkgo

Features: summer and fall foliage, habit, fruit, bark **Habit:** conical (in youth) to variable, deciduous tree **Height:** 40–120' **Spread:** 25–100' **Planting:** container; spring, fall **Zones:** 3–9

ONE THINKS THAT 'ONLY IN BERKELEY' CAN SOMETHING LIKE THIS happen. In 1936 seedling ginkgoes—which turned out to be female trees—were planted as street trees in Berkeley. The trees were planted to prepare the area for the 1939 and 1940 world's fair. During this time period, Berkeley and Oakland were using the bay as their sewage disposal. At low tide the odor was unpleasant, to say the least. President Franklin Delano Roosevelt came to Berkeley to open the fair. Unfortunately, the ripe fruit from the female ginkgo and the low tide in the bay left a very unfavorable impression on President Roosevelt and he said so. Not long after his visit, the trees were removed, and male ginkgo trees were planted in their stead.

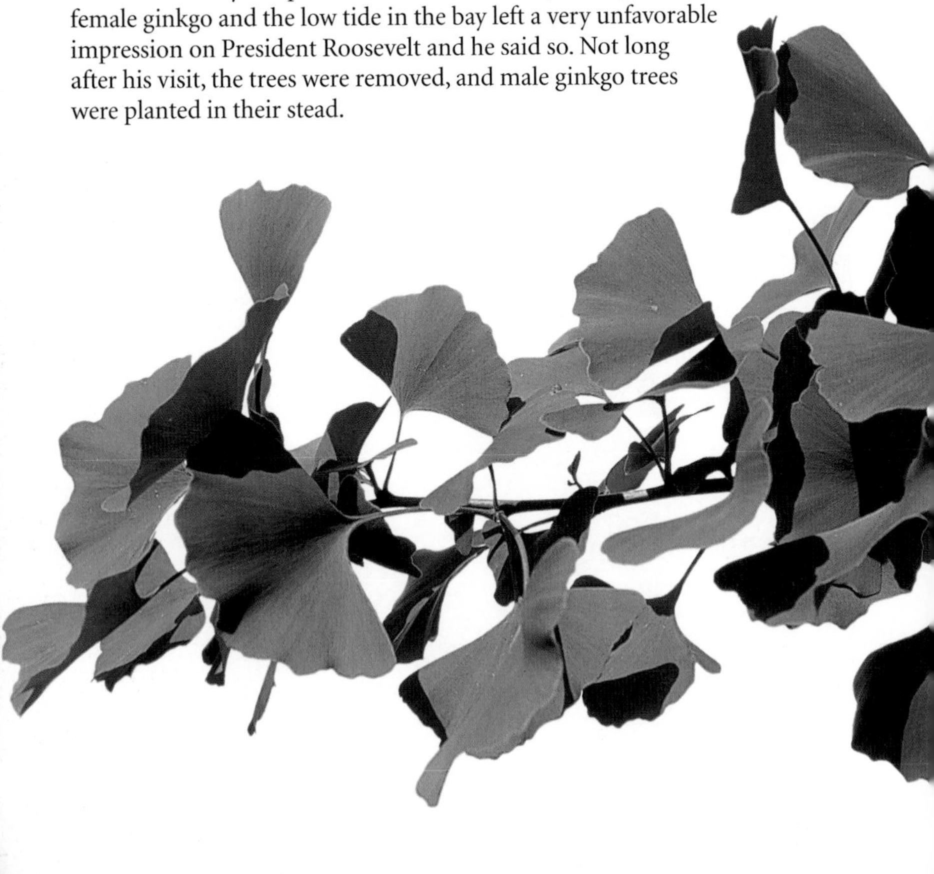

Growing

Ginkgo prefers **full sun.** The soil should be **fertile, sandy** and **well drained,** but this tree adapts to most conditions. It is also tolerant of urban conditions and cold weather. Little or no pruning is necessary.

Tips

Although its growth is very slow, ginkgo eventually becomes a large tree that is best suited as a specimen tree in parks and large gardens. It can be used as a street tree.

If you buy an unnamed plant, be sure it has been propagated from cuttings. Seed-grown trees may prove to be female, and the stinky fruit is not something you want dropping all over your lawn, driveway or sidewalk.

G. biloba (all photos this page)

This ancient tree is classed as a gymnosperm ('naked seed' plant), along with coniferous trees. The 'fruits' are actually fleshy seed coats.

Recommended

G. biloba is variable in habit. It grows 50–80' tall and 30–60' wide. In ideal conditions, it can reach 120' in height and 100' in width. The leaves can turn an attractive shade of yellow in fall, after a few cool nights. Female plants are generally avoided because the fruits have a very unpleasant odor. Several male cultivars are available. **'Autumn Gold'** is a broadly conical tree that grows 40–50' tall and 30' wide. The fall color is bright yellow-gold. **'Princeton Sentry'** is narrow and upright. It grows 50–80' tall and spreads 25'. **'Saratoga'** resembles 'Autumn Gold,' growing to 40' tall. It has a distinct central leader. (Zones 3–9)

The genus name Ginkgo *arises from the Chinese word,* ngin-ghang, *meaning silver apricot. The pronunciation is from the Japanese word* ginkyo, *also meaning silver apricot.*

Problems & Pests

This tree seems to have outlived most of the pests that might have afflicted it. A leaf spot may affect ginkgo, but it doesn't cause any real trouble.

Ginkgo appears to have been saved from extinction by its long-time use in Asian temple gardens. Today this 'living fossil' grows almost entirely in horticultural settings.

G. biloba (all photos both pages)

Goldenchain Tree

Laburnum

Features: late-spring to early-summer flowers
Habit: spreading, deciduous tree
Height: 15–25'
Spread: 15–25'
Planting: container; spring
Zones: 5–9

I HAVE SEEN GOLDENCHAIN TREE used as covering for a pergola that led into an entry of a water garden. I saw this tree in the garden of the Impressionist painter Claude Monet on a trip I made to France. The tree was in bloom and quite spectacular. Goldenchain tree can be used as a lawn tree if provided with proper drainage. Removing the seedpods will aid the tree's vigor because the production of seeds sidetracks the tree's energy for other growth.

Growing

Goldenchain tree grows in **full sun** or **light shade.** The soil should be of **moderate fertility** and **well drained.** This tree tolerates alkaline soils. Plant it in light or afternoon shade in the hot interior valleys.

This tree needs very little pruning, but it responds well to training and can be encouraged to grow over arbors, pergolas and other structures. All structural pruning should be done before the third season because large wounds tend to heal slowly, and structures that weaken the tree may be created.

Tips

Goldenchain tree can be used as a specimen tree in small gardens. Plant an annual or perennial vine, such as a morning glory, at the foot of your goldenchain tree, and let the vines climb up to provide summer flowers once the golden chains have faded.

All parts of this tree, but especially the seeds, contain a poisonous alkaloid. Children can be poisoned by eating the seeds, which resemble beans or peas.

Recommended

L.* x *watereri bears bright yellow flowers in pendulous clusters up to 10" long. This plant lives longest in climates with cool summers. **'Vossii'** has a denser growth habit and bears flower clusters up to 24" long. This cultivar can be trained to form an espalier. (Zones 5–9)

Problems & Pests

Goldenchain tree may have occasional difficulties with aphids, canker, laburnum vein mosaic, leaf spot, mealybugs and twig blight.

'Vossii' (all photos this page)

The species L. *x* watereri *is a hybrid of* L. alpinum *and* L. anagyroides. *The name honors the Waterer Nursery, where a form of this hybrid was raised.*

Grevillea

Spider Flower

Grevillea

Features: winter to spring flowers, foliage, habit **Habit:** evergreen, upright, rounded shrub or compact, pyramidal to broadly open tree **Height:** 4–120' **Spread:** 4–70' **Planting:** container; spring, fall **Zones:** 8–11

GREVILLEA IS A SHRUB THAT HAS A FINITE LIFE. IN IDEAL locations, it is at its best the first 10–15 years. When it starts looking undesirable, remove and plant a new one-gallon plant in its place. Because of grevillea's fast growth, the vacant spot will fill in within a couple of years. *G. robusta* is an exception in that it is considered a long-lived tree. New varieties appear in local nurseries almost weekly. Most grevilleas are planted for the blooms that can last for up to six months.

Growing

Grevillea prefers **full sun.** *G.* 'Canberra' and *G. rosmarinifolia* will tolerate partial shade. Plant in **well-drained, neutral to acidic, moderately fertile** soil. This plant does not like salt, poor-water quality or over-irrigation in heavy soil. It is frost hardy to 25° F. Grevillea tolerates and/or thrives in hot, arid conditions. *G. robusta* can handle regular watering during summer as long as there is good drainage. Plant *G. robusta* out of areas that experience high winds because wind can damage the brittle branches.

Grevillea dislikes having its roots disturbed. It will perform best when planted as a young plant and left in place. Do not transplant grevillea after it is established.

Grevilleas need only minimal pruning. Prune shrubs immediately after flowering to promote healthy new growth and to maintain a compact growth habit. When removing branches, always cut back to the point of origin of the branch being removed. Do not shear grevilleas.

Tips

Grevillea is an excellent choice for xeriscaping, and both tree and shrub selections are wonderful specimen plants. The shrub species of grevillea work well as screening and in shrub or mixed borders. *G. robusta* is useful as a fast-growing, tall screen. It is sometimes grown as a houseplant and is discarded when it becomes too large.

All parts of grevillea may aggravate skin allergies.

'Constance' (above), 'Canberra' (below)

G. rosmarinifolia (above), G. robusta (below)

Recommended

G. 'Canberra' ('Canberra Gem') is a vigorous, bushy shrub that reaches 6–8' tall and spreads 6–12'. It has rich, dark green, needle-like leaves and produces clusters of waxy, bright pink to pinkish red flowers in spring and occasionally throughout the year. This cultivar can take hard pruning but is often short-lived. (Zones 8–10)

G. 'Constance' is much like 'Canberra' but can tolerate more summer watering. The foliage is broader that 'Canberra' with a deep green surface and an almost white underside. It produces bright orange-red blooms twice a year in spring and fall. Is among the longest-lived. (Zones 8–10)

G. 'Noelii' is a dense, rounded shrub with glossy, needle-like, mid-green leaves. It grows 4–5' tall and wide and bears clusters of pink and white flowers in spring. This selection needs moderate water during the growing season. (Zones 9–10)

G. robusta (Silk Oak, Silky Oak) is a vigorous, dense, erect to pyramidal tree in youth, becoming broad, open and stately with age. In gardens, *G. robusta* reaches an average height of 50–60' tall and spreads 30–35', but it can grow 100–120' tall and 70' wide in ideal conditions. It bears dark green, fern-like leaves with silver hairs underneath. Large clusters of bright golden orange flowers bloom in early spring. *G. robusta* experiences some leaf drop just before the tree comes into full flower. Do not locate this plant near walkways, where the bloom and leaf drop might present a problem. (Zones 9–11)

G. rosmarinifolia (Rosemary Grevillea) is an upright to spreading shrub that grows 6' tall and wide, sometimes with gently arching stems. It has bright green, needle-like, often prickly foliage and clusters of red to pink and cream flowers that bloom in fall and winter, with scattered blooms throughout the year. Unlike other varieties, this form will tolerate shearing. (Zones 8–10)

'Canberra' (above)

Problems & Pests

Grevillea may experience scale insects, mealybugs and leaf spot. Root rot is infrequent but can pose problems when drainage is poor.

Grevillea is deer resistant and suitable for garden settings where wildlife is prominent.

G. rosmarinifolia (below)

Hardy Hibiscus

Rose-of-Sharon

Hibiscus

Features: mid-summer to fall flowers **Habit:** bushy, upright, deciduous shrub **Height:** 8–12' **Spread:** 6–8' **Planting:** container (spring, fall), bare-root (January, February) **Zones:** 5–10

RECENTLY DEVELOPED TYPES OF HARDY HIBISCUS HAVE LARGER flowers and more color than were previously available. Many shrubs have blooms that can grow to more than 12" across, and over 100 colors and sizes are available at local nurseries and by mail order from Gilberg Farms in Missouri. Gilberg Farms can also be found at <www.hibiscuscentral.com>. Hardy hibiscus is disease resistant and hardy from –25° F to 100° F.

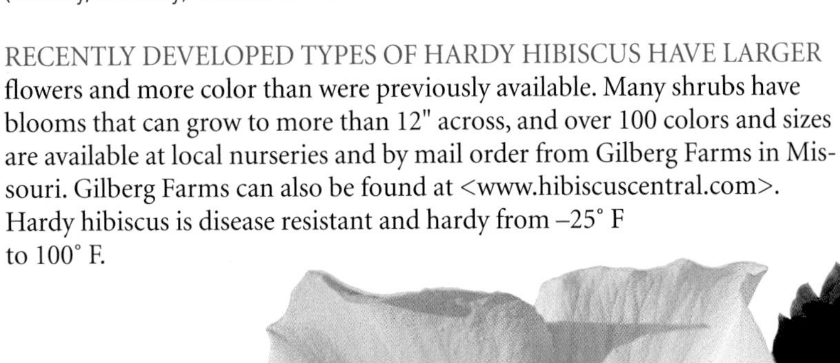

Growing

Hardy hibiscus prefers **full sun** and tolerates partial shade. It responds well in fertile soil that is **humus rich, moist** and **well drained,** but it can tolerate poor soil and wet spots.

Pinch young shrubs to encourage bushy growth. Young plants can be trained to form a single-stemmed tree by selectively pruning out all but the strongest stem. The flowers form on the current year's growth; prune back the tip growth in late winter or early spring for larger but fewer flowers.

Tips

Hardy hibiscus is best used in shrub borders or mixed borders.

This shrub develops unsightly legs as it matures. Plant low, bushy perennials or shrubs around the base to hide the bare stems.

The leaves emerge late in spring and drop early in fall. Planting hardy hibiscus along with evergreen shrubs will make up for the short period of leafiness.

Recommended

H. syriacus is an erect, multi-stemmed shrub that bears dark pink flowers from mid-summer to fall. Many cultivars are available. **'Aphrodite'** bears rose pink flowers with dark red centers. **'Blue Bird'** bears large, blue flowers with red centers. **'Diana'** bears large, white flowers. **'Helene'** has white flowers with red petal bases. (Zones 5–10)

Problems & Pests

Hardy hibiscus can be afflicted with aphids, mealybugs, root rot, scale insects, whiteflies and ringspot virus.

This species is believed to have originated in Syria; the species name, syriacus, *means 'of Syria.' Hibiscus is the Greek name for 'mallow.'*

'Blue Bird' (above), 'Diana' (below)

Heavenly Bamboo

Sacred Bamboo

Nandina

Features: flowers, fruit, foliage **Habit:** upright to rounded, evergreen or semi-evergreen shrub **Height:** 18"–8' **Spread:** 18"–5' **Planting:** container; spring, fall **Zones:** 7–9

THIS SHRUB IS OFTEN CONFUSED WITH MANY FORMS OF BAMBOO, which can be very invasive of your neighbors' gardens. Heavenly bamboo is not a relative of bamboo. It is so named because of the similarity to bamboo in its foliage. Heavenly bamboo is a well-behaved, non-invasive plant. Many landscapers use this shrub to give a garden an oriental accent. It can stand by itself, and some of the dwarf forms can create a close-knit groundcover. The larger varieties make good container plants, giving an oriental accent to any entryway; this usage is a refreshing relief from those gardeners who insist that the 'juniper bush' is the ultimate landscape material.

Growing

Heavenly bamboo prefers **full sun** to **partial shade** in **humus-rich, moist, well-drained** soil. It prefers afternoon shade in the hot interior valleys. Heavenly bamboo is prone to chlorosis when planted in alkaline soils. Add fertilizers containing some form of iron. It prefers regular water but can tolerate drier conditions. Shrubs in full sun that experience some frost will produce the best fall and winter color. Heavenly bamboo appreciates a location out of any cold, drying winds.

Heavenly bamboo needs only minimal pruning. Older, neglected shrubs can be rejuvenated by cutting up to one-third of the oldest stems to the ground before new growth begins in spring. Young stem tips may be damaged by hard frost and can be pruned back at this time as can the naked skeletons of the fruit clusters.

Tips

Heavenly bamboo adds an oriental feel to your garden. It can be used in shrub borders and as background plants, and it can make open, informal hedges and screens. It is a great plant for containers and for mass planting. Heavenly bamboo can make handsome houseplants.

Heavenly bamboo produces male and female flowers on the same plant. Isolated specimens will produce limited amounts of fruit, but planting a few plants together will ensure a good quantity of the shiny, red berries.

N. domestica (above), 'Firepower' (below)

Recommended

N. domestica produces clumps of thin, upright, lightly branched stems and fine-textured foliage. It grows 6–8' tall and spreads 3–5' wide and wider, spreading slowly by suckering. Large, loose clusters of small, white flowers are borne in late spring to early summer, followed by persistent, spherical, glossy, bright red fruit. New foliage is tinged bronze to red, becoming light to medium green in summer, with many varieties turning red to reddish purple in fall and winter. **'Compacta'** grows 4–5' tall and 3–4' wide. It produces more stems and denser foliage than the species. **'Firepower'** is a dwarf form growing 24" tall and wide. Its leaves are bright red in fall and winter and tinted red throughout the year. **'Harbor Dwarf'** grows 24–36" tall and spreads indefinitely by suckers. It has orange-red to bronze-red fall and winter color. **'Nana'** ('Pygmaea') is a dense, mound-forming shrub with very little to no flower or fruit production. It grows 24–36" tall and wide. Its large leaves are purple-green in summer and purple-red to bright red in fall and winter. **'Wood's Dwarf'** is a slow-growing, compact shrub with dense, light golden green summer foliage. The leaves turn bright red-orange to bright red in fall and winter. This cultivar grows 18" tall and wide. 'Nana,' 'Harbour Dwarf' and 'Wood's Dwarf' can be planted in mass to make an interesting groundcover pattern. (Zones 7–9)

'Harbor Dwarf' (below)

Problems & Pests

Heavenly bamboo may have problems with mealybugs and scale insects. It is resistant to oak root fungus.

Heavenly bamboo is infected with a virus that causes the leaves to be different colors and sometimes distorted. The virus does no harm to the plant, and the effects are considered ornamental. The virus usually infects only the hybrids.

The Japanese like to plant this shrub in their gardens and especially by the front door, because it's said that heavenly bamboo wards off danger and evil. People who experience nightmares are said to benefit from heavenly bamboo planted near the entrance of their home.

N. domestica (above)

'Wood's Dwarf' (below)

Hebe

Hebe

Features: flowers, fragrance, foliage, habit **Habit:** mounded, evergreen shrub with dense foliage **Height:** 2–5' **Spread:** 2–5' **Planting:** container; spring, fall **Zones:** 8–10

HEBE IS A MUST-HAVE FOR THE COASTAL AND COOLER REGIONS OF Northern California because it blooms regardless of fog, wind and other inclement weather. It does require adequate water, however, and good drainage. The many forms of this shrub make it appropriate for various landscapes. Several of these forms contrast well with other similar-growing shrubs. 'Patty's Purple,' for example, makes a great combination with *Pittosporum* 'Wheeler's Dwarf' as a border behind a perennial or annual bed. One of the workhorses is an old-time favorite called *H. speciosa* 'Imperialis.' It will tolerate the heat of the Sacramento Valley provided it receives adequate moisture.

Growing

Hebe grows well in **full sun** in coastal gardens but prefers **partial to light shade** in the hot valleys. This shrub does best in the Sacramento Valley when exposed to morning sun only. It will not tolerate full sun and heat there. The ideal soil is **well drained, moderate** to **poor, moist** and **neutral** to **slightly alkaline,** though hebe will tolerate a variety of soils. It is also tolerant of urban pollution. Plant in a spot out of cold, drying winds. Dry summer heat and winter frosts can shorten this shrub's lifespan.

Pruning is not required unless a more compact form is desired. Flowering stems can be cut back by half when flowering is complete. Hebe can be cut back hard—if it becomes rangy and ugly looking—because it easily rejuvenates from leafless, old wood. Hebe propagates readily from new wood cuttings.

'Veronica Lake' (above)

H. buxifolia *is sometimes confused with* H. odora *and* H. anomala *(two other very similar hebe species). No matter, any of these three species makes a wonderful addition to a garden.*

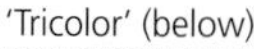

'Tricolor' (below)

Tips

Hebe can be used as short hedges, groundcovers or topiary. It works well in shrub and mixed borders, rock gardens and containers.

Hebe is easily transplanted at anytime. Some gardeners grow extra plants in a nursery to fill in gaps when they occur in the garden.

Recommended

H. buxifolia (Boxleaf Hebe, New Zealand Flame Bush) is a fast-growing, rounded and symmetrical shrub that grows 3–5' tall and wide. It bears a plethora of small, glossy green leaves and showy clusters of white flowers on reddish yellow stems. The summer blossoms are followed by capsule-like fruits in fall. This species is considered the most heat resistant, but it still does best in coastal gardens. (Zones 8–10)

***H.* 'Coed'** is a compact, 36" tall and wide shrub. The reddish stems are densely covered with dark green foliage. Clusters of small, pinkish purple flowers top the stems in summer. (Zones 8–10)

***H.* 'Patty's Purple'** is a spreading, mounding shrub that grows 24–36" tall and wide, bearing clusters of purple flowers in spring and summer. The flowers fade to white with age. The wine red stems are densely covered with small, dark green, glossy leaves. (Zones 8–10)

H. speciosa is a stout shrub with thick branches and large, shiny, dark green leaves. It grows 3–5' tall,

H. speciosa (below)

spreads 4' and bears red-purple to blue-purple flowers in summer. **'Imperialis'** has crimson-purple flowers. **'Tricolor'** has cream-edged foliage tinged purple or pink underneath. (Zones 8–10)

H. **'Veronica Lake'** is a compact, mounding shrub growing 36" tall and wide. Clusters of lilac purple flowers bloom profusely in summer. (Zones 8–10)

Problems & Pests

Fusarium wilt is a problem in parts of California. Do not replant a hebe where you previously had a problem with *Fusarium* wilt, because this particular pest lives in the soil. Leaf spot, root rot, aphids and downy mildew are also potential problems.

'Coed' (all photos this page)

Holly

Ilex

Features: foliage, fruit, variable habit **Habit:** erect, pyramidal or spreading, evergreen shrub or tree **Height:** 3–50' **Spread:** 3–40' **Planting:** container; spring, fall **Zones:** 6–10

I HAVE ALWAYS THOUGHT OF HOLLY, DOUGLAS-FIR AND MISTLETOE as the mainstays of Christmas decorations. Next to the Safeway store in Willits was a 20' tall, conical-shaped English holly that dependably produced the red berries on cue as the holidays arrived. I found out that if I was really nice and said please, the owner would clip off some branches and give them to me as a most wonderful gift. Those clippings added a lot to my holidays. I shared them with my grandmother, who felt very special when I gave them to her. It made up for many past transgressions.

Using the leaves as mulch is a great deterrent in areas where you want to keep neighborhood cats at bay.

Growing

These plants prefer **full sun** but tolerate partial shade. The soil should be of **average to rich fertility, humus rich, moist, slightly acidic** and **well drained**. Shelter from harsh wind helps prevent the leaves from drying out. Apply mulch to keep the roots cool and moist.

Holly requires little pruning. Damaged growth and growth that spoils the symmetry can be removed in spring. If you are growing it as a hedge, trim it in summer. Dispose of all the trimmings to prevent the spiny leaves from puncturing bare feet and paws.

Tips

Holly can be used in groups, as hedges, in woodland gardens and in shrub or mixed borders. It makes a wonderful specimen plant. The best time to purchase holly is in late fall so you can see if the plant produces colorful fruit.

I. aquifolium cultivar (above)

I. crenata cultivar (below)

I. cornuta (all photos this page)

Male and female flowers occur on separate plants, and both must be present for the female to set fruit. One male will adequately pollinate two to three females. It is best to have male and female plants of the same species. Some female plants have male limbs grafted into them so that pollination can take place on one plant. Other available cultivars set fruit without pollination. All varieties of holly are deer resistant.

Recommended

I. aquifolium (English Holly) is a dense, pyramidal shrub or tree. It grows 30–40' tall and 15–25' wide. Its red berries last into winter. Many cultivars are available, some with yellow berries, weeping or dwarf habits, variegated foliage and other features. These plants are best on the coast and may suffer from the heat inland. This species is resistant to oak root fungus. (Zones 7–10)

I. cornuta (Chinese Holly, Horned Holly) is a densely branched, rounded shrub or small tree growing 10–12' tall and 10–15' wide. The dark green leaves are leathery and rectangular in shape, and many have spines. The fruit is large, bright red and persistent. *I. cornuta* needs a long warm season to produce fruit. Many of the female cultivars do not need a male to produce fruit. **'Bufordii'** grows 15' tall and spreads 10–12'. The glossy, pea green leaves cup downward. 'Bufordii' is self-pollinating. *I. cornuta* and its cultivars are useful as tub or container plants. (Zones 7–10)

I. crenata (Japanese Holly, Box-leaved Holly) is a densely branched, variable shrub or small tree. It can reach 15' tall and 12' wide, but it is usually smaller in gardens. The leaves are small, narrow, glossy and dark green, with scalloped edges, and the fruit is glossy black. The species and its cultivars are frost hardy and are excellent for topiary, hedges, espalier and bonsai. (Zones 6–10)

I. wilsonii (*I.* x *altaclerensis* 'Wilsonii') is an evergreen tree that reaches 10–20' in height and spreads 10', or an evergreen shrub that grows 6–8' tall and wide. It has smooth-edged, glossy, dark green leaves and spherical, red fruit. This self-fertile variety is best used where summer temperatures hover in the high 90s to 100s. It will tolerate coastal winds. (Zones 8–10)

I. wilsonii (above), *I. aquifolium* cultivar (below)

Problems & Pests

Aphids may attack young shoots. Scale insects, beetles, caterpillars, spider mites, whiteflies, leaf miners, powdery mildew, leaf spot and canker can present problems. Crown and root rot are problems in poorly drained soils.

The showy, scarlet berries look tempting, especially to children, but they are not edible. Ingestion can cause stomach cramps.

Horsechestnut

Aesculus

Features: early-summer flowers, foliage, spiny fruit **Habit:** rounded or spreading, deciduous tree **Height:** 10–70' **Spread:** 25–50' **Planting:** container; spring, fall **Zones:** 4–9

IN 1992 WHEN BEV AND I VISITED THE JAMES MADISON ESTATE IN Montpelier, Virginia, we were treated to the sight of a 60' tall horsechestnut. I was only familiar with the California buckeye, which is a small tree, and did not know this stately beauty. I was surprised to see some of these more than 200-year-old trees with lightening rods in them to protect them. Our landscapes in Northern California are at the most 150 years old, so we have yet to realize the mature growth of many of our trees. It is always a thrill to see the older, more mature plantings in the older estates in the East. It lets us know the ultimate growth that we have yet to experience.

Growing

Horsechestnuts grow well in **full sun** or **partial shade.** The soil should be **fertile, moist** and **well drained.** These trees dislike excessive drought. Little pruning of this tree is required. Remove wayward branches in winter or early spring. Remove dead or diseased branches anytime.

Tips

Horsechestnuts are used as specimen and shade trees and in the background. The roots of horsechestnuts can break up sidewalks and patios if planted too close.

The smaller, shrubby horsechestnuts grow well near ponds and also make interesting specimens. They need lots of space because they can form large colonies.

A. x *carnea* (above)

A. californica (below)

A. x *carnea* (all photos this page)

Horsechestnuts give heavy shade, which is excellent for cooling buildings but makes it difficult to grow grass beneath. Consider a shade-loving groundcover as an alternative.

The entire tree and especially the seeds contain a poisonous compound that breaks down blood proteins. People are commonly poisoned when they confuse the nuts with edible sweet chestnuts (*Castanea*).

Recommended

A. californica (California Buckeye) is a rounded, low-headed tree that is often multi-stemmed. It grows 10–25' tall (occasionally to 40'), with a spread of 30' or more. Large, upright clusters of fragrant, white, cream or pink-tinged flowers are produced in spring. This tree loses its leaves early (August) and becomes bare for the rest of the year. It is deer proof, except for occasional browsing on the new foliage in spring. It is best used as a background with other trees and tall shrubs where their silvery white trunks makes striking silhouettes against a background of dark green. This tree will self-seed. The seedlings are in popular demand for bonsai specimens. (Zones 6–9)

A.* x *carnea (Red Horsechestnut) is a dense, rounded to spreading tree. It grows 30–70' tall, with a spread of 30–50'. It is smaller than common horsechestnut—*A. hippocastanum*—but needs more regular watering in summer. Spikes of dark pink flowers are borne in late spring and early summer. **'Briotii'** has large leaves and stunning red flowers in spring.

It grows 25–40' tall and wide. It is not as hardy as *A.* x *carnea*, growing in Zones 5–9. **'O'Neill'** bears bright red, single flowers. It grows slowly to 35' in height. (Zones 4–8)

Problems & Pests

Horsechestnuts are most susceptible to disease when under stress. Canker, leaf scorch, leaf spot, scale insects, anthracnose, rust and powdery mildew can all cause problems.

Horsechestnut flowers attract hummingbirds to the garden. Squirrels eat the apparently safe embryos in the otherwise poisonous seeds. The seeds are used in many floral arrangements and dried Christmas arrangements.

A. carnea (above)

A. californica (below)

Hydrangea

Hydrangea

Features: flowers, habit **Habit:** deciduous, mounding or spreading shrub, woody climber or tree **Height:** 3–80' **Spread:** 2–20' **Planting:** container; spring, fall **Zones:** 3–11

THE LOWLY, YET PRODUCTIVE *H. MACROPHYLLA* IS ONE OF THE most ignored plants in the garden. It is misunderstood, abused, mismanaged, decapitated needlessly and stressed. Every year I watch in horror when I see 'professional' landscapers cut the entire plant to the ground. Even when it recovers from this abuse, it is a wonder if it gets watered, much less fed or mulched. Let me emphasize that hydrangeas do need some regular care and should never be pruned to the ground every January or whenever someone gets around to it. I would love to see this plant able to again hold its head up high, and take its rightful place in the shade garden.

Growing

Hydrangeas grow well in **full sun** or **partial shade**. In the hot interior valleys, provide all species with afternoon shade to reduce leaf and flower scorch. The soil should be of **average to high fertility, humus rich, moist** and **well drained**. Hydrangeas

perform best in cool, moist conditions. An organic mulch will help lower your water bill. The flower buds of *H. macrophylla* and *H. quercifolia* can be damaged by a hard frost. A sheltered spot will help minimize the damage.

Tips

Hydrangeas come in many forms and have many uses in the landscape. They can be included in shrub or mixed borders, used as specimens or informal barriers and planted in groups or containers. Climbing varieties can be trained up walls, pergolas and arbors. Tie them in place for the first couple of years of growth until the aerial roots anchor themselves.

Hydrangea flowerheads contain both inconspicuous fertile flowers and showy sterile flowers. They come in two basic arrangements: **hortensia** flowerheads consist

H. quercifolia (above)

Softwood cuttings of H. arborescens *are easy to root.*

H. paniculata (above)

H. anomala subsp. *petiolaris* (below)

almost entirely of showy sterile flowers clustered together to form a globe; **lacecap** flowerheads have a loose ring of showy sterile flowers around the fertile ones, giving the flowerhead a delicate, lacy appearance.

By pruning this shrub properly, you can have blooms as early as April, and it will continue to bloom through fall.

The leaves and buds of some hydrangeas, but apparently not those of *H. paniculata* 'Grandiflora,' can cause cyanide poisoning if eaten or if the smoke is inhaled. Avoid burning hydrangea clippings.

Recommended

H. anomala* subsp. *petiolaris (*H. petiolaris*) (Climbing Hydrangea) is considered by some gardeners to be the most elegant climbing plant available. It clings to any rough surface by means of little rootlets that sprout from the stems. It can climb 50–80'. Although this plant is shade tolerant, it will produce the best flowers when exposed to some direct sun each day. The leaves are a dark, glossy green and sometimes show yellow fall color. White lacecap flowerheads cover the plant for over a month in summer. The entire plant appears to be veiled in a lacy mist. This climber can be pruned after flowering, if required, to restrict its growth. It will also grow over rocks and can be used as a groundcover in shady areas. With careful pruning and some support when young, it can be trained to form a small tree or shrub. (Zones 4–10)

H. arborescens (Smooth Hydrangea) forms a rounded shrub 6–10' tall, with an equal spread. It is tolerant of shady conditions. The flowers appear on new growth each year, and they will look most attractive if the shrub is cut right back to the ground in spring before new growth begins. The flowers of the species are not very showy, but the cultivars have large, showy blossoms. **'Annabelle'** bears large, white, ball-like hortensia flowerheads. A single flowerhead can be up to 12" in diameter. This cultivar is more compact than the species, growing 3–4' tall and wide, and it is useful for brightening up a shady wall or corner of the garden. (Zones 3–10)

H. macrophylla (Bigleaf Hydrangea, Garden Hydrangea) is a large, rounded shrub growing 6–10' tall and wide. It has large, shiny, dark green leaves and lacecap flowerheads of red, blue, pink or white flowers that bloom in summer. The many cultivars can have either hortensia or lacecap flowerheads. The species and cultivars bloom on older wood. Prune stems that have finished flowering back to just above a pair of fat, healthy buds close to the base of the shrub. Overgrown or neglected plants can have up to one-third of the stems removed. Cut these close to the ground below any visible buds. **'All Summer Beauty'** grows 3–4' tall and produces flowers on new growth. Prune in the late dormant season. **'Nikko Blue'** has the darkest blue flowers of any variety, all on 4–6' tall plants. **'Tricolor'** is a lacecap variety grown for its strongly variegated,

H. quercifolia (above), *H. macrophylla* (below)

dark green, light green and white foliage. This shrub is perfect for darker areas of the garden. It grows 3–4' tall. (Zones 6–11)

H. paniculata (Panicle Hydrangea) is a spreading to upright, large shrub or small tree. It grows 10–22' tall and spreads to 8'. It bears white flowers from late summer to early fall. This plant requires little pruning. When young, it can be pruned to encourage a shrub-like or tree-like habit. The entire shrub can be cut to within 12" of the ground in spring before growth begins to encourage vigorous new growth the following summer. **'Grandiflora'** (Pee Gee Hydrangea) is a spreading, large shrub or small tree that is 15–25' tall and 10' wide. The mostly sterile flowers are borne in hortensia clusters up to 18" long. (Zones 3–10)

H. quercifolia (Oak-leaf Hydrangea) is a mound-forming shrub with attractive, cinnamon brown, exfoliating bark. It grows 4–8' tall, with an equal spread. The large leaves are lobed like an oak's and often turn bronze or bright red in fall. Conical clusters of sterile and fertile flowers bloom from late spring to midsummer. Pruning can be done after flowering. Remove spent flowers and cut out some of the older growth to encourage young replacement growth. **'Snowflake'** bears clusters of double flowers 12–15" long that open white and fade to pink as they age. The flowers are so heavy that they cause the stems to arch towards the ground. This cultivar prefers partial shade. (Zones 5–10)

Hydrangeas have an unusual reaction to the pH level of the soil. In an acidic soil the flowers will tend to be blue; the same plant grown in an alkaline soil will tend to have pink to red flowers. Cultivars develop their best color in one or the other soil type. You can intensify pink colors by adding oystershell lime to the soil. Blue is intensified by the addition of aluminum sulfate.

H. paniculata 'Grandiflora' (below)

Problems & Pests

Occasional problems for hydrangeas include slugs, snails, aphids, scale insects, powdery mildew, rust, bacterial wilt, root rot and leaf spot. Hot sun and excessive wind will dry out petals and leaves, turning them brown.

All flowerheads can be used in dried or fresh flower arrangements. For the longest-lasting fresh flowers, deeply water the soil around the plant the evening before to help keep the petals from wilting when the flowers are cut. Make a second cutting under warm water before placing in your flower arrangement.

H. macrophylla (above)

Japanese Pagoda Tree

Chinese Scholar Tree

Sophora

Features: fragrant summer flowers, habit **Habit:** dense, rounded, deciduous tree or shrub **Height:** 10–80' **Spread:** 10–80' **Planting:** container; spring, fall **Zones:** 4–10

JAPANESE PAGODA TREE IS ONE OF THE FEW TREES OR SHRUBS I can recommend for growing in lawns—it doesn't have the habit of surface rooting that is usually associated with lawn watering. Also, the loose foliage allows adequate sun to reach the ground, so that lawns do quite well underneath. The blooms and seedpods can be somewhat messy on concrete patios, but they will not stain permanently. This tree does well in the Sacramento Valley and up to 5000' elevation in the Sierras. It is a perfect tree for locations that are difficult to water, and it rarely needs pruning.

Growing

Japanese pagoda tree grows best in **full sun**. The soil should be of **average fertility** and **well drained.** Once established, this species tolerates most conditions, even polluted urban settings. Provide moderate water during the growing season.

Tips

Use Japanese pagoda tree as a specimen tree or a shade tree. The cultivar 'Pendula' can be used in borders.

Plant in a sheltered location and provide some protection to young trees, which can be quite tender until they are established.

The seeds are poisonous and can even be fatal if eaten.

Recommended

S. japonica may reach heights of 100' in the wild, but it usually grows to about 50–80' tall and wide in garden settings. It grows quickly to about 20', then growth is much slower. It bears large, pendant clusters of fragrant, white flowers in summer, followed by attractive seedpods. The dark green foliage may turn yellow in fall. **'Pendula'** has long, drooping branches that are usually grafted to a standard, creating a small but dramatic weeping tree. The size depends on the height of the standard, usually 10–25' in height, with an equal or greater spread. This cultivar rarely flowers. (Zones 4–10)

Problems & Pests

Japanese pagoda tree can be affected by twig blight, *Verticillium* wilt, canker, rust, powdery mildew and leafhoppers. It is resistant to oak root fungus.

S. japonica (all photos this page)

Some people might consider this tree messy when the flowers drop, but the blanket of delicate petals beneath the tree is really quite attractive.

Kalmia

Mountain Laurel

Kalmia

Features: foliage, late-spring to mid-summer flowers **Habit:** large, dense, bushy, evergreen shrub **Height:** 3–10' **Spread:** 3–10' **Planting:** container; spring, fall **Zones:** 4–9

WHEN MY GRANDCHILDREN WERE VERY YOUNG, I WOULD ASK them to put their hands over kalmia blooms and then watch very closely. The shrub would react by puffing out a spray of pollen from the open blooms. My grandchildren were thrilled, as if they had just become wizards. Harry Potter had nothing on them! The puff my grandchildren witnessed resulted from the kalmia flower's fertilization mechanism. The pollen is held under tension and is released when an insect touches a bloom. The puff of pollen coats the insect, which then takes that pollen to the next flower it visits.

Growing

Kalmia prefers **light or partial shade.** The soil should be of **average to high fertility, moist, acidic** and **well**

drained. Kalmia does not perform well in alkaline soil. A mulch of leaf mold or pine needles will keep the roots of this drought-sensitive plant from drying out.

Little pruning is required, but spent flowerheads can be removed in summer and awkward shoots removed as needed.

Tips

Use kalmia in a shaded part of a shrub or mixed border, in a woodland garden or combined with other acid- and shade-loving plants, such as rhododendrons. It makes a good container plant.

Do not make tea from kalmia or otherwise ingest its flowers or foliage, which are extremely poisonous.

'Ostbo Red' (above), *K. latifolia* (below)

Recommended

K. latifolia grows 6–10' tall with an equal spread. It has glossy green leaves and pink or white flowers that bloom in late spring. Cultivars are more commonly grown than the species. **'Alpine Pink'** has a very dense habit and dark pink buds that open to light pink flowers. **'Elf'** is a dwarf cultivar that grows to 36" tall and wide. It has pink buds, white flowers and quite small leaves. **'Ostbo Red'** is an older cultivar with bright red buds and light pink flowers. **'Silver Dollar'** has large, white flowers. (Zones 4–9)

Problems & Pests

Kalmia can be affected by borers, lace bugs, leaf gall, leaf spot, powdery mildew, scale insects and weevils.

Kerria
Japanese Kerria
Kerria

Features: mid- to late-spring flowers, habit **Habit:** suckering, mounding or arching, deciduous shrub **Height:** 4–10' **Spread:** 6–10' **Planting:** B & B, container; spring, fall **Zones:** 4–9

THIS LARGE SHRUB NEEDS AT LEAST 6' TO SPREAD ITS GRACEFUL stems and foliage. The long, arching branches can be used in many floral arrangements, even when they are dormant. Kerria is a dependable early bloomer that might take the place of forsythia, which needs a cooler climate than Northern California's to bloom at its best. I have never figured out why a plant native to China would be called *K. japonica.*

Growing

Kerria prefers **light to partial shade.** The soil should be of **average fertility, moist** and **well drained.** Fewer flowers will appear on a shrub grown in soil that is too fertile. This shrub has naturalized in many coastal areas throughout Northern California, requiring little or no water in summer. In these areas, it can be grown in full sun. Kerria requires some protection in the warmer climates of the state.

Prune after flowering. Cut the flowering shoots back to young side shoots, strong buds or right to the ground. Remove all thin, weak shoots. Kerria spreads by suckers. Remove unwanted suckers to keep the shrub compact. The entire plant can be cut back to the ground after flowering if it becomes overgrown and needs rejuvenating.

Tips

Kerria is useful in group plantings, woodland gardens and shrub or mixed borders.

Recommended

K. japonica grows 4–6' tall, and it spreads 6–8'. It has single yellow flowers that bloom in spring and occasionally into early summer. **'Aureo-variegata'** has yellow leaf margins. **'Pleniflora'** grows 10' tall and wide and has yellow, double flowers. Its habit is more upright than that of the species. **'Variegata'** ('Picta') has white-edged foliage. (Zones 4–9)

Problems & Pests

Leaf spot, leaf blight, twig blight, canker and root rot may occur, but they are not serious.

'Pleniflora' (above)

The distinct yellow-green to bright green, arching stems of kerria add interest to the winter landscape and to winter flower arrangements.

K. japonica (below)

Lilac

Syringa

Features: fragrant, early-spring to early-summer flowers **Habit:** rounded or suckering, deciduous shrub or small tree **Height:** 6–30' **Spread:** 4–25' **Planting:** bare-root, container; late winter, early spring **Zones:** 3–10

MANY PEOPLE WHO MIGRATE FROM THE EAST TO THE PACIFIC Coast of Northern California have fond memories of 15' tall lilac trees in full bloom that hedged their property or served as specimen plants. They are quite disappointed when they find that in the mild winters of Northern California, *S. vulgaris* will be quite a lot smaller. The Descanso Hybrids, however, are grown for our milder climates, and though they don't reach the height of their eastern cousins, they will bloom dependably. If you are determined to have a lilac that reminds you of your grandma's, reduce watering in September and don't water at all after the end of the month. The plant won't look great, but that isn't what you grow them for in the first place. If all else fails, *S. persica* will reward you with dependable, fragrant lilac blooms each and every spring. Bi-weekly watering will keep this plant quite content once it is established.

Growing

Lilacs grow best in **full sun** in areas that have a distinct, chilling winter. The soil should be **fertile, moist, neutral** to **alkaline** and **well drained.** These plants tolerate open, windy locations, and the improved air circulation helps keep powdery mildew at bay. Clean up leaves in fall to help discourage overwintering pests.

Most lilacs need little pruning. Deadhead as much as possible to keep plants neat. On established French and Persian lilacs, one-third to one-half of the growth can be cut right back each year after flowering. This treatment will make way for vigorous young growth and prevent the plants from becoming leggy, overgrown and unattractive. You can also prune during blooming to collect the fragrant flowers for a wonderful spring treat. For grafted varieties, remove all suckers from below the grant union.

'Angel White' (above), *S. vulgaris* cultivar (below)

Ghosts at home? Keep a vase full of the wonderfully fragrant flowers of S. vulgaris*; this species is reputed to keep ghosts away from your house.*

S. persica & *S. vulgaris* (above), 'Ivory Silk' (below)

Tips

Include lilacs in a shrub or mixed border or use them to create an informal hedge. Japanese tree lilac can be used as a specimen tree.

Lilacs grown from small plants or cuttings can take up to five years to begin flowering.

Don't be concerned when your lilac starts to decline in September—it is a normal transition. Fall clean-up is necessary to give the plant a new start in spring.

Recommended

S. persica (Persian Lilac) is a densely branched shrub growing 6' tall and wide. It produces clusters of pale violet flowers all along its branches in spring. **'Alba'** has fragrant, white flowers. (Zones 5–9)

S. reticulata (Japanese Tree Lilac) is a rounded, large shrub or small tree that grows 20–30' tall and spreads 15–25'. It bears white flowers in early summer. The species and its cultivars are resistant to powdery mildew, scale insects and borers. **'Ivory Silk,'** which grows 10–15' tall and spreads 6–12', has a more compact habit and produces more flowers than the species. It is a recommended small patio tree and is not a problem if planted near concrete. (Zones 3–9)

S. vulgaris (French Lilac, Common Lilac) is the plant most people think of when they think of a lilac. It grows 10–20' tall and wide, bearing fragrant flowers from mid- to late spring. This suckering, spreading shrub has an irregular habit, but consistent maintenance pruning will keep it neat and in good condition. **Descanso Hybrids** were bred in Southern California to handle the lack of chilling temperatures. They grow to 8–12' tall and 4–5' wide and flower 7–10 days before the species. **'Angel White'** bears a profusion of fragrant, white flowers. **'Blue Skies'** has blue flowers. **'California Rose'** has pink flowers with a sweet fragrance. **'Lavender Lady'** has very large, very fragrant, lavender flowers. (Zones 3–10)

Problems & Pests

Powdery mildew, leaf spot, leaf miners, borers, caterpillars, scale insects and bacterial blight are all possible troublemakers for lilacs.

'Ivory Silk' (above)

The wonderfully fragrant flowers have inspired the development of 800 or 900 cultivars of S. vulgaris. *Check with your local nursery to see what is available.*

S. persica (below)

Loquat

Eriobotrya

Features: fragrant flowers, foliage, fruit **Habit:** upright to rounded, evergreen shrub or tree **Height:** 15–30' **Spread:** 15–30' **Planting:** container; spring to fall **Zones:** 8–11

THIS EVERGREEN, TROPICAL-LOOKING PLANT HAS MANY USES throughout one's garden. Loquat is well behaved in its root system, but because it bears fruit it is not recommended as a street tree or near swimming pools, cement patios or sidewalks. My friend Alice Waters, of Chez Panisse—a world-famous restaurant in Berkeley—has written a wonderful book called *Chez Panisse Fruit.* Regarding the standard everyday loquat, Alice recommends letting it fully ripen on the tree, at which point you can eat it right out of your hand. Loquats do not preserve well, so they must be used right after harvest. They combine well with strawberries and can be used in pies, jams, compotes and sauces for meats. One of the benefits of loquats is that they ripen at a time of year when other fruit is not readily available. If you aren't interested in the fruit but like the tropical effect of the tree, try *E. deflexa* (bronze loquat). It blooms in spring with fragrant, mostly sterile, white blooms.

Growing

Loquat grows well in **full sun** to **partial shade** in **moist, well-drained, moderately fertile** soil with a **neutral** pH. It can tolerate coarse, alkaline soils and a touch of drought, but it requires a site sheltered from cold, drying winds. Water *E. japonica* regularly when the fruit is forming. All species of loquat respond well to fertilizers that are used for citrus trees.

Loquat needs only minimal pruning to maintain the plant shape. Prune it in late winter or early spring while it is still dormant. Loquats are best when trained as small trees with short trunks. Crowded growth can be thinned by removing excess shoots completely. When growing *E. japonica* for fruit, thin the branches to allow light to penetrate the crown. If the tree is heavily laden with fruit, remove the tip of each fruit cluster. The remaining fruit will grow larger, and the branches will be protected from breaking under too much weight. When harvesting the fruit, remove the entire cluster back to a strong bud or shoot.

Tips

Loquat is suitable for growing in a container, as a specimen, as a street, patio or shade tree, as an accent or background tree or espaliered onto a fence or trellis. It combines well with other tropical-looking trees, shrubs and perennials, such as banana palms, canna and tree ferns.

E. japonica (all photos this page)

Recommended

E. deflexa (Bronze Loquat) is a vigorous, low-branched, vase-shaped shrub or small tree. It bears clusters of fragrant, creamy white flowers in spring, followed infrequently by fleshy, yellow to green, inedible fruit. Its large, shiny leaves start out a bright bronze color, turning deep green with age. The effect of the bright young foliage against the dark mature foliage makes this loquat a wonderful show piece. The healthier the plant, the better the contrast between the new and old foliage. (Zones 9–11)

E. japonica (Japanese Loquat) is a small, rounded tree with large, showy, dark green leaves with prominent veins. It bears clusters of small, creamy white flowers in fall to early winter, followed by sweet to tart, orange to yellow, edible fruit that ripens in winter to spring. If the fruit

is more seed than fruit, you can separate out the seeds by mashing the fruit in a kitchen ricer. The extracted fruit can then be used for making a delicious jam. **'Gold Nugget'** is a grafted variety grown for its dependable fruit crop. (Zones 8–11)

Problems & Pests

Loquats are subject to fire blight, fungal spots, blights, cankers and root rots. The fruit may be damaged by birds and fruit flies. Use liquid copper spray in January to eliminate any fungal disease and blight. Fruit infected with fruit flies should be destroyed and not allowed to stay on the ground.

E. japonica *is widely and frequently grown commercially for fruit production. The fruit is used in preserves and pies or eaten fresh, and it is also attractive to birds.*

E. japonica (all photos both pages)

Magnolia

Magnolia

Features: flowers, fruit, foliage, habit, bark **Habit:** upright to spreading, deciduous or evergreen shrub or tree **Height:** 8–80' **Spread:** 10–60' **Planting:** B & B for deciduous varieties, container; late winter, early spring **Zones:** 4–11

MOST MAGNOLIA VARIETIES ON THE MARKET WILL NEVER BE LARGE shade trees like *M. grandiflora*, but they all have their place. Most magnolias are fragrant and bear spectacular tulip-like flowers in the early spring. The flowers vary from star-shaped to giant saucer-shaped ones. To purchase the color you wish, it is best to see them in bloom in your local nurseries. Many arboretums feature these trees in early spring, where they make the perfect background for beds of tulips and other bulbs.

M. liliiflora (above)

Growing

Magnolias grow well in **full sun** or **partial shade**. The soil should be **fertile, humus rich, neutral** to **acidic, moist** and **well drained**. A summer mulch will help keep the roots cool and the soil moist, especially when the plants are young. Staking is necessary when planting in windy areas or when planting in fall before winter rains. Evergreen magnolias will show stress in overly windy locations.

Magnolias are sensitive to excess salts. They may experience chlorosis in alkaline soils. Excess salts from overfertilizing, salty soil or salty irrigation water may cause leaf burn. Deep watering can help leach excess salts down below the root zone.

Very little pruning is needed. Prune evergreen magnolias in spring before new growth begins. When plants are young, thin out a few branches to encourage an attractive habit. Remove all but the strongest stem to train as a single-stemmed tree. Always prune twigs and branches back to their point of origin. Prune deciduous magnolias when blooming is complete, and remove only dead, diseased or crossing branches.

M. x *soulangiana* (above), *M. liliiflora* (below)

Tips

The larger magnolias are useful as specimens and shade trees. The smaller deciduous magnolias are used in containers, shrub beds and borders, and they may be trained as espalier.

Avoid planting deciduous magnolias where the morning sun will encourage the blooms to open too early in

M. grandiflora at Marin Art & Garden Center

Despite their often fuzzy coats, magnolia flower buds are frost sensitive. On rare occasions, excessive rain can spoil open blooms.

the season. The blossoms can be damaged by cold, wind and rain.

Magnolias are susceptible to leaf scorch in late fall, but because they go dormant, it is rarely a problem that needs attention.

The root systems of magnolias are shallow and resent any kind of disturbance or damage. Select an open location that minimizes potential damage and foot traffic. Avoid transplanting. The shallow roots and dense crown makes growing anything underneath difficult, especially lawns.

Recommended

M. grandiflora (Southern Magnolia, Bull Bay) is a large, single or multi-stemmed tree with a broadly pyramidal crown and glossy, leathery, dark green leaves that have rust-colored undersides. It grows 60–80' tall and 50–60' wide at maturity.

M. grandiflora

The large, fragrant flowers are white to cream colored, fading to beige, and bloom from summer to fall. **'Russet'** is a narrow, upright, pyramidal tree reaching 60–80' in height and spreading 20'. The leaves are russet to beige colored underneath. The large, cream flowers bloom earlier than the species. **'St. Mary'** is a large shrub or small tree growing 20' tall and wide. It also tends to be multi-stemmed. It has large leaves and freely produces many large, white to cream flowers. (Zone 7–11)

M. stellata (above)

M. liliiflora (*M. quinquepeta*) (Lily Magnolia) is a large, rounded shrub that grows 8–12' tall and 10–15' wide. The outsides of the petals are purple, and they open to reveal white insides. The species can look scruffy by the end of the season. (Zones 5–10)

M.* x *soulangiana (Saucer Magnolia) is a rounded, spreading, deciduous shrub or tree. It grows 20–30' tall and wide and bears pink, purple or white flowers. **'Alexandrina'** is an upright tree. Its flower petals are pink on the outside and white on the inside. (Zones 5–10)

M. x *soulangiana* cultivar (above), *M. grandiflora* (below)

M. stellata (Star Magnolia) is a compact, bushy or spreading, deciduous shrub or small tree with fragrant, white flowers. It grows 10–20' tall and spreads 10–15'. (Zones 4–10)

Problems & Pests

Possible problems affecting magnolias include aphids, scale insects, spider mites, slugs and snails. They may also experience leaf spot, canker, dieback, treehoppers, powdery mildew, thrips and weevils.

Manzanita

Arctostaphylos

Features: branches, bark, fruit, foliage **Habit:** upright or low-growing, mat-forming, evergreen shrub **Height:** 4"–5' **Spread:** 18"–10' **Planting:** container; spring, fall **Zones:** 2–11

WHEN I USED TO BACKPACK IN THE CASCADE MOUNTAINS OF Northern California, I would search for the dead wood of manzanita because it would make a small but extremely hot cooking fire. It was always amusing to me that fellow campers would build huge fires out of pine and other softwoods. They would spend the larger part of the night trying to get water to boil. That wasn't their only problem—cleaning the bottom of their pot would take forever, too.

Growing

Manzanitas grow well in **full sun** or **partial shade.** Although they prefer a soil that is of **poor to average fertility, acidic, light** and very **well drained,** they adapt to heavier soils as long as there is good drainage.

Ensure you provide adequate water when the shrubs are establishing. In ideal conditions, one good soaking a week during the first summer should be sufficient. Manzanitas prefer deep, infrequent watering once established.

Pruning is not generally required. Prune only to remove branches that affect the overall form. Do not cut into old, bare wood because manzanitas do not generate new growth from those areas.

Tips

The low-growing manzanitas are good choices for groundcover. They can be included in a large rock garden, but you might have to prune a little more to keep them inbounds. Use the shrub species in beds and shrub borders and as specimen plants. Manzanitas easily cross-pollinate, so there is a great variation in seedlings. It is best to purchase container plants that have been cloned or cutting grown.

Forty-three of the 50 or so species of manzanita are native to California, and they are found in dry areas from the coast to elevations of 10,000'. Bears, birds and many other animals use the fruit as a food source.

A. densiflora 'Howard McMinn' (all photos this page)

A. uva-ursi 'Vancouver Jade' (below)

When growing manzanitas as groundcover, use mulch to keep the weeds down while the shrubs become established. Pinch the tips of the new growth off in spring to stimulate more branching.

Recommended

***A. densiflora* 'Howard McMinn'** is a dense, low, spreading shrub that is 3–6' tall and 6–7' wide. It roots where nodes on the stems touch the ground. The flowers are a sharper pink than most. (Zones 8–11)

***A.* 'Emerald Carpet'** is a dense, low-growing, groundcover shrub that reaches 8–14" tall and spreads about 5'. The foliage is bright emerald green, even in hot, dry areas. It has inconspicuous pink flowers. (Zones 7–10)

***A.* 'Pacific Mist'** is a low-growing, groundcover shrub that grows to 30" tall and spreads to 10' wide. It has gray-green foliage on dark reddish brown stems. It produces white flowers, but not in an appreciable quantity. (Zones 8–10)

***A.* 'Sunset'** is a mounding shrub that grows 4–5' tall and 4–6' wide and has pinkish white flowers. The new foliage is flushed orange-red, turning to bright green with age. (Zones 7–10)

A. uva-ursi (Bearberry, Kinnikinnick) is a prostrate shrub with white flowers that appear in late spring, followed by berries that ripen to bright red. It grows 4–6" tall and spreads 2–4'. It roots where nodes on the stems touch the ground. It will keep spreading forever if allowed to root at the nodes. The following cutting-grown cultivars share the white flowers and red fruit but also have leaves that turn shades of red in winter. **'Vancouver Jade'** is a low-growing shrub with arching stems. It grows 6" high and spreads 18". This cultivar is resistant to the leaf spot that can afflict manzanitas. **'Wood's Compact'** spreads about 3–4'. (Zones 2–10)

Problems & Pests

Possible problems include bud and leaf galls, as well as fungal diseases of the leaves, stems and fruit. The leaf galls do not hinder the growth of the shrub and are thought by some to be attractive.

A. uva-ursi (above)

'Kinnikinnick' is said to be an Algonquian term meaning 'smoking mixture,' reflecting that traditional use for the leaves of A. uva-ursi.

A. densiflora 'Howard McMinn' (below)

Maple

Acer

Features: foliage, bark, fruit, fall color, habit, flowers **Habit:** small, multi-stemmed, deciduous tree or large shrub **Height:** 6–80' **Spread:** 6–50' **Planting:** B & B (December, January), container (spring, as soon as possible after purchase) **Zones:** 3–9

I LOVE JAPANESE MAPLES BECAUSE THEY HAVE SO MANY LANDSCAPE uses. The more exotic varieties, such as the lace-leaved maples, are red, green or variegated and are wonderful specimen plants. One of the very special plants that I took with me when I sold the nursery is a beautiful, weeping, red lace-leaf variety I had grafted onto an 8' green Japanese maple. The red foliage cascades from the graft to the ground. One year an 80' California live oak fell into the crown and destroyed half of the graft, but it recovered nicely and is still bringing me joy.

Growing

Maples generally do well in **full sun** or **light shade**, but preferences vary from species to species. The soil should be **fertile, moist, high in organic matter** and **well drained**.

Maples respond well to pruning, with the amount depending on what purpose the tree will serve in the garden. In general, pruning should take place in early January to early February because the heavy sap flow makes it unwise to prune in spring. As well as being messy, the sap will attract ants. You can actually begin pruning as soon as the leaves are completely gone in late fall.

Tips

Maples can be used as specimen trees, as large elements in shrub or mixed borders or as garden delineators (informal hedges). Some are useful as understory plants bordering wooded areas; others can be grown in containers on patios or terraces.

Great blue heron on *A. palmatum* var. *dissectum* cultivar (above)

A. palmatum (below)

A. palmatum var. dissectum (above), A. palmatum (fall color)

Few Japanese gardens are without the attractive smaller maples. Almost all maples can be used to create bonsai specimens.

A good time to purchase maples is in fall as the leaf color starts to change. They can be planted at this time. To improve the coloring of any maple, treat the soil with a solution of iron sulfate in August.

Recommended

A. buergeranum (Trident Maple) can grow 20–35' tall, with an equal spread. It is drought and heat tolerant and prefers full sun and acidic soil. It may suffer winter damage if temperatures drop below –20° F. As the bark ages, it develops scales that flake off, revealing lighter bark beneath. The fall color ranges from yellow to red. (Zones 5–9)

A. circinatum (Vine Maple, Oregon Vine Maple) is a Pacific Northwest native that closely resembles *A. palmatum*. It grows naturally as an understory tree or shrub in damp areas and along streambanks. It often becomes a multi-stemmed tree 10–20' in height, with a greater spread. This maple is elegant in form and texture, with bright red-green bark and lovely layered foliage. The fall color ranges from golden in the shade to fire-engine red in open sites. (Zones 6–9)

A. davidii (Father David's Maple) is an excellent four-season tree. Its distinctive, shiny, olive green bark with silver gray stripes is a great winter feature. It grows 20–35' tall and wide and may grow to 50' in ideal conditions. Clusters of chartreuse flowers bloom in spring. The shiny green foliage is tinted bronze in spring and is awash in bright purple, red, orange and yellow in fall. (Zones 6–9)

A. griseum (Paperbark Maple) is attractive and adaptable to many conditions. It grows slowly to 20–35' tall, with a width half or equal the height. The orange-brown bark peels and curls away from the trunk in papery strips. Unfortunately, this popular species is difficult to propagate, so it can be quite expensive and sometimes hard to find. It grows well from seed. (Zones 4–8)

A. macrophyllum (Bigleaf Maple, Canyon Maple) is a large, deciduous tree. It grows 50–80' tall and 30–50' wide. It can grow to 100' tall and 70' wide in ideal conditions. The common name comes from the size of the dark green leaves, which turn yellow to orange in fall. Pendulous clusters of yellow flowers bloom in spring. It makes a great shade tree for large gardens, estates and parks—it works well on large hillsides—but it should not be used in yards with limited space. (Zones 6–9)

A. palmatum (Japanese Maple) is considered by many gardeners to be one of the most beautiful and versatile trees available. Although many cultivars and varieties are quite small, the species itself generally grows 15–25' tall, with an equal or greater spread. With enough space, this tree can even reach 50'. Because it leafs out early in spring, this maple can be badly damaged or killed by a late-spring frost. The red varieties need to have more sun in order to keep the red in their

A. buergeranum (above)

A. buergeranum bark (above), *A. macrophyllum* (below)

A. palmatum var. *dissectum* cultivar (above)

foliage. The green and variegated varieties need partial shade. They make spectacular container plants that can grow for years in the same pot, and they are root pruned every three years. Two distinct groups of cultivars have been developed from *A. palmatum* varieties. Types without dissected leaves, derived from **var. *atropurpureum*,** are grown for their purple foliage, though many lose their purple coloring as summer progresses. Two that keep their color are **'Bloodgood'** and **'Moonfire,'** both of which grow to about 15' tall. Types with dissected leaves, derived from **var. *dissectum*,** have foliage so deeply lobed and divided that it appears fern-like or even thread-like. The leaves can be green, as in the cultivar **'Waterfall,'** or red, as in **'Red Filigree Lace.'** These trees are generally small, growing to 6–10' tall. (Zones 5–8)

Maple wood is hard and dense and is used for fine furniture construction and for some musical instruments.

A. palmatum var. *atropurpureum* (below)

Problems & Pests

Anthracnose, *Verticillium* wilt, aphids, caterpillars, leaf cutters, leafhoppers, borers, leaf spots, scale insects and cankers can afflict maples. Iron deficiency (chlorosis) can occur in alkaline soils. Leaf scorch can be prevented by watering young trees during hot, dry spells and ensuring the soil pH is not too alkaline. If the problem is ongoing, apply an antidesiccant prior to the heat spell.

A. circinatum (above)

The wings of maple samaras act like miniature helicopter rotors and help in seed dispersal.

A. buergeranum (below)

Mimosa Tree

Jacaranda, Green Ebony

Jacaranda

Features: flowers, foliage, habit **Habit:** deciduous to semi-evergreen tree with rounded to irregular crown **Height:** 25–40' **Spread:** 15–30' **Planting:** container; spring, after all risk of frost has passed **Zones:** 9–11

MIMOSA TREE IS OFTEN CONFUSED WITH BAILEY ACACIA BECAUSE their fern-like foliage is similar. When the trees are in flower, however, mimosa tree's bluish purple blooms are easily distinguished from the yellow acacia flowers. Mimosa tree can survive frost providing it has matured. The specimen in Courthouse Square in San Rafael is a great example—it has survived through several Alaskan-type winters. Because hard frosts (below 15° F) happen so rarely in Northern California, this tree can become a showpiece for many coastal as well Bayside gardens.

Growing

Mimosa tree thrives in **full sun** in **well-drained, moderate** to **fertile** soil, though it will tolerate heavy clay soil. It has a low tolerance to salt. Ensure moderate water during the growing season. Trees in coastal areas may not produce flowers because of low summertime temperatures.

Young plants are frost tender and should be protected the first couple of winters. Older trees can be damaged when temperatures reach 15° F or lower. Most will come back from the root, but they will have to be retrained to take tree form.

Mimosa tree needs only minimal pruning. Remove any wayward branches, cutting back to the branch's point of origin. When a mimosa tree is planted as a street tree, remove the lower branches to allow enough room under the crown for cars to pass. Prune in mid- to late winter before new growth begins.

Tips

Mimosa tree is used as a street tree, a shade tree and a specimen tree. Its roots are well behaved, so it can also make an interesting patio tree. It is a great tree when allowed the space to fully mature.

Mimosa tree is normally evergreen in mild climates, but it drops its leaves where winter temperatures drop below 25° F. The seedpods are ornamental and can be used as accents in flower arrangements.

Mimosa tree has a shallow root system that makes underplanting difficult. Try an organic mulch out to the dripline.

Recommended

J. mimosifolia has fern-like, bright green foliage that drops in late winter. Large clusters of fragrant, bluish purple, trumpet-shaped flowers are produced in mid- to late spring at the tips of the light gray branches. There may be occasional blooming through summer. The flowers are followed by leathery, flat, disk-like seedpods. (Zones 9–11)

Problems & Pests

Aphids may be a problem, and mimosa tree can also experience crown gall, leaf spot and root rot where drainage is poor. It is resistant to oak root fungus.

Mockorange

Philadelphus

Features: early-summer flowers **Habit:** rounded, deciduous shrub with arching branches **Height:** 8–12' **Spread:** 4–12' **Planting:** container; spring, fall **Zones:** 4–10

WHEN MY MOTHER AND GRANDMOTHER PLANTED SOME CUTTINGS of this plant and told me it was 'mock' orange I was pretty excited. That is until I discovered that its fragrance is the only thing citrus-like about it. The plants did not bear any fruit that even resembled an orange. Young boys aren't the best judges of how great a plant is, however. You can bring sprays of this shrub into the house to add fragrance to any room. Mockorange combines well with forsythia and rarely fails to bloom in abundance. It makes a great background for early- and late-blooming bulbs.

Growing

Mockoranges grow well in **full sun, partial shade** or **light shade.** The soil should be of **average fertility, humus rich, moist** and **well drained.** Mockoranges will adapt to a variety of soils as long as they are well drained.

Once the shrub is established, remove one-third of the old wood each year after flowering. Overgrown shrubs can be rejuvenated by cutting them right back to within 6" of the ground. Established mockoranges transplant readily.

Tips

Include mockoranges in shrub or mixed borders, foundation plantings or woodland gardens. Use them in groups to create barriers and screens.

'Minnesota Snowflake' (above)

P. coronarius (below)

Recommended

P. coronarius (Sweet Mockorange) is an upright, broadly rounded shrub with fragrant, white flowers that bloom in late spring to early summer. It grows 8–12' tall, with an equal spread. **'Aureus'** has bright yellow, young foliage that matures to yellow-green. It grows 8' tall and spreads 5'. **'Variegatus'** has leaves with creamy white margins. It grows 8' tall and spreads 6'. (Zones 4–10)

P.* x *virginalis is a stiff, upright shrub growing 8–10' tall and wide. It is seldom grown in favor of its cultivars. **'Minnesota Snowflake'** is a hardy, dense, upright shrub that is slightly

P. coronarius (above), 'Aureus' (below)

'Minnesota Snowflake' (below)

smaller than the species. It bears fragrant, white, double flowers in late spring to early summer. **'Natchez'** grows 8–10' tall and 4–8' wide. It bears slightly fragrant, single, white flowers in late spring. (Zones 5–10)

Problems & Pests

Mockoranges can be affected by fungal spots, gray mold, powdery mildew, rust and scale insects, but these problems are rarely serious.

'Natchez' (above)

Monkey Puzzle Tree

Araucaria

Features: habit, branches, foliage, fruit **Habit:** broadly pyramidal, coniferous, evergreen tree **Height:** 70–100' **Spread:** 25–60' **Planting:** container; spring **Zones:** 7–10

AT OLOMPALI STATE HISTORIC PARK IN NORTHERN MARIN COUNTY, a specimen of monkey puzzle tree that is over 100 years old stands proudly next to 100-year-old palm trees and California pepper trees. These proud trees exist in what was once California's most elegant 'Victorian' garden. Monkey puzzle trees have a surprise about them: always watch for falling cones if you walk under one of these trees. A cone can weigh as much as a bowling ball—a bowling ball covered in spikes. For these two reasons, a cone could cause serious injury to someone who is struck by one.

Growing

Monkey puzzle tree grows best in **full sun** to **partial shade** in **moist, well-drained, moderately fertile** soil. Provide it some shelter from the wind.

No pruning is required. The tree requires little if any water after the first two years in the ground.

Tips

This unique tree can be used as a specimen in larger areas, but it is very impractical for smaller gardens. Use it where close contact with the armored branches can be avoided. The branches are densely packed with sharp-pointed, triangular, scale-like foliage that persists for many years. These scales are produced in whorls around the trunk, giving a tiered effect. The tree loses its lower branches with age.

Recommended

A. araucana grows slowly to 70–90' tall and 30' wide. The male and female cones are produced on separate trees after a number of years. The cones are about 6" long, they weigh 10–15 pounds each and they are covered with stiff spines. The seeds are edible. (Zones 7–10)

A. heterophylla (Norfolk Island Pine, Hawaiian Christmas Tree) has very soft foliage, especially when compared to *A. araucana*. It can reach 100' tall and 25–60' wide. In ideal conditions, this species can reach 150' tall. It is well adapted to growing in containers and is well behaved as a houseplant. It will tolerate temperatures to 25° F without damage. As the plant grows, it will drop lower branches if they are not receiving sufficient sunlight. (Zones 7–10)

Problems & Pests

Monkey puzzle trees are subject to attacks by mealybugs and scale insects.

A. heterophylla (above)

Monkey puzzle tree is native to tropical rain forests in the southern hemisphere that experience a definite dry season.

A. araucana (below)

New Zealand Christmas Tree

Pohutukawa

Metrosideros

Features: flowers, foliage, habit **Habit:** erect, freely branching, evergreen tree
Height: 30–40' **Spread:** 15–30' **Planting:** container; spring, fall **Zones:** 9–11

THE GRAY FOLIAGE AND BRIGHT RED BOTTLEBRUSH BLOOMS make this drought-resistant tree a must for gardens that are striving for low-water usage. It is best in areas within 80 miles of the coast, but I've seen it in the Sierra foothills where there is plenty of summer heat. It can be burned if temperatures drop below 15° F, but it recovers with only a modest pruning of the frozen and dead branches. New Zealand Christmas tree is used as a street tree in San Francisco and has appeared along the freeways throughout the northern part of the state. It is best used as a tree, but if it is damaged it can serve as a multi-stemmed background shrub. Sandankwa viburnum *(Viburnum suspensum)* is a wonderful contrast shrub to use in front of this tree.

Growing

New Zealand Christmas tree is most prolific in **full sun,** but it will tolerate partial shade. Grow it in **moist, fertile, neutral** to **slightly acidic, well-drained** soil. This tree prefers normal watering and fertilizing for best results, but it is tolerant of nutrient-poor, alkaline or salty soils, wind, salt spray and moderate drought when established. It is hardy to 20° F. Mature plants will resprout after a killing frost, much like mimosa tree.

New Zealand Christmas tree needs only minimal pruning. Prune immediately after flowering to remove crowded and weak branches. Pruning is not necessary to maintain its natural form.

Tips

New Zealand Christmas tree is an excellent specimen. It can also be used as a street or shade tree. Ensure you provide plenty of space for the roots to grow.

Recommended

M. excelsus (*M. tomentosus*) starts out as a dense, multi-stemmed shrub, later evolving into a tree with one or two thickened main stems and an umbrella-like crown. It has oblong, leathery leaves and produces large clusters of scarlet flowers with crimson stamens in July and August. **'Aureus'** has rich yellow flowers. **'Variegata'** has cream- to yellow-edged leaves. (Zones 9–11)

M. excelsus (all photos this page)

Olive

Olea

Features: fruit, foliage **Habit:** evergreen tree with rounded to spreading crown
Height: 25–30' **Spread:** 25–30' **Planting:** container, B & B; spring, fall
Zones: 8–11

OLIVE TREES ARE WELL KNOWN FOR GROWING AROUND THE missions of California. At one time these lovely trees were largely grown for fruit processing and eating. Now 45% of olives are grown for their oil. Often used in cooking oils and salad dressings, olive oil is a monosaturate oil, which makes it a healthier choice for consumption than some oils. Because the olive fruit fly 'spoils' the ripe fruit of the olive—its appearance isn't as attractive for packaging—many farmers are happier to avoid this problem and just press the olive for its oil.

Olive wood is treasured by woodworkers and hobbyists for carving and turning.

Growing

Olive performs best in **full sun** in **deep, well-drained, fertile** soil but will tolerate infertile, dry and alkaline soils. Olive does not tolerate poorly drained soils. This species only needs 100 hours of chill at 42° F to produce a bountiful harvest. It bears fruit every other year with heavy, then light crops. When the fruit is forming in areas with inadequate rainfall, ensure the tree gets adequate watering. A tree in Zone 8 does best along a south or west wall. Olive is easily transplanted. If you can grow a fruiting fig, you can produce olives.

O. europaea (all photos this page)

Olives can be trained as single- or multi-stemmed trees and are best trained when young—prune minimally as the plant matures. Stake the main stem or stems in the direction you want them to grow. Remove the lower branches to 3–5' and remove suckers. On mature olive trees, remove old, unproductive branches and keep the center of the crown open so sunlight can reach all the branches. It has been said that an olive tree should be pruned so that the birds can fly through it. Cut frost-damaged branches back to live wood. Olives produce flowers and fruit on one-year-old branches, so any pruning will reduce the amount of flowers and fruits for that year. Olives can take hard pruning and can be completely cut to the ground for rejuvenation. Olives can be pruned to restrict the height. Prune in spring before new growth begins. Never prune olive trees in summer or fall.

Tips

Olives are suitable for use as shade or street trees, as specimens, in borders and for fruit production. Fallen fruit can stain paved surfaces.

If you have an olive tree and don't want the fruit, use a spray that is applied while the tree is in bloom—it sterilizes the flowers. The other alternative is to harvest the fruit while green, take it to one of the many olive oil processors and have your own oil made. Contact the California Olive Oil Council in Berkeley, California, P.O. Box 7520, 94707-0520, or check the website at <www.cooc.com>.

Recommended

O. europaea is a slow-growing, long-lived tree with narrow, gray-green leaves. The trunk has smooth, gray bark when young, becoming

blackened and gnarled with age. Tiny, fragrant, creamy white flowers are produced in clusters in summer and are followed by green fruit in fall, which ripens to black and eventually fall off the tree for easy harvest or clean-up. Fruit production does not begin until the tree is at least 10 years old. **'Manzanillo'** is grown for its large fruit. **'Mission'** is a vigorous and cold-hardy selection, growing slightly larger than the species. It is grown for its fruit and oil. **'Sevillano'** is grown for its oil.

Problems & Pests

Olive is susceptible to *Verticillium* wilt, root rot, scale insects and borers. In Northern California, the olive fruit fly is now a serious pest. No cure is known at this time.

The most common and important species is O. europaea, *which many cultivars have come from. The fruits of this species are pressed for the oil.*

O. europaea (all photos both pages)

Oregon Grape

Mahonia

Features: spring flowers, summer fruit, late-fall and winter foliage **Habit:** upright, spreading, evergreen shrub **Height:** 1–12' **Spread:** 2–10' **Planting:** container; anytime **Zones:** 5–10

A BOTANIST FROM OREGON MUST HAVE WON THE RACE TO NAME this plant because it is more common in Northern California than it is in Oregon. Be that as it may, this shrub can be used by itself or, better yet, as a transition plant between a woodland garden and a more formal garden. It does best where it has adequate moisture and some relief from afternoon sun, which is particularly important in the warmer valley regions of California. The black berries are edible and make a wonderful jelly. Snails and slugs are the major problems for it, but they are easily controlled. The occasional invasion of small looper caterpillars is easily dealt with; they can be handpicked to prevent the new foliage from being eaten.

Growing

Oregon grapes grow in **full sun** to **light shade.** The soil should be **well drained** and **neutral** to **slightly acidic.** *M. lomariifolia* needs light to partial shade, but in the hot valleys ensure that this shrub gets afternoon shade. Its soil should also be humus rich and moist. *M. aquifolium* does best when given regular moisture and afternoon shade in the hot valleys. *M. repens* prefers full sun and little to no water and is one of the best groundcovers under walnut, oak and native trees.

Use an organic fertilizer once a month from March to September to promote flowers and fruit in spring.

Prune these shrubs after flowering is complete. Cut old, damaged, diseased or awkward stems to the ground. Avoid topping the shoots. These shrubs put out only very minimal side shoots, if any at all.

M. lomariifolia (above & below))

Birds are attracted to the fruit. This plant is deer resistant.

Tips

Use these shrubs in mixed or shrub borders and in woodland gardens. Low-growing specimens can be used as groundcovers.

Recommended

M. aquifolium is a suckering shrub that grows 3–6' tall, with an equal spread. Bright yellow flowers appear in spring and are followed by clusters of purple or blue berries. The foliage turns a bronze-purple color in late fall and winter. **'Compactum'** is a low, mounding shrub with bronze foliage. It grows 24–36" tall, with an equal or greater spread. (Zones 5–10)

M. lomariifolia is an erect shrub 6–12' tall and 6–10' wide. The stems are either minimally branched or branchless. The large, compound, dark green leaves are held horizontally near the ends of the stems. Erect clusters of fragrant, yellow flowers are held just above the foliage and bloom in mid-winter. Blue berries follow the flowers. This species can make a exotic houseplant if provided with sufficient light. Don't place it where there is heavy traffic—the leaves have spines. (Zones 7–10)

M. repens (Creeping Mahonia) is a creeping shrub 12" tall and 36" wide with erect stems. It spreads by suckers. The dull green leaves turn a bronze color in late fall and winter. Small clusters of lightly fragrant, deep yellow flowers are produced in mid- to late spring and are followed by blue-black berries. (Zones 6–10)

Problems & Pests

Rust, leaf spot, gall, loopers and scale insects may cause occasional problems. Shrubs in exposed locations may develop leaf scorch in winter. New foliage can be eaten by slugs and snails.

The juicy berries are edible but very tart. They can be eaten fresh or used to make jellies, juices or wine. The wine can be mixed with sweet red wine; the combination makes an excellent and fragrant dessert wine.

M. aquifolium (all photos both pages)

Photinia

Fraser Photinia, Red Tip

Photinia

Features: foliage **Habit:** upright, evergreen shrub or small tree **Height:** 5–15'
Spread: 5–15' **Planting:** container; spring, fall **Zones:** 8–10

WHEN USED AS A HEDGE, PHOTINIA MAY GROW FOR SEVERAL YEARS without any problems. Then, without any warning, part of it will die off. Unfortunately, there is no correction for this problem. Planting a new photinia to replace the part that died is a good idea unless there is poor drainage in the location. Deer like to eat all members of the rose family, including this plant.

Growing

Photinia grows well in **full sun** to **partial shade** in **moist, well-drained, fertile** soil. It provides afternoon shade in the hot interior valleys and protects other

plants from cold, drying winds. Photinia tolerates heat and lime soils and is easily transplanted. It is also tolerant of serpentine soils.

Photinia needs only minimal pruning and can be pruned before new growth begins in spring or after flowering is complete. The stem tips of new growth can be pinched, or the older stems can be pruned back to an outward facing bud to encourage colorful, bushy growth. Hedges can be trimmed in spring and summer. For rejuvenation, photinia can be cut back hard into old wood.

'Birmingham' (above)

Tips

Photinia can be used for a formal or informal hedge or screen. It can be trained into small, single-trunked trees, standards or espalier. It works well in lawns, shrub borders and woodland gardens, and it makes a great background plant.

Recommended

P.* x *fraseri is an upright shrub or small tree that grows 10–15' tall and wide. The foliage is a bronze-red color that matures to dark green. Greenish brown bark releases a fragrance reminiscent of cherries when bruised or crushed. Flat clusters of small, white flowers are produced in the early spring. Persistent red to black fruit ripens in fall and is enjoyed by birds. **'Birmingham'** is the most common cultivar and is often sold as the species. It rarely produces fruit. **'Red Robin'** is a compact shrub that grows 5–8' tall and wide. It produces bright red new leaves. (Zones 8–10)

Problems & Pests

Photinia is susceptible to aphids, scale insects, fungal leaf spot and fire blight.

Photinia *comes from the Greek word* photeinos, *which means 'shining.' The name refers to the glossy leaves.*

P. x *fraseri* (above & below)

Pineapple Guava

Guava, Feijoa, Guavasteen

Feijoa

Features: late-spring flowers, late-summer fruit, foliage, habit
Habit: multi-stemmed, evergreen shrub **Height:** 18–25' **Spread:** 18–25'
Planting: container; spring, fall **Zones:** 9–11

THE FLOWERS ARE AMONG THE MOST SPECTACULAR OF ANY TREE or shrub. They attract hummingbirds as well as butterflies and bees. Many people grow pineapple guava for its fruit and are disappointed when, after several years and many blooms, no fruit appears. Many of these shrubs require cross-pollination before fruit production can take place. Some varieties are self fertile, but more fruit is produced with cross-pollination. The elongated fruit has a very tangy flavor and can be eaten raw or used in jams and jellies. It can also be used in a tropical drink by combining the juice with pineapple juice.

Growing

Grow pineapple guava in **full sun** in **well-drained, humus-rich** soil. It can tolerate partial shade, exposure to salt spray and mild frost to 25° F. The shrub should be sheltered from cold, drying winds. Pineapple guava is drought resistant, but the fruit may drop prematurely without ample moisture.

Pineapple guava can be pruned into a variety of forms, including hedges, screens, single-stemmed small trees and espalier. Shrubs grown for ornamental purposes can be pruned after flowering. Shrubs grown for fruit production are pruned before the new growth begins in spring. Remove frost-damaged growth in spring.

Tips

Pineapple guava is grown for fruit production or as hedging, screening and foundation plantings. It can be used in large shrub beds or as a specimen.

When growing pineapple guava for fruit production, it is recommended to plant two different varieties for cross-pollination. Fruit is not produced until the shrubs are at least three years old.

Recommended

F. sellowiana (*Acca sellowiana*) is a fast-growing, large shrub, with a spreading habit. Pendulous, showy flowers are produced on the new season's growth. The flowers have red, fleshy petals with white undersides and prominent red stamens. The gray-green to red-tinged green, oval fruits need a long, hot summer

to ripen and may be damaged by an early frost. The fruit emits a strong and long-lasting fragrance, even before the fruit is completely ripe. (Zones 9–11)

Problems & Pests

Pineapple guava may be affected by fruit fly in some areas. Occasionally, it is attacked by black scale, root rot and fungal leaf spot.

Pineapple guava was named after the Brazilian botanist Don de Silva Feijo.

Podocarpus

Plum Pine

Podocarpus

Features: foliage, habit **Habit:** upright, evergreen shrub or tree **Height:** 8–70' **Spread:** 2–25' **Planting:** container, B & B; spring, fall **Zones:** 7–11

PODOCARPUS IS ONE OF THE MOST VERSATILE AND DEER-RESISTANT plants around. The major uses of it are numerous. Podocarpus can be trained as a 6' hedge, or it can be allowed to grow to its full height as a shade tree or screen—which might mean 60–80' for some species! It can be grown as a hardy house plant in a bright sunny window, or it can make a wonderful evergreen espalier on shady or sunny walls. Podocarpus will require substantial staking in its youth, but after it is established, it will withstand winds. This plant will tolerate very brief temperatures of 15° F as long as it doesn't stay that cold.

Growing

Podocarpus grows in **full sun** to **partial shade** in a variety of soils. The leaves may turn yellow in alkaline soil or heavy, wet soil. Provide shelter from cold and drying winds. Podocarpus need no pruning unless you are growing it for a formal hedge.

Tips

Podocarpus is useful in containers and borders and as screens, hedges, backgrounds or specimens.

Recommended

P. gracillior (*Afrocarpus elongatus, Nageia falcatus*) (Fern Pine) is considered one of the cleanest and most pest-free trees for just about any setting. The spirally arranged, long, narrow leaves are produced sparsely on younger plants. The foliage becomes more dense and darkens with age. Male plants have catkin-like, yellow pollen cones; female plants produce naked seeds that are borne on short stalks. The seeds evolve into fleshy, bluish black-red fruits. Seedling-grown trees will need staking until a strong trunk develops. These trees will grow more upright than cutting-grown plants. Cutting-grown plants are more willowy and make the best specimens for espalier. (Zones 7–11)

P. henkelii (Long Leafed Podocarpus, Long-Leaved Yellowwood) is the most dramatic of the podocarpus species, having very dark green, almost black, foliage. In its youth, leaves will reach 5–7" long. It is a slow-growing, pyramidal tree that reaches 20–50' tall and 8–20' wide in gardens. In its native South

P. 'Maki' (above)

The name 'podocarpus' is derived from the Greek words podos *(foot) and* karpos *(fruit), referring to the fleshy receptacle at the foot of the seed.*

P. macrophyllus (above), P. gracillior (below)

Africa, it can grow 120' tall. It is exceptionally hardy to cold and maintains its dark green foliage under all circumstances. These plants are always cutting grown and are usually male and fruitless. (Zones 7–11)

P. macrophyllus (Buddhist Pine, Yew Pine, Southern Yew) is a narrow, upright tree that reaches heights of 20–50' and widths of 8–20'. It prefers a long, hot, humid summer and moist, fertile soil to achieve its largest size. This species bears long, thick, dark green leaves. The female plants may bear small, black fruit. *P. macrophyllus* responds well to pruning, and it makes great hedges and topiary. It is also a good plant for espalier and for growing in containers. This variety is the best for a windbreak or hedge. It tolerates shearing without showing dead wood. It will sprout from old wood. This plant does well in the heat of the Sacramento Valley. (Zones 7–11)

Male and female flowers are borne on different plants, and it is the female plants that produce naked seeds. These seeds develop into fleshy blue-black to red fruits, giving rise to the common name 'plum pine.'

***P.* 'Maki'** (Shrubby Yew Pine) is an erect plant, with vertically oriented branching. It grows 8–15' tall and 2–4' wide and bears waxy, dark green leaves. This cultivar is excellent in containers and makes a great low hedge. This species is the best podocarpus for use as a house plant or specimen container plant. It grows more slowly than the other species. (Zones 9–11)

Problems & Pests

Podocarpus has very infrequent problems with root rot and scale insects.

P. macrophyllus (above)

P. 'Maki' (below)

Pomegranate

Punica

Features: flowers, fruit, foliage **Habit:** rounded, deciduous, multi-stemmed shrub or small tree **Height:** 2–20' **Spread:** 2–20' **Planting:** container; spring, fall **Zones:** 9–11

MAKING POMEGRANATE JUICE THAT WILL BE USED IN JELLY CAN BE an insurmountable and time-consuming task. Do not try to use a juicer that grinds the seeds—they are bitter. First, you must separate the seeds from the husk; do so underwater. You merely rub the seeds loose, which then sink to the bottom while the husk floats. Once you have separated the seeds, you must place them in a food processor for a couple of twirls. Don't process longer than a couple of seconds. Place seeds and processed juice in a potato ricer that then squeezes out the juice. The juice can be drank or used in jelly-making or basting a leg of lamb. I once donated some 4 ounce jars of jelly to a church bazaar, and the organizers priced them at $1. I couldn't believe that they didn't realize the effort I had made in preparing the jelly. I bought them all back.

Growing

Pomegranate prefers **full sun** in **fertile, moist, well-drained** soil, with shelter from cold, drying winds. It can adapt to quite a variety of soils, including alkaline soil, and it is drought tolerant. Pomegranate needs long, hot summers and regular moisture for good fruit production. It is easily transplanted. In the colder parts of its range, grow pomegranate against a south- or southwest-facing wall.

Pomegranate needs only minimal pruning in late winter or early spring before new growth begins. It can be pruned to control the height. Old, unproductive growth can be removed from trees and shrubs. Remove suckers that grow at the base of the tree, unless a new stem is required. Pomegranate can be trained as a single-stemmed tree, with a low-branching crown. Use hand pruners when harvesting fruit to avoid damaging the fruiting spur.

'Wonderful' (above), *P. granatum* (below)

Pomegranates ripen in fall. Harvest when the color is rich and dark. Fruits tend to rot when left on the tree.

P. granatum var. nana (above), P. granatum (below)

Pomegranate is native from Iran to the Himalayas.

Tips

Pomegranate can be grown for the juicy fruit or used in the landscape as a specimen or hedge. It grows well in containers and can be used as a foundation planting or fan-trained against a wall. The dwarf selections can be used in mixed and shrub borders and do well in containers.

Recommended

P. granatum is a rounded, sometimes spiny shrub or small tree that grows 15–20' tall and wide. The foliage begins copper tinged, matures to bright green in summer and turns bright yellow in fall. Showy orange-red flowers bloom for an extended period in summer, followed by red-yellow to pink-yellow fruit. **'Chico'** is a dwarf, fruitless selection with double, orange-red flowers. It grows 3–6' tall and wide. **'Legrellei'** ('Madame

Legrelle,' 'Variegata') grows 8–10' tall and wide and bears double, orange-red flowers that are striped with creamy white. It does not bear fruit. **Var. *nana*** (Dwarf Pomegranate) grows 2–6' tall and wide and bears orange-red flowers followed by small, inedible, red fruit. It is known to bloom when only 12" tall. **'Wonderful'** is a great fruiting selection that grows the same size as the species. It produces orange-red, double flowers and red fruit. 'Wonderful' is the most popular variety. The fruit can be left on the tree until it splits. When it splits, it is telling you it's harvest time. (Zones 9–11)

The rind and bark have been used medicinally as an astringent for 1000s of years.

Pomegranate juice has been used to make grenadine syrup, a flavoring for wines, cocktails, carbonated beverages, preserves and confectioneries.

Problems & Pests

Pomegranate is susceptible to dieback, powdery mildew, leaf blotch, gray mold, scale insects and thrips. It is resistant to oak root fungus.

'Wonderful' (below)

Princess Flower

Pleroma, Brazilian Spider Flower, Glory Bush

Tibouchina

Features: flowers, foliage **Habit:** bushy, erect to rounded, evergreen shrub
Height: 10–15' **Spread:** 5–10' **Planting:** container; spring, fall
Zones: 9 (with frost protection) to 12

THIS WONDERFUL PLANT CAN BE USED AS A BLOOMING background for dwarf pomegranates. The combination of the pomegranate's orange flowers in front of the royal purple flowers of princess flower is a knockout. Princess flower is also a wonderful colorful accent plant in a semi-tropical garden that contains canna lilies, banana trees or tree ferns.

Growing

Princess flower prefers **full sun** in **well-drained, moist, fertile, slightly acidic** soil. In the interior valleys, it likes shade from the hot afternoon sun. Provide princess flower with protection from strong winds to keep the blooms from shattering. Feed once a month from March through October with a rhododendron fertilizer. The top of the shrub freezes when temperatures are below 25° F. Princess flower can be grown as a perennial in Zone 8 if mulched in winter.

Princess flower needs only minimal pruning. Pinch young stem tips to promote bushy growth. Once the flowering is finished, princess flower can be pruned lightly to shape. Princess flower can be cut back to within two pairs of buds on last year's growth. Try cutting back one-third of the stems at one time and allow the rest to continue to bloom. Doing so will allow a longer flowering cycle.

Tips

Princess flower is useful as a specimen, as an accent or in a shrub border. It can be trained into a small tree. It can be grown in containers, which can be moved indoors in frostier climates. Make sure it is in a sunny window for winter bloom.

Princess flower can be grown from cuttings to increase the number of plants.

Recommended

T. urvilleana (*Pleroma macrantha, T. semidecandra, Lasiandra semidecandra*) is a fast-growing, erect to rounded shrub. The dark green, velvety leaves may have red margins, and older foliage may be marked and spotted yellow, orange and red. Fat, rounded, red-tinged buds open to reveal vivid, royal purple flowers in late spring to winter. (Zones 9–12)

Problems & Pests

Gray mold, mushroom root rot, leaf spots, spider mites and geranium budworm are all potential problems for this shrub.

Redbud

Cercis

Features: spring flowers, fall foliage **Habit:** rounded or spreading, multi-stemmed, deciduous tree or shrub **Height:** 10–35' **Spread:** 10–35' **Planting:** B & B, container; spring, fall **Zones:** 5–9

MY FATHER WAS IN LOVE WITH DRIVING A CAR. ON WEEKENDS, when it wasn't time to garden, he would load up anyone who was interested and go for miles. Lake County in Northern California has fields and hills literally covered with the native redbud. Because of Dad's natural interest in driving, it was easy for my Mom to ask him to drive from Willits to the appointed areas in Lake County where the profusely blooming plants could be viewed. I went along, not giving a 'diddly' for the show. Lake County was known at that time for having the best hamburgers and milkshakes around. The hamburger buns were made fresh each day. When you entered a restaurant, the aroma of fresh bread overpowered any smell of the cooking burgers.

Growing

Redbuds grow well in **full sun, partial shade** or **light shade**. The ideal soil should be a **fertile, deep loam** that is **moist** and **well drained.** Proper planting is a must. In heavy soil, use a large amount of planting mix.

Pruning is rarely required. Growth of young plants can be thinned to encourage an open habit at maturity. Awkward branches can be removed after flowering.

These plants have tender roots and do not like being transplanted. When planting from B & B stock, make sure that the soil in the rootball is absorbing water.

Tips

Redbuds can be used as specimen trees, in shrub or mixed borders and in woodland gardens. The best flowering is in areas that experience some winter chill. Redbuds are not good container plants.

C. canadensis (above)

Select a redbud from a locally grown source. Plants that are from seeds produced in the south are not hardy in the north.

C. occidentalis (below)

C. *canadensis* (all photos this page)

Recommended

C. canadensis (Eastern Redbud) is a spreading, multi-stemmed tree that grows 25–35' tall and wide. It bears red, purple or pink flowers in spring, before the leaves emerge. The young foliage is bronze but fades to green over the summer and turns bright yellow in fall. **Var. *alba*** has white flowers. **'Forest Pansy'** has purple or pink flowers and reddish purple foliage that fades to green over the summer. The best foliage color is produced when this shrub is cut back hard in early spring, but plants cut back this way will not produce flowers. In the interior valleys, keep this cultivar out of the hot afternoon sun. It makes a great companion plant with green Japanese maples and other pale green, small trees. Daylilies make a good groundcover underneath these trees and take the same type of watering. This species will tolerate heavy soils, but make sure the soil does not remain saturated. (Zones 5–9)

C. chinensis (Chinese Redbud) is an open, rounded, multi-stemmed shrub or tree that grows 10–12' tall, with an equal spread. It bears deep pink or purple flowers from early to mid-spring. This species performs best in partial shade. (Zones 7–9)

C. occidentalis (Western Redbud) is a very drought-tolerant, multi-stemmed shrub or small tree that grows 10–18' tall and wide. Deep purple-pink flowers are borne in spring before the leaves appear. The leaves are blue-green, turning to yellow or red in fall. The seedpods are deep purple-pink, fading to reddish brown and persisting through winter. This species is resistant to oak root fungus. (Zones 6–9)

Problems & Pests

Verticillium wilt, blight, canker, caterpillars, dieback, downy mildew, leafhoppers, leaf spot, scale insects, and weevils are potential problems for redbuds.

C. canadensis (above)

C. occidentalis (below)

Rhododendron

Azalea

Rhododendron

Features: late-winter to early-summer flowers, foliage **Habit:** upright, mounding, rounded, evergreen or deciduous shrub **Height:** 1–8' **Spread:** 1–8' **Planting:** B & B, container; spring, fall **Zones:** 4–10

THE KNAP HILL–EXBURY HYBRIDS OF RHODODENDRON ARE THE best color that you can put into a garden. Planting these hybrids in mass and mixing the colors will take the winter blues out of any garden. They can be inter-planted with the evergreen varieties. These hybrids take the same conditions as other azaleas and rhododendrons. Kurume Hybrids—when forced to bloom—are very popular and given as gifts. These gift azaleas can be a successful part of the landscape, but first they must be slowly acclimated to the outside environment. It is best to keep them in a cool location in bright light for a full month before transplanting into the garden. Evergreen azaleas tolerate shearing after each bloom cycle.

Growing

Rhododendrons prefer **partial shade** or **light shade** but tolerate full sun in mild summer climates. The soil should be **fertile, humus rich, acidic, moist** and **well drained.** Good drainage is essential. Rhododendrons are sensitive to alkaline soil, salinity, frost damage and winter injury. These shrubs prefer a location sheltered from strong winds. Feed these plants with an acid fertilizer once a month from March, when the flower buds are swelling, through the end of August. If fed any later, they may not bloom.

Shallow planting with a good mulch is essential, as is excellent drainage. In most soils, elevate the crown of rhododendrons 1" above soil level when planting to ensure good surface drainage of excess water. In heavy, poorly drained soil, plant these shrubs several inches above soil level. Dig a hole four times as wide as the rootball and twice as

Knap Hill-Exbury Hybrids (above)

Rhododendrons and azaleas are generally grouped together. Extensive breeding and hybridizing are making it more and more difficult to apply one label or the other.

deep as the rootball. Fill the hole with an acid-loving planter mix. Place the rootball on top of the mix and cover it with a mound of the same mix. Planting baby tears around this area will keep soil from eroding. Using raised beds is another option when you have heavy soil. Don't dig or cultivate deeply under rhododendrons and azaleas; they have shallow roots that resent being disturbed.

Dead and damaged growth can be removed in early spring once the danger of frost has passed. Spent flower clusters should be removed if possible. Grasp the base of the cluster between your thumb and forefinger and twist to remove the entire cluster. Be careful not to damage the new buds that form directly beneath the flowerheads.

Tips

Take advantage of these gorgeous shrubs in almost any shady location. Use them in shrub or mixed borders, in woodland gardens, as specimen plants, in group plantings, as hedges and informal barriers, in rock gardens or in planters on a shady patio or balcony. Never plant these shrubs under established trees.

The flowers and foliage of rhododendron species are poisonous, as is honey produced from the nectar. Rhododendrons are deer resistant.

Recommended

Hundreds of species and thousands of cultivars and hybrids of rhododendrons and azaleas are available. The following is a very short list of some of the wonderful plants

R. yakushimanum (below)

available. Check with your local nursery or garden center to see what is available where you live. Don't be blinded by the wonderful blooms; check the plant tag for growth habit and hardiness.

R. catawbiense (Catawba Rhododendron, Mountain Rosebay) is a large, rounded, evergreen rhododendron. It grows 6–8' tall, with an equal spread. Clusters of reddish purple flowers appear in mid- to late spring. This species can take cold and heat. **'Album'** has light purple buds and green-marked, white flowers. **'Christmas Cheer'** grows 4' tall and wide and produces light pink flowers in winter to early spring. **'Cilpinense'** has early spring-blooming, frost-tender, white flowers that are flushed with pink. It grows 36" tall and wide or slightly wider. These plants tolerate the heat of the Sacramento Valley. (Zones 4–9)

R. **Knap Hill–Exbury Hybrids** are a large group of rounded to upright, deciduous azaleas. They grow 5–8' tall and wide. The flowers bloom in mid- to late spring, and the color varies with cultivar selection. **'Cockatoo'** has fragrant, pink-yellow to orange-yellow flowers. **'Dawn's Chorus'** has pink buds and white flowers with pink veins. **'Fireball'** is a vigorous plant with bronze new foliage that matures to dark green. The flowers are orange-red. **'Firefly'** has red flowers. **'Gibraltar'** has bright orange flowers. **'Gold Dust'** has fragrant, bright yellow flowers. (Zones 5–9)

R. **Kurume Hybrids** are dwarf, evergreen azaleas with small, dark green leaves. They grow 12–24" tall, with an equal spread, and they are often used

R. Kurume Hybrids (above)

R. catawbiense cultivar (above)

Mixed rhododendron & azalea planting (below)

R. 'PJM' (above)

The clusters of flowers that appear at the tips of the branches are known as 'trusses.'

R. Kurume Hybrids (below)

for bonsai and mass plantings. The color of the abundant spring flowers varies with the cultivar. Keep out of hot, drying winds. These hybrids lend themselves to shearing after the bloom cycle is over. **'Hexe'** bears crimson flowers and is the most common variety to use for this effect. **'Hino-crimson'** has a dense habit and red flowers. **'Sherwood Red'** has orange-red blooms. **'Ward's Ruby'** has dark red flowers. (Zones 5–10)

***R.* 'PJM'** is a dense, rounded, evergreen rhododendron that grows 3–5' tall, with an equal spread. It bears abundant trusses or purple-pink flowers in early spring. It is somewhat weevil resistant and can take the heat. (Zones 4–9)

R. yakushimanum (Yakushima Rhododendron) is a dense, mounding, evergreen rhododendron. It

grows 36" tall, with an equal spread. Rose red buds open to reveal white flowers in mid- to late spring. The underside of the foliage is soft and fuzzy. This rhododendron is resistant to root weevils. (Zones 5–9)

Problems & Pests

Rhododendrons planted in good conditions, such as well-drained soil, suffer few problems. When plants are stressed, however, aphids, caterpillars, lace bugs, leaf galls, leafhoppers, petal blight, powdery mildew, root rot, root weevils, rust, scale insects, vine weevils, Japanese beetles and whiteflies can cause problems. Thrips are especially bad on rhododendrons in Northern California. One of the most common problems is *Phytophthora,* which is caused by a incurable soil fungus. To avoid this problem, make sure the drainage is perfect.

R. yakushimanum (above)

Rhododendron translates as 'rose tree'—an apt description of these beautiful plants.

Rockrose

Cistus

Features: foliage, mid-spring through mid-summer flowers **Habit:** upright, rounded, evergreen shrub **Height:** 2–6' **Spread:** 2–8' **Planting:** container; spring **Zones:** 8–10

THIS PARTICULAR SHRUB IS TYPICALLY PLANTED IN AREAS WHERE nothing else grows. It usually does not require any water after the second year. Although short-lived, it has its place in the landscape—it is hardy and tolerates even the most difficult locations, soils and exposure. Most rockroses have foliage that is gray and a profusion of single blooms in spring. The longest-lived rockrose is *C. salviifolius* (sageleaf rockrose). This species is the most dependable variety to use as a groundcover on hot, dry banks. Shearing the new growth after the completion of the bloom cycle will keep this species and most other rockrose varieties looking fresh for longer periods of time. *C. laurifolius* has been used in roadside hydroseeding and has naturalized in several of these areas. The flowers resemble matilija poppy *(Romneya coulteri)*.

Growing

Rockroses grow best in a **sheltered** site in **full sun.** The soil should be of **poor to average fertility** and **well drained.** These plants are drought tolerant once established. Transplanting or relocating is not recommended because the roots dislike being disturbed. Rockroses will require mulching in the hot interior valleys.

It is important that young plants can be pinched to shape them and to encourage bushy growth. It's best to do so after they bloom. These shrubs respond poorly to hard pruning. Remove only dead, diseased or damaged wood.

Tips

Rockroses are used in shrub or mixed borders, on sunny banks, against warm walls and in planters. They are excellent plants for any dry areas. They need little or no water after being in the ground for two or more years.

These plants can look unattractive when they become old and leggy. It is best to remove such specimens and plant new ones. Most varieties are at their best for the first three to five years.

Recommended

C. **'Doris Hibberson'** grows 36" tall and wide and produces gray-green foliage and a plethora of clear, pale pink flowers. It is one of the longest-lived rockroses. (Zones 8–10)

C. x ***hybridus*** (*C.* x *corbariensis*) (White Rockrose) grows 3–4' tall and 5–8' wide. It produces dark green to gray-green foliage and white flowers with a yellow spot at the base of each petal. (Zones 8–10)

C. x *purpureus* (below)

C. *laurifolius* (above & right)

C. *laurifolius* (Rockrose) is a stiff, upright shrub that grows 3–6' tall, with an equal spread. It has blue-green foliage and bears white flowers. (Zones 8–10)

C. x *purpureus* (Orchidspot Rockrose) forms a rounded mound, 2–4' tall, with an equal or greater spread. The flowers, borne in clusters, are dark pink with purple spots at the bases. It is an excellent shrub for seaside planting. (Zones 9–10)

Certain Cistus *species produce an aromatic resin that was used by the Greeks and Romans for perfume and incense. Crush a leaf to release the fragrance.*

C. salviifolius (Sageleaf Rockrose) is a mounding shrub that grows 24–30" tall and up to 6' wide. This species is another long-lived rockrose that is great on hot, dry hillsides. It can cover a hillside more quickly than most junipers or other groundcovers. It is also a profuse bloomer with white flowers and a yellow dot at the base of each petal; it has interesting, crinkly gray foliage. (Zones 8–10)

These short-lived shrubs have an extended flowering period; sometimes they flower all year long. Individual flowers are very short-lived, and all rockrose flowers have a center of golden stamens.

Russian Olive

Elaeagnus

Features: fragrant flowers, summer foliage, fruit **Habit:** upright to rounded, evergreen or deciduous tree or shrub **Height:** 6–20' **Spread:** 6–20' **Planting:** container; spring, fall **Zones:** 2–10

RUSSIAN OLIVE IS THE PERFECT PLANT FOR THE HOT INTERIOR valleys of Northern California, but it is not for the coast. Very cold to very hot weather makes the ideal challenge for this very hardy plant. Russian olive will naturalize in most areas of Northern California if the weather is cold and/or hot. *E. pungens* does exceptionally well in mild winter areas or cool summer areas. It actually does quite well in all areas of the state. Russian olive is ideal for hedging around gardens where browsing animals, especially deer, are a problem. It is fire retardant, making an ideal barrier between native forests and formal yards. The inedible fruit resembles miniature olives. All *Elaeagnus* species are deer resistant.

Growing

Grow the deciduous species in **full sun**. The evergreen species can be grown in **full sun** to **partial shade**. Preferably, the soil should be a **well-drained, sandy loam** of **average to high fertility**. These plants adapt to poor, heavy clay soil because they can fix nitrogen from the air. They also tolerate salty and dry conditions, which makes them useful for plantings along highways and other salted roads. The evergreen varieties will require little if any watering after the second year.

These trees or shrubs tolerate hard pruning. One-third of the old growth can be removed each year from multi-stemmed specimens, making them useful as hedges or screens. The evergreen varieties will tolerate coastal conditions.

E. angustifolia (all photos this page)

E. multiflora (above), *E. pungens* 'Maculata' (below)

Tips

These tough plants are used in shrub or mixed borders, as hedges and screens and as specimen plants. The fruits are edible but dry and mealy.

Recommended

E. angustifolia (Russian Olive) is a rounded, spreading, deciduous tree. It grows 12–20' tall, with an equal spread. The fragrant, yellow, early summer flowers are often obscured by the foliage, as is the silvery yellow fruit. The main attractions of this species are its tolerance of adverse conditions and its narrow, silver gray leaves. This species is resistant to oak root fungus. (Zones 2–9)

E. commutata (Silverberry) is an upright, thicket-forming, deciduous shrub that spreads by suckers. It grows 10–12' tall and spreads to 6' wide. Tiny, fragrant, silvery yellow flowers are borne in spring. The silvery fruit follows in fall. It is a good plant for wild, out-of-the-way gardens and is the best plant for attracting birds. This species is best used on hillsides or in areas that have a wild look. (Zones 2–9)

E. multiflora (Cherry Elaeagnus) is a wide-spreading, rounded, deciduous shrub with somewhat arching branches. It grows 6–10' tall, with an equal spread. The bright red fruits are hidden by the silvery green foliage. (Zones 5–10)

E. pungens (Silverberry) is a spiny, evergreen shrub that grows 10–15' tall and wide. The foliage is dark, silvery green on top and silvery white beneath. Tiny, fragrant, silvery white flowers are produced in fall. The flowers are followed by brown fruit that ripens to red. **'Fruitlandii'** has larger leaves with silver undersides. **'Maculata'** ('Aureovariegata') (Golden Elaeagnus) has golden blotches on silver gray leaves. **'Marginata'** has silver leaves with white margins on the leaves. **'Variegata'** has yellow leaf margins. All have fruit that is attractive to wildlife, and all are resistant to deer and, surprisingly, rabbits. (Zones 7–10)

Problems & Pests

In stressful conditions, these plants are susceptible to canker, dieback, fungal leaf spot, nematodes, root rot and rust.

E. angustifolia (above)

E. multiflora (below)

Salal

Shallon

Gaultheria (Pernettya)

Features: spring to early-summer flowers, foliage, fruit **Habit:** compact, bushy, spreading, evergreen shrub **Height:** 6"–10' **Spread:** 1–10' **Planting:** container; spring **Zones:** 3–9

THE MORE I SEE THIS PLANT IN ITS NATIVE HABITAT, THE MORE I respect its ability to add to the beauty of other shrubs, such as azaleas and rhododendrons, that like shade and acid soil conditions. In Northern California's Douglas-fir forest, you will find this plant covering a shady group of dogwood and native rhododendron. It is an ideal groundcover for a shady spot or rock garden and will crowd out pesky baby tears where they are not invited.

Growing

Salal prefers **partial shade** in **moist, well-drained, humus rich, acidic** soil. Salal will tolerate full sun if the soil remains somewhat moist.

Salal needs little pruning. When necessary, remove deadwood and weak growth in spring. Salal benefits from mulching with acidic organic matter, such as leaf mold or peatmoss.

Tips

Salal is a woodland shrub and is commonly used in woodland gardens. The creeping underground stems mean it is suitable for stabilizing hillsides.

Although the fruits are edible, eating other parts of salal may cause mild stomach upset.

Recommended

G. procumbens (Wintergreen, Checkerberry, Teaberry) spreads by creeping underground stems. It grows 6" tall and spreads 36" or more, and it bears pinkish white flowers in summer. The persistent scarlet berries are edible and have the flavor of wintergreen, as does the crushed or bruised foliage. The foliage turns purple red to bronze in winter. (Zones 3–9)

G. shallon is a bushy shrub with erect branches. It grows 4–6' tall and wide and up to 10' tall and wide in ideal conditions. When planted in dry, poor soil and full sun, it only grows 12–24" tall and wide. It bears clusters of bell-shaped, pink-tinged, waxy, white flowers in spring. When ripe, the edible, berry-like fruits are purple to black. Salal spreads vigorously by suckers. (Zones 6–9)

Problems & Pests

Salal may be afflicted with leaf gall, fungal leaf spots and powdery mildew.

G. shallon (all photos this page)

Gaultheria *was named after Dr. Jean François Gaulthier, a mid-18th century physician and botanist from Quebec.*

Spirea

Bridal Wreath

Spiraea

Features: spring, summer, fall flowers, habit **Habit:** round, bushy, deciduous shrub **Height:** 18"–7' **Spread:** 2–6' **Planting:** container; spring, fall **Zones:** 3–10

MANY WONDERFUL *S. JAPONICA* CULTIVARS CAN BRIGHTEN YOUR garden with their colorful summertime foliage. Most of them are mounding, well-behaved shrubs that combine well with perennials. *S.* x *vanhouttei* is the classical spirea, with long, arching branches covered with many white blooms from late winter to early spring. *S. douglasii*, a useful plant near woodsy, damp areas of the garden, is a good companion plant to shade-loving California natives and hydrangeas.

Growing

Spireas grow well in **full sun** to **partial shade.** These plants prefer **fertile, acidic, moist, well-drained** soil but will tolerate a wide range of soils as long as they are moist. To help prevent foliage burn, provide protection from the very hot sun in the interior valleys. Mulching in hot interior valleys will protect the sensitive root system.

S. douglasii (above)

Pruning is necessary to keep spireas neat and graceful. Prune *S. douglasii* in early spring before new growth begins. Remove all weak and old wood to the ground. Remove enough of the stems to keep the plant open. Cut back one-third of the stems to within two healthy buds of the previous year's growth.

Before new growth begins, prune *S. japonica* and its selections in early spring. Cut stems back to within two healthy buds of last year's growth. The low-growing selections can be lightly sheared after flowering.

Under a magnifying glass, the flowers of these rose family members do resemble tiny roses.

S. japonica cultivar (below)

Prune *S. trilobata* and *S.* x *vanhouttei* in summer when flowering is complete. From established plants, remove one-quarter of the oldest stems and any weak growth. Cut back stems that have flowered by one-half. Cut the flowered stems of young plants back to a healthy bud and remove any weak growth.

Tips

Spireas are used in shrub or mixed borders, in rock gardens and as informal screens and hedges.

Recommended

S. douglasii (Hardhack, Western Spirea) is an erect, suckering shrub that is native to western North America. This vigorous species grows 5–7' tall and spreads up to 6'. Clusters of pink to deep rose flowers appear in summer. This species can grow well in wet places and needs moist, acidic soil. It may become invasive. (Zones 4–10)

S. japonica (Japanese Spirea) forms a clump of erect stems. It grows 4–6' tall and spreads up to 5'. Clusters of pink or white flowers are borne in summer to fall. Many varieties, cultivars and hybrids have been developed from this species. **'Anthony Waterer'** grows 3–4' tall and spreads 4–5'. The new foliage is reddish, turning blue-green over the summer and red again in fall. **'Coccinea'** grows 24–36" tall and wide. It has purple-red foliage and red flowers. **'Goldmound'** has bright yellow foliage and bears pink flowers in late spring and early summer. **'Limemound'** grows about 36" tall and spreads about 6'. The stems are red, and the foliage is yellow with good fall color. **'Little Princess'** forms a dense mound 18" tall and 3–6' wide. The flowers are rose pink. (Zones 4–10)

S. trilobata (Dwarf Bridal Wreath Spirea) is an intricately branched shrub with three-lobed, blue-green

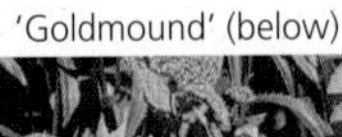

'Goldmound' (below)

foliage that is especially blue-green on the undersides. It grows 4–5' tall and wide and bears clusters of small, white flowers at the tips of leafy branches in mid- to late spring. **'Swan Lake'** grows 3–4' tall and wide. It has dark green foliage and abundant clusters of tiny, white flowers on arching branches. (Zones 5–10)

S.* x *vanhouttei (Bridal Wreath Spirea, Vanhoutte Spirea) is a dense, bushy shrub with arching branches. It grows 6–8' tall and spreads 8–12'. White flowers are borne profusely in abundant clusters in early summer. (Zones 3–10)

Problems & Pests

Aphids, fire blight, leaf spot, powdery mildew, scale insects and weevils can cause occasional problems.

'Limemound' (above)

S. x *vanhouttei* (below)

Spruce

Picea

Features: foliage, cones, habit **Habit:** broad to narrowly pyramidal, evergreen tree or shrub **Height:** 2–160' **Spread:** 2–40' **Planting:** B & B, container; spring, fall **Zones:** 2–10

DWARF ALBERTA SPRUCE (*P. GLAUCA ALBERTIANA* 'CONICA') IS ONE of my favorite trees to use as a Christmas tree. Its denseness makes it difficult to decorate, but it will last several years as a Christmas tree, as well as a decorative container plant on the patio or deck. The slow growth of this cultivar makes this spruce one of the most cost-effective trees for the holidays. I kept one for 12 years. The original high cost of $85, when amortized over 12 years, was only $7 a year. Compare that with the $45 it costs to buy a cut tree, which you toss at the end of the season.

Growing

Spruce trees or shrubs grow best in **full sun** but will tolerate light shade. The soil should be **moist, well drained** and **neutral** to **acidic**. These trees generally don't like hot, dry or polluted conditions. They have shallow roots and easily succumb to drought conditions. Pruning is rarely needed.

Spruce trees are best grown from small, young stock because they dislike being transplanted when larger or more mature.

Tips

Spruces are used as specimen trees. The dwarf and slow-growing cultivars can also be used in shrub or mixed borders, in foundation plantings and in containers.

Oil-based pesticides such as dormant oil can take the blue out of your blue-needled spruces.

P. abies (above)

Spruce is the traditional Christmas tree in Europe.

'Mission Blue' (below)

'Hoopsii' (above), *P. pungens* var. *glauca* (below)

Recommended

P. abies (Norway Spruce) is a fast-growing, pyramidal tree with dark green needles. It grows 70–100' tall and spreads about 20'. Branchlets in older specimens hang straight down. This species is also wind resistant. **'Nidiformis'** (Nest Spruce) is a slow-growing, low, compact, mounding form. It grows about 3–4' tall and spreads 3–5'. This cultivar is an ideal plant for use in oriental style gardens. (Zones 2–8)

***P. glauca albertiana* 'Conica'** (Dwarf Alberta Spruce) is a slow-growing, compact, pyramidal tree with dense, dark green foliage. It grows 6–10' tall and 4–6' wide but can reach 20' tall and 8' wide in ideal conditions. Give this plant shelter from drying winds and reflected sunlight. (Zones 3–10)

P. pungens (Colorado Spruce) is a conical or columnar tree with stiff, blue-green needles and dense growth. This drought-tolerant,

hardy tree grows 30–60' tall, with a spread of 10–20'. **Var. *glauca*** (Colorado Blue Spruce) is similar to the species but with blue-gray needles. Some smaller cultivars have been developed from this variety. **'Hoopsii'** grows up to 60' tall. It has a dense, pyramidal form and even more blue-white foliage than var. *glauca*. **'Mission Blue'** is a broad-based, compact form, 4–8' tall, with bold blue foliage. (Zones 2–8)

P. sitchensis (Sitka Spruce) is a narrowly pyramidal tree that grows 80–160' tall and 20–40' wide, with horizontal branching and slightly drooping branchlets. The dark green needles are flattened and prickly, and they are silvery blue on the undersides. *P. sitchensis* performs best in areas with higher humidity. **'Papoose'** ('Tenas') is a slow-growing, broadly conical, dwarf selection that grows 2–4' tall and wide with blue and green bicolored foliage. (Zones 7–9)

P. glauca albertiana 'Conica' (above)

Problems & Pests

Possible problems include aphids, borers, budworms, canker, gall insects, needle cast, needle miners, root rot, rust, sawflies, scale insects and spider mites.

'Nidiformis' (below)

Sweetbox

Sarcococca

Features: early-spring flowers, fruit, foliage **Habit:** dense, suckering, evergreen shrub **Height:** 18"–6' **Spread:** 3–8' **Planting:** container; anytime **Zones:** 6–9

SWEETBOX IS AN IDEAL PLANT FOR NORTHERN EXPOSURES WHERE the sun never shines, but there is some light. This shrub also has a great smell. When I first experienced the fragrance, I couldn't figure where it came from. It was in late January, and nothing I could see was in bloom. As I came closer to my shade garden near the deck, I located the tiny, white blooms with the giant-sized fragrance. The very dark green foliage is a great contrast to shade-loving perennials such as hostas, lungworts and Christmas roses.

Growing

Sweetboxes grow well in **partial, light or full shade.** The soil should be of **average fertility, humus rich, moist** and **well drained.** These plants are drought tolerant once established.

They need only minimal pruning in spring. If a groomed appearance is required, deadhead *S. hookeriana* after flowering is complete.

Tips

Sweetboxes can be used in shady borders, as groundcovers, in woodland gardens or as low hedges. They can also be combined with plants in the heather family, such as rhododendrons.

If sweetbox is under the eaves of houses or where winter rains do not wash off the foliage, it is a good idea to give it a good cleaning after the blooming cycle.

Recommended

S. hookeriana (Sweetbox, Himalayan Sarcococca) is a dense, bushy, suckering shrub that grows 4–6' tall, with an equal or greater spread. Fragrant flowers appear in late winter to early spring. Some dark blue fruits may form if spent flowers are not removed. **Var. *humilis*** is a dwarf, clump-forming shrub that grows 18–24" tall and spreads 6–8' and wider with age. It bears fragrant, white flowers tinged with pink. (Zones 6–9)

S. rusticifolia (Fragrant Sarcococca) is a dense, bushy shrub with arching shoots. It grows 3–6' tall, with an equal or greater spread. It bears clusters of fragrant, white flowers in late winter to early spring, followed by showy red fruits. **Var. *chinensis*,** more commonly available than the species, is similar but has narrower leaves. (Zones 6–9)

S. rusticifolia (above)

Problems & Pests

Sweetbox could get scale insects.

S. hookeriana var. *humilis* (below)

Sweetgum

Liquidambar

Features: habit, fall color, spiny fruit, corky bark **Habit:** pyramidal to rounded, deciduous tree **Height:** 60–80' **Spread:** 20–30' **Planting:** B & B; spring **Zones:** 5–10

THIS TREE IS ADDED TO MOST LANDSCAPES FOR ITS AUTUMN-colored foliage. It is best to shop for these trees in fall. The majority of sweetgums are seedling grown, which means that fall color variations are not guaranteed. Grafted varieties, on the other hand, are true to the parent. Cultivars, such as 'Festival' and 'Palo Alto,' were developed in Northern California and are the best choices to give dependable fall color. People often know this tree from their childhoods—when they chewed the gum. The resinous gum is used medicinally in the treatment of dysentery and diarrhea and as a perfuming agent in soaps and perfumes.

Growing

Sweetgum grows equally well in **full sun** or **partial shade,** but it develops the best color in full sun. The soil should be of **average fertility, slightly acidic, moist** and **well drained**. Fall color can be intensified by the addition of an iron product to the soil in July.

This tree has gained a bad reputation for destroying more sidewalks than can be counted because of its roots. Sweetgum requires lots of room for roots to develop. If you just stick the tree into a hole, the roots have no other choice but to go on the surface. If this tree is being used as a street tree, it is important to plant it properly. At the minimum, have a mulched area out to the dripline.

Little pruning is required. Remove dead, damaged, diseased or awkward branches in spring or early summer. Lower branches can be removed to expose the trunk.

The interesting growth on the bark is quite normal and not some sort of exotic disease.

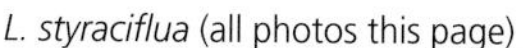

L. styraciflua (all photos this page)

L. *styraciflua* cultivar (above)

Tips

Sweetgum is attractive as a shade tree, street tree or specimen tree or as part of a woodland garden. The falling spiny fruit makes sweetgum inappropriate near patios or decks or where people may be walking in bare feet. This tree is also hard on lawn mowers. The roots can lift paved areas and create a nuisance in lawns.

Recommended

L. styraciflua is a neat, symmetrical, pyramidal tree with attractive, star-shaped foliage. The crown opens up with age. Spiny, capsular fruit drop off the tree over the winter and often into the following summer. The fall color of the glossy, dark green leaves varies, often from year to year, from yellow to purple or brilliant red. Young bark may develop corky ridges, but it loses them as the bark ages. **'Festival'** is narrower in habit than the species and has yellow,

peach, pink, orange or red fall color. **'Palo Alto'** is similar to the species and has orange-red to bright red fall color. **'Rotundiloba'** has rounded leaf lobes and does not bear any fruit. (Zones 5–10)

Problems & Pests

Occasional problems with borers, caterpillars, leaf spot, rot and scale insects can occur. Iron chlorosis can occur if the soil is too alkaline.

This beautiful tree would be more popular except for the messy and potentially dangerous falling fruit. Although some people do find the spiked fruit attractive, it can be avoided by spraying the tree, as the blooms appear, with Florel® brand growth regulator put out by Monterey Bay Lawn and Garden. The product also eliminates mistletoe.

L. styraciflua (below & bottom left)

Tulip Tree

Liriodendron

Features: early-summer flowers, foliage, fruit, habit **Habit:** large, rounded to pyramidal, deciduous tree **Height:** 70–80' **Spread:** 35–40' **Planting:** container; spring, summer **Zones:** 4–10

WHEN BEV AND I VISITED GEORGE WASHINGTON'S HOME IN Mt. Vernon in 1992, we saw a specimen of this tree that was well over 100' tall. It was such a prominent tree that it had to be protected with lightning rods. Seedlings from this tree are available from American Forests' Historic Tree Nursery in Jacksonville, Florida. Their website is <www.historictrees.org> or call 1–800–320–TREE (8733). When planting this tree, keep in mind its size. In my daughter Edie's home, the whole front yard was taken up with one tulip tree and one sycamore tree. Removing these two trees provided enough room to plant an incredibly charming small garden.

Growing

Tulip tree grows well in **full sun** or **partial shade**. Soil should be **average to rich, slightly acidic, well drained** and **moist**. Tulip tree needs plenty of room for the roots to grow. Frequent periods of drought can eventually kill the tree. Many of these trees were lost during the 1975–77 drought. Always deep water tulip tree.

Little pruning is required. Remove dead, damaged or diseased growth as needed and awkward growth in winter.

Tips

This beautiful, massive tree needs lots of room to grow. Parks, golf courses and home owners with large gardens can use this tree as a specimen or group planting; its susceptibility to drought and need for root space make it a poor choice as a specimen, shade tree or street tree on smaller properties.

Recommended

L. tulipifera is native to eastern North American. It is known more for its unusually shaped leaves than for its tulip-like flowers; the flowers are often borne high in the tree and go unnoticed until the falling petals litter the ground. The foliage turns golden yellow in fall. **'Aureomarginata'** has yellow-green margins to the leaves. (Zones 4–10)

Problems & Pests

Aphids, borers, leaf miners, leaf spots, powdery mildew, scale insects and sooty mold. Drought stress can cause the leaves to drop early.

L. tulipifera (all photos this page)

Viburnum

Viburnum

Features: flowers, summer and fall foliage, fruit, habit **Habit:** bushy or spreading, evergreen or deciduous shrub **Height:** 2–15' **Spread:** 2–12'
Planting: bare-root, B & B, container; spring, fall **Zones:** 2–11

MANY OF THE MOST IMPORTANT VIBURNUMS HAVE HAD THEIR names changed over the years, and that bothers me. My grandmother once took a cutting of her favorite plant—*Viburnum opulus* 'Sterile,' which was called a snowball bush—and this wonderful plant became her pride and joy. She reproduced by cuttings and gave them as presents to all of her four, then living, daughters. My Dad placed it in the landscape of our new home in Willits for my Mom, and it was a showpiece in the oversized lawn. Mom grew cuttings of this plant in the two homes she and Dad owned—one in Lincoln and one in Loomis. These shrubs liked the heat of the Sacramento Valley and the coolness of the coastal regions. The name, after a couple of readjustments, wound up being called *V. o.* 'Roseum.' The name doesn't fit because the only time it turns to a rose color is when the blooms die.

Growing

Viburnums grow well in **full sun, partial shade** or **light shade**. The soil should be of **average fertility, moist** and **well drained.** Viburnums tolerate both alkaline and acidic soils.

These plants will look neatest if deadheaded, but this practice will, of course, prevent fruits from forming. Fruiting is better when more than one plant of a species is grown.

Tips

Viburnums can be used in borders and woodland gardens. They are a good choice for plantings near swimming pools.

The edible but very tart fruits of *V. opulus* are popular for making jellies, pies and wine. They can be sweetened somewhat by freezing or by picking them after the first frost or two.

V. x *burkwoodii* (above)

Grow V. davidii *and* V. tinus *'Spring Bouquet' as hedges.*

'Spring Bouquet' just beginning to open its flowers

V. *opulus* (above), *V. davidii* (below)

Recommended

V. x ***burkwoodii*** (Burkwood Viburnum) is a rounded shrub that is evergreen in warm climates. It grows 6–10' tall and spreads 5–8'. Clusters of fragrant, pinkish white flowers appear in late winter to early spring and are followed by red fruits that ripen to black. Occasional shaping will result in a more full and usable landscape shrub. (Zones 4–10)

V. ***davidii*** (David Viburnum) is a low, rounded, compact, evergreen shrub. It grows 3–5' tall, with an equal spread. White spring flowers are followed by showy, metallic blue fruit. This species and its cultivars are not self fertile, so two different plants (sometimes sold as 'male' and 'female') must be present for the fruit to set. Protect these plants from strong winds and plant in partial shade. The deeply veined leaves are showpieces in any garden. This species will tolerate full sun in

coastal areas but requires shade in the Sacramento Valley. (Zones 7–10)

V. japonicum is a rounded, evergreen shrub that grows 8–15' tall and 6–12' wide. It has large, dark green, glossy leaves. It produces clusters of fragrant, white flowers in spring followed by showy red fruit, which can persist through winter. Provide this species with afternoon shade in the hot interior valleys. (Zones 7–10)

V. opulus (European Cranberrybush, Guelder-Rose) is a rounded, spreading, deciduous shrub with leaves that resemble maple leaves. It grows 8–15' tall and spreads 8–12'. The flower clusters consist of an outer ring of showy sterile flowers surrounding the inner fertile flowers. The two rings give the plant a lacy look in spring, which is

V. davidii (above)

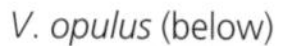

V. opulus (below)

followed by showy, persistent, red fruit. The fall foliage ranges from yellow to red to reddish purple. **'Compactum'** is dense and slow growing, reaching 2–5' in height and spread. **'Roseum'** ('Sterile') (Snowball Bush) is a large, rounded shrub that produces snowball-like clusters of sterile, white flowers in spring. The foliage turns red and orange in fall. (Zones 3–10)

V. suspensum (Sandankwa Viburnum) is a rounded, evergreen shrub that grows 6–10' tall and wide. This selection is subject to damage in freezing weather. Freezing affects only the newer growth, and the plant recovers rapidly. It produces clusters of foul-scented, pink-tinged, white flowers in early to mid-spring, followed by red fruit that ages to black. When established, this species is tolerant of mild drought. (Zones 9–11)

V. opulus (all photos both pages)

V. tinus **'Spring Bouquet'** is a dense, compact shrub, growing 4–6' tall and wide and bearing clusters of white flowers from fall to spring. Bright to indigo blue fruit ripens to black and persists into summer. This species is one of the most usable varieties in that it requires little if any pruning to keep its dense shape. The wonderful blooming pattern gives this plant a boost of color in the early spring. This species combines well with many round-growing shrubs, such as *Pittosporum* 'Wheeler's Dwarf.' It also works well as a low background to annual beds. (Zones 7–10)

Many species of birds are attracted to viburnums for the edible fruit and the shelter they provide.

Problems & Pests

Anthracnose, aphids (especially on *V. opulus*), beetles, borers, crown gall, leaf spot, mealybugs, powdery mildew, root rot, rust, scale insects and weevils can affect viburnums. Do not use sulfur spray on the leaves because they will be damaged.

Weeping Willow

Salix

Features: weeping habit **Habit:** rounded, deciduous tree with weeping branches **Height:** 30–50' **Spread:** 30–50' **Planting:** container; spring, after frost danger has passed **Zones:** 5–10

OF ALL THE WEEPING TREES IN OUR WORLD, WEEPING WILLOW IS the most beautiful. There is something about this tree that demands a large pond of water with at least two white swans afloat on it and two lovers on a white marble bench. When Bev and I were at the Keukenhoff Bulb Gardens in the Netherlands, we saw this sight. Well, without the lovers.

Growing

Weeping willow prefers **full sun** in **deep, moist, well-drained** soil. Weeping willow does not do well in shallow, alkaline soil. Ensure plenty of water

during the growing season. Give young trees shelter from frosts below 15° F. Willows have weak wood and are subject to breakage in high winds.

Weeping willow needs minimal to no pruning. Do not remove the erect top growth. The tree gains height this way, and the upright growth will eventually weep. The crown may be thinned occasionally in spring before new growth begins. Deadwood can be removed in summer.

Tips

Weeping willow is a graceful and elegant tree, and it can be used as a single specimen or as a shade tree in a larger setting. Weeping willow is especially effective when planted near water features.

The shallow, aggressive roots may invade water and sewer pipes. The roots also make it difficult to garden under the tree. It is a good idea to apply an organic mulch out to the dripline.

Recommended

S. babylonica is a short-lived, fast-growing tree, with a short, thick-set trunk and long, narrow leaves on delicate, weeping branches that reach the ground. It leafs out early and keeps its leaves to late in the season. **'Crispa'** ('Annularis') (Ringleaf Willow, Corkscrew Willow) is slightly narrower than the species. The interesting leaves are curled into rings. (Zones 5–10)

Willow bark produces salicylic acid. It was the original source for aspirin.

Problems & Pests

Willows are subject to a number of insect and disease pests, including aphids, beetles, borers, canker, caterpillars, crown rot, heart rot, root rot, scale insects and spider mites. Willow is also subject to damage by yellow-bellied sapsuckers.

S. babylonica (all photos this page)

Witch-Hazel

Hamamelis

Features: flowers, foliage, habit **Habit:** spreading, deciduous shrub or small tree
Height: 8–20' **Spread:** 8–20' **Planting:** container; spring, fall **Zones:** 3–10

THE BEST USE OF THIS PLANT IS TO BRIGHTEN UP DRAB WINTER gardens. The sparkling yellow whorls of flowers bring interest to even the most bland of landscapes. To spark floral excitement, use as a background to winter-blooming annuals. Use this plant in combination with evergreen shrubs, such as juniper, privet and other common shrubs, to add fall coloring to an otherwise dull landscape. The flowering branches make a wonderful fragrant bouquet when cut and brought into the winter home.

Growing

Witch-hazels will grow in **full sun** or **light shade**. The soil should be of **average fertility, neutral** to **acidic, moist** and **well drained**. Pruning is rarely required. Remove awkward shoots once flowering is complete. Remove any suckers from below the graft union on grafted plants.

Tips

Witch-hazels work well individually or in groups. They can be used as specimen plants, in shrub or mixed borders or in woodland gardens. As small trees, they are ideal for space-limited gardens.

The unique flowers have long, narrow, crinkled petals that give the plant a spidery appearance when in bloom. If the weather gets too cold, the petals will roll up, protecting the flowers and extending the flowering season.

The twigs of witch-hazel are used for divining water. The word 'witch' in Old English referred to a pliable branch.

H. virginiana (both photos this page)

H. mollis (above), 'Arnold Promise' (below)

Recommended

H.* x *intermedia is a vase-shaped, spreading shrub. It grows 10–15' tall, with an equal spread. Fragrant clusters of yellow, orange or red flowers appear in mid- to late winter. The leaves turn attractive shades of orange, red and bronze in fall. **'Arnold Promise'** has large, fragrant, bright yellow or yellow-orange flowers. **'Diane'** ('Diana') has dark red flowers in late winter and good fall color of yellow, orange and red. **'Jelena'** has a horizontal, spreading habit. The fragrant flowers are coppery orange, and the fall color is orange-red. **'Pallida'** is a more compact plant, growing to 9–12' tall and wide. Its flowers are bright yellow, and the fall leaf color is yellow. (Zones 5–10)

H. japonica (Japanese Witch-Hazel) is an open, wide-spreading tree. It grows 15–20' tall, with an equal or greater spread. Yellow flowers appear in mid- to late winter. The fall color comes in red, purple or yellow. The angular branches form an attractive criss-cross pattern. (Zones 5–10)

H. mollis (Chinese Witch-Hazel) is a rounded, spreading shrub that is more dense and compact than the other species. The branches lie in an attractive zig-zag pattern. This species grows 8–15' tall, with an equal spread. It bears very fragrant, yellow flowers in mid- to late winter. The fall color is orange or yellow. (Zones 5–10)

H. virginiana (Common Witch-Hazel) is a large, rounded, spreading shrub or small tree. It grows 12–20' or more in height, with an equal spread. Yellow fall flowers are often hidden by the foliage that turns yellow at the same time, but this species is attractive nonetheless. (Zones 3–9)

Problems & Pests

Aphids, leaf rollers, leaf spot, powdery mildew, scale insects and wood rot are possible, but rarely serious, problems.

A witch-hazel extract was used traditionally as a general remedy for burns and skin inflammations. Today it is often sold as a mild astringent in facial products.

H. virginiana (all photos this page)

Yesterday, Today, Tomorrow

Brunfelsia

Features: flowers **Habit:** open, rounded, multi-stemmed shrub **Height:** 3–10' **Spread:** 3–8' **Planting:** container; spring, fall **Zones:** 10–11

YESTERDAY, TODAY, TOMORROW IS ONE OF THOSE PLANTS THAT should be in a container—using it as an entry container plant is most effective while it is in bloom. Put it in a less visible location during winter. It becomes almost bare in the cool weather, but its flowers are spectacular from May through October. It does well in the morning sun, but flowers fade in the hot afternoon sun. Fertilizing this shrub, either in a container or in the ground, will guarantee its blooming success. It will take the same fertilizer as azaleas, amellias and other acid-loving plants. Once-a-month feeding is my recommendation. This shrub is deer resistant.

Growing

Brunsfelsia will tolerate some shade, but it needs at least **five hours of direct sun** to bloom properly. The soil should be **fertile, humus rich, moist, well drained** and **neutral** to **slightly acidic**. Alkaline soils may need the addition of iron to prevent plant chlorosis. Shrubs in the hot afternoon sun may experience scorched leaves. Prune lightly after flowering to maintain shape.

The common name 'yesterday, today, tomorrow' arises from the fading habit of the flowers. Yesterday, they were deep purple; today, they are light purple; tomorrow, they will be white. They combine well with shade-loving annuals, such as dwarf impatiens.

Tips

Use yesterday, today, tomorrow in mixed beds or shrub beds and borders. Put the plant in a location where the flower show can be enjoyed. Pinching the tips off the young growth will encourage bushiness. When the tips of one- to two-year-old plants are pinched they will develop a better overall form.

Recommended

B. pauciflora is an open, semi-evergreen shrub. In spring and early summer it bears white-throated, deep purple flowers that fade to white over a couple of days. It will lose its leaves for a short time in winter. **'Floribunda'** resembles the species, except it has smaller leaves and more abundant flowers. (Zones 10–11)

B. pauciflora (below)

QUICK REFERENCE CHART

TREE HEIGHT LEGEND: Short: < 7.5 m (25') • Medium: 7.5–15 m (25–50') • Tall: > 15 m (50')

SPECIES by Common Name	FORM					FOLIAGE									
	Tall Tree	Med. Tree	Short Tree	Shrub	Groundcover	Evergreen	Semi-evergreen	Deciduous	Variegated	Blue/Green	Purple/Red	Silver/White	Yellow/Gold	Dark–Mid-green	Light Green
Abelia				*		*	*							*	
Acacia		*	*	*	*	*						*			
Angel's Trumpet			*	*				*						*	
Arbutus	*	*	*	*		*								*	
Aucuba				*		*			*					*	
Beautyberry				*				*						*	
Beech	*	*						*	*		*			*	
Birch	*	*						*						*	
Bird-of-Paradise Bush				*		*	*							*	
Bluebeard				*				*				*	*	*	
Bog Rosemary				*		*				*				*	
Bottlebrush		*	*	*		*					*			*	*
Boxleaf Azara			*	*		*								*	
Butterfly Bush				*				*						*	
California Lilac				*	*	*								*	*
California Pepper Tree		*	*			*								*	*
Camellia			*	*		*								*	
Cape Plumbago				*		*	*							*	*
Cedar	*	*	*	*		*				*				*	
Chinese Pistache	*	*						*						*	
Coast Redwood	*	*	*	*		*				*				*	
Common Quince			*	*				*						*	
Crape Myrtle			*	*				*			*			*	*
Cypress	*	*	*			*				*			*	*	*
Daphne				*		*	*		*					*	
Dawn Redwood	*							*						*	*

SPECIES
by Common Name

FEATURES								BLOOMING						
Habit	Flowers	Foliage	Bark	Fruit/Cones	Scent	Spines	Fall Color	Spring	Summer	Fall	Winter	Zones	Page Number	
	*	*	*				*		*			5–9	76	Abelia
	*	*			*						*	8–11	80	Acacia
	*	*			*				*	*		10–12	84	Angel's Trumpet
*	*		*	*					*	*		7–9	88	Arbutus
		*		*				*				6–9	92	Aucuba
				*			*		*			6–10	96	Beautyberry
*		*	*	*			*	*				4–9	100	Beech
*		*	*				*	*			*	2–10	104	Birch
	*								*			9–11	108	Bird-of-Paradise Bush
	*	*			*				*	*		5–9	110	Bluebeard
	*	*						*	*			2–6	112	Bog Rosemary
*	*							*	*	*		9–11	114	Bottlebrush
*	*	*			*						*	7–9	116	Boxleaf Azara
*	*	*						*	*			5–10	118	Butterfly Bush
*	*	*			*			*	*			7–10	122	California Lilac
*	*	*		*				*	*			9–11	126	California Pepper Tree
*	*	*						*		*	*	7–9	128	Camellia
*	*							*	*	*		9–11	134	Cape Plumbago
*		*	*	*								7–9	136	Cedar
	*	*		*	*		*	*				7–10	140	Chinese Pistache
*		*	*	*								6–10	142	Coast Redwood
*	*			*			*	*				5–9	146	Common Quince
	*	*	*				*		*			7–10	148	Crape Myrtle
*		*	*	*								7–10	152	Cypress
	*	*			*			*				4–10	156	Daphne
*		*	*	*								4–10	160	Dawn Redwood

TREE HEIGHT LEGEND: Short: < 7.5 m (25') • Medium: 7.5–15 m (25–50') • Tall: > 15 m (50')

SPECIES by Common Name	FORM					FOLIAGE									
	Tall Tree	Med. Tree	Short Tree	Shrub	Groundcover	Evergreen	Semi-evergreen	Deciduous	Variegated	Blue/Green	Purple/Red	Silver/White	Yellow/Gold	Dark–Mid-green	Light Green
Dogwood		*	*	*				*	*					*	*
Douglas-Fir	*		*	*		*				*				*	
Dove Tree	*	*						*							*
False Cypress	*	*	*	*		*				*		*	*	*	
Fir	*	*	*	*		*				*		*		*	
Firethorn				*		*	*							*	
Flannel Bush			*	*		*								*	
Flowering Quince				*				*						*	
Forsythia				*	*			*						*	
Fringe Tree			*	*				*						*	*
Ginkgo	*	*						*							*
Goldenchain Tree			*					*						*	
Grevillea	*	*		*		*								*	
Hardy Hibiscus				*				*						*	
Heavenly Bamboo				*		*	*				*		*	*	*
Hebe				*	*	*			*					*	
Holly		*	*	*		*			*					*	
Horsechestnut	*	*	*					*						*	
Hydrangea			*	*				*						*	
Japanese Pagoda Tree	*		*	*				*						*	
Kalmia				*		*								*	
Kerria				*				*	*					*	
Lilac			*	*				*						*	
Loquat			*	*		*					*			*	
Magnolia	*		*	*		*	*							*	
Manzanita				*	*	*					*	*		*	

SPECIES
by Common Name

FEATURES								BLOOMING						
Habit	Flowers	Foliage	Bark	Fruit/Cones	Scent	Spines	Fall Color	Spring	Summer	Fall	Winter	Zones	Page Number	
*	*		*	*			*	*	*			2–9	162	Dogwood
*		*		*								4–9	166	Douglas-Fir
	*		*					*				6–10	168	Dove Tree
*		*		*								4–9	170	False Cypress
		*		*								3–7	174	Fir
	*	*		*		*		*				6–10	178	Firethorn
	*	*						*	*	*		8–10	182	Flannel Bush
	*			*		*		*				4–9	186	Flowering Quince
	*							*				4–10	190	Forsythia
*	*		*		*			*	*			4–9	194	Fringe Tree
*		*	*	*			*					3–9	198	Ginkgo
	*							*	*			5–9	202	Goldenchain Tree
*	*	*						*		*	*	8–11	204	Grevillea
	*								*	*		5–10	208	Hardy Hibiscus
	*	*		*			*	*	*			7–9	210	Heavenly Bamboo
*	*	*			*			*	*			8–10	214	Hebe
*		*		*				*	*			6–10	218	Holly
	*	*		*	*			*	*			4–9	222	Horsechestnut
*	*						*	*	*	*		3–11	226	Hydrangea
*	*				*				*			4–10	232	Japanese Pagoda Tree
	*	*						*	*			4–9	234	Kalmia
*	*							*				4–9	236	Kerria
	*				*			*	*			3–10	238	Lilac
	*	*		*	*			*		*	*	8–11	242	Loquat
*	*	*	*	*	*			*	*	*	*	4–11	246	Magnolia
*		*	*	*				*			*	2–11	250	Manzanita

TREE HEIGHT LEGEND: Short: < 7.5 m (25') • Medium: 7.5–15 m (25–50') • Tall: > 15 m (50')

SPECIES by Common Name	FORM					FOLIAGE									
	Tall Tree	Med. Tree	Short Tree	Shrub	Groundcover	Evergreen	Semi-evergreen	Deciduous	Variegated	Blue/Green	Purple/Red	Silver/White	Yellow/Gold	Dark–Mid-green	Light Green
Maple	*	*	*	*				*			*			*	
Mimosa Tree		*					*	*						*	
Mockorange				*				*	*				*	*	
Monkey Puzzle Tree	*					*								*	*
New Zealand Christmas Tree		*				*			*			*		*	
Olive		*	*			*						*		*	
Oregon Grape				*		*								*	
Photinia			*	*		*					*			*	
Pineapple Guava				*		*						*		*	
Podocarpus	*	*	*	*		*								*	
Pomegranate			*	*				*			*				*
Princess Flower				*				*	*		*			*	
Redbud		*	*	*				*		*	*			*	
Rhododendron				*		*		*						*	
Rockrose				*		*				*		*		*	
Russian Olive			*	*		*		*	*			*		*	
Salal				*		*								*	
Spirea				*				*		*	*		*	*	
Spruce	*	*	*	*		*				*				*	
Sweetbox				*		*								*	
Sweetgum	*							*						*	
Tulip Tree	*							*	*					*	
Viburnum				*		*		*						*	
Weeping Willow		*						*				*		*	
Witch-Hazel			*	*				*						*	*
Yesterday, Today, Tomorrow				*			*							*	

SPECIES
by Common Name

FEATURES								BLOOMING						
Habit	Flowers	Foliage	Bark	Fruit/Cones	Scent	Spines	Fall Color	Spring	Summer	Fall	Winter	Zones	Page Number	
*	*	*	*	*			*	*				3–9	254	Maple
*	*	*			*			*				9–11	260	Mimosa Tree
	*				*			*	*			4–10	262	Mockorange
*		*		*								7–10	266	Monkey Puzzle Tree
*	*	*							*			9–11	268	New Zealand Christmas Tree
		*		*	*				*			8–11	270	Olive
	*			*	*		*	*			*	5–10	274	Oregon Grape
		*						*				8–10	278	Photinia
*	*	*		*				*				9–11	280	Pineapple Guava
*		*										7–11	282	Podocarpus
	*	*		*			*		*			9–11	286	Pomegranate
	*	*						*	*	*	*	9–12	290	Princess Flower
	*						*	*				5–9	292	Redbud
	*	*			*			*	*		*	4–10	296	Rhododendron
	*	*						*	*			8–10	302	Rockrose
	*	*		*	*			*	*			2–10	306	Russian Olive
	*	*		*				*	*			3–9	310	Salal
*	*						*	*	*	*		3–10	312	Spirea
*		*		*								2–10	316	Spruce
	*	*		*	*			*			*	6–9	320	Sweetbox
*		*	*	*			*	*				5–10	322	Sweetgum
*	*	*		*			*		*			4–10	326	Tulip Tree
*	*	*		*	*		*	*	*			2–11	328	Viburnum
*								*				5–10	334	Weeping Willow
*	*	*			*		*			*	*	3–10	336	Witch-Hazel
	*							*	*			10–11	340	Yesterday, Today, Tomorrow

GLOSSARY

B & B: abbreviation for balled-and-burlapped stock; i.e., plants that have been dug out of the ground and have had their rootballs wrapped in burlap

Bonsai: the art of training plants into miniature trees and landscapes

Candles: the new, soft spring growth of needle-leaved evergreens such as pine, spruce and fir

Crown: the part of a plant at or just below the soil where the stems meet the roots; also, the top of a tree, including the branches and leaves

Cultivar: a cultivated plant variety with one or more distinct differences from the species; e.g., *Hedera helix* is a botanical species, of which 'Gold Heart' is a cultivar distinguished by leaf variegation

Deadhead: to remove spent flowers in order to maintain a neat appearance, encourage a longer blooming period and prevent the plant from expending energy on fruit production

Dieback: death of a branch from the tip inwards; usually used to describe winter damage

Dormancy: an inactive stage, often coinciding with the onset of winter

Double flower: a flower with an unusually large number of petals, often caused by mutation of the stamens into petals

Dripline: the area around the bottom of a tree, directly under the tips of the farthest-extending branches

Dwarf: a plant that is small compared to the normal growth of the species; dwarf growth is often cultivated by plant breeders

Espalier: the training of a tree or shrub to grow in two dimensions

Gall: an abnormal outgrowth or swelling produced as a reaction to sucking insects, other pests or diseases

Genus: a category of biological classification between the species and family levels; the first word in a Latin name indicates the genus; e.g., *Pinus* in *Pinus mugo*

Girdling: a restricted flow of water and nutrients in a plant caused by something tied tightly around a trunk or branch, or by an encircling cut

Grafting: a type of propagation in which a stem or bud of one plant is joined onto the rootstock of another plant of a closely related species

Heartwood: the wood in the center of a stem or branch consisting of old, dense, non-functional conducting tissue

Hybrid: a plant resulting from natural or human-induced cross-breeding between varieties, species or genera; often sterile, but may be more vigorous than either parent and have attributes of both

Inflorescence: a flower cluster

Leader: the dominant upward growth at the top of a tree; may be erect or drooping

Nodes: the places on the stem from where leaves grow; when cuttings are planted, new roots grow from the nodes under the soil

pH: a measure of acidity or alkalinity (the lower the pH, the higher the acidity); the pH of soil influences availability of nutrients for plants

Pollarding: a severe form of pruning in which all the younger branches of a tree are cut back virtually to the trunk to encourage bushy new growth

Procumbent, prostrate: terms used to describe plants that grow along the ground

Rootball: the root mass and surrounding soil of a container-grown or dug-out plant

Rhizome: a modified stem that grows underground, horizontally

Single flower: a flower with a single ring of typically four or five petals

Species: simply defined as a group of organisms that can interbreed to yield fertile offspring; the fundamental unit of biological classification

Standard: a shrub or small tree grown with an erect main stem; accomplished either through pruning and training or by grafting the plant onto a tall, straight stock

Subspecies (subsp.): a naturally occurring, regional form of a species, often geographically isolated from other subspecies but still potentially interfertile with them

Sucker: a shoot that comes up from a root, often some distance from the plant; it can be separated to form a new plant once it develops its own roots

Topiary: the training of plants into geometric, animal or other unique shapes

Variegated: describes foliage that has more than one color, often patched or striped or bearing differently colored leaf margins

Variety (var.): a naturally occurring variant of a species; below the level of subspecies in biological classification

Flowering quince

Further Reading

Brickell, Christopher, and David Joyce. 1996. *Pruning and Training.* Dorling Kindersley, Limited, London.

Dirr, Michael A. 1997. *Dirr's Hardy Trees and Shrubs: An Illustrated Encyclopedia.* Timber Press, Portland, Oregon.

Editors of Sunset Books and Sunset Magazine. 2001. *Sunset Western Garden Book.* Sunset Books Inc., Menlo Park, California.

Ellis, B.W., and F.M. Bradley, eds. 1996. *The Organic Gardener's Handbook of Natural Insect and Disease Control.* Rodale Press, Emmaus, Pennsylvania.

Thompson, P. 1992. *Creative Propagation: A Grower's Guide.* Timber Press, Portland, Oregon.

INDEX

Entries in **bold** type indicate the main tree and shrub headings.

A

B

C

G

H

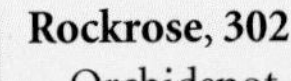

T,V

W

Y